Alexandra Tătăran

Contemporary Life and Witchcraft

Magic, Divination, and Religious Ritual in Europe

Alexandra Tătăran

CONTEMPORARY LIFE AND WITCHCRAFT

Magic, Divination, and Religious Ritual in Europe

ibidem-Verlag
Stuttgart

Bibliographic information published by the Deutsche Nationalbibliothek
Die Deutsche Nationalbibliothek lists this publication in the Deutsche Nationalbibliografie; detailed bibliographic data are available in the Internet at http://dnb.d-nb.de.

Bibliografische Information der Deutschen Nationalbibliothek
Die Deutsche Nationalbibliothek verzeichnet diese Publikation in der Deutschen Nationalbibliografie; detaillierte bibliografische Daten sind im Internet über http://dnb.d-nb.de abrufbar.

Cover picture: Painting on the outer wall of Rila Monastery church, Bulgaria. Wikimedia Commons. Licensed under CC BY 2.5 (s. https://creativecommons.org/licenses/by/2.5/deed.en)
Cover design by Sergiu Moldovan

ISBN-13: 978-3-8382-0778-0

Stuttgart, Germany 2016

Printed in the United States of America

Contents

Introduction

In the summer of 2005, my colleague Iulia Hossu and I were beginning our doctoral field research projects in the village of Râşca in the Apuseni Mountains of western Romania. My research at the time was focused on rituals of defense and protection that are part of religious celebrations and seasonal crossings. Armed with carefully selected theories and sharp analytical distinctions, we presented the scope and purpose of our investigations to our neighbor and future key informant Rodica (woman, age 53). She nodded approvingly and said she would be glad to help but then gave us a stark and unexpected warning:

> *You have to be careful about what you ask and how you ask it. Don't you ever, by any chance, start asking about* ***those things****. If you do, people will start thinking that you are actually seeking some sort of spells or whatnot. And ... if that's the talk in the village, nobody will ever talk to you. You can count on it.*

This announcement was a big surprise to me. At that time, I could not imagine any direct connection between our research subjects and 'those things,' by which Rodica meant the magic/witchcraft discourse. This warning made very clear to me the extent of the difficulties that come with open-field inquiries on witchcraft. Especially in rural Romania, ethnologists who research magical interventions are perceived as suspect individuals, and it is near-impossible for them to establish community contacts. As Dominique Camus wrote in the context of his research in rural France, 'the ethnologist is perceived as someone who comes to seek power. This relates to the very staging of witchcraft. There is no space for an innocent inquirer'[1]; there is no space for small talk or for casual exchange of information. Jeanne Favret-Saada issued the same caution: in witchcraft, words represent war rather than shar-

1 Dominique Camus, *Puteri şi practici vrăjitoreşti. Anchetă asupra practicilor actuale de vrăjitorie* (Iaşi: Polirom, 2003), p. 11.

ing knowledge; so, 'there isn't a place for a neutral observer.'[2] Because magic is *praxis*, the only imaginable purpose of talking about it is to acquire magical knowledge that can subsequently be put into effect. In a discourse universe where talking necessarily means already acting or preparing to act, protected by strict guidelines of taboos and secrecy, the gathering of information for its own sake—so intrinsic to any anthropological research—comes as something completely foreign, parallel, and contrary to the witchcraft discourse's internal logic.

Three years later, my research focused exclusively on *those things*.[3] Given the extraordinary recurrence of witchcraft discourses I discovered during my field investigations, I was surprised that this issue is so little represented in contemporary academic studies. The epistemological purview of anthropological research is the analysis of social and cultural phenomena that are both significant and recurrent, which *those things* certainly are. Although there is a small number of significant contributions,[4] the contemporary manifesta-

---

2 Jeanne Favret-Saada, *Les mots, la mort, les sorts* (Paris: Gallimard, 1977), p. 27.

3 When discussing a witchcraft situation in contemporary Transylvania, the terms tend to be euphemisms or surrogate collocations: 'those things' ('*de-acelea*') signify spells, charms, or any conceivable magical operations. The word 'witch' ('*vrăjitoare*') is hardly used as such. When referring to a suspected magical aggressor, people rather say 'that woman (or person) who knows how to handle *those things*' ('*femeie ce ştie a umbla cu de-acelea*'). The verbal evasiveness is consistent with the convention of taboos, always present within the witchcraft discourse.

4 Dominique Camus' and Jeanne Favret-Saada's field research projects in rural France are among the most detailed and thorough accounts of specific forms of contemporary (traditional) witchcraft. Galina Lindquist's anthropological studies on contemporary magic and religion in today's Russia offer a fascinating glimpse into the manifestations, functions, and reshaping of both fields after the demise of former Soviet Union. Willem de Blécourt's comparative approaches on contemporary European witchcraft discourse and the key actors in the witchcraft triangle are, to my knowledge, singular attempts to shape the field of research and open relevant lines of inquiries. However, as suggested by the latter, one issue might actually be the relative linguistic inaccessibility of regional research: 'It takes a linguist rather than an anthropologist to read them all.' 'The Witch, her Victim, the Unwitcher

tions of the witchcraft discourse throughout Europe, its forms, functions, and regional traits still require a great deal of further fieldwork and theoretical considerations. It is entirely possible that sociocultural phenomena relevant to the witchcraft discourse are completely absent in some European regions. It is equally possible that they are more present in Europe than suggested by contemporary social sciences research, simply because the efforts were not made to record them. Whatever the case may be: where, how, and why they do function can offer valuable insights into those contemporary European practices and mentalities that can be individually accessed, in times of need, as strategies of warding off adversity.

The majority of studies of witchcraft in contemporary Europe focus on New Age, neo-pagan, Wiccan practices, and beliefs,[5] but there are no comparable phenomena in modern Romanian society. As a post-communist development, the Romanian market of pseudo religious products flourished after 1989,[6] when a vast category of religious/magical/mystical/occult concepts inspired by Western thought started to be circulated in the media. Actual beliefs and practices in post-communist Romania may incorporate idiosyncratic elements of ancient rural magic and mentalities, religious orthodox practice, modern and urban divination techniques, and pseudoscientific explanations that follow New Age concepts or a belief in the paranormal. Although the span and impact of these new concepts are significant and their emergence in the media probably enabled the reinvigoration of witchcraft discourse in post-communist Roma-

---

and the Researcher: the continued existence of traditional witchcraft', *Witchcraft and Magic in Europe. The Twentieth Century,* ed. by Bengt Ankarloo and Stuart Clark (University of Pennsylvania Press, 1999), 141–219, p. 146.

5 About the Neo-Pagan witch, De Blécourt writes that although 'presented as timeless, she reveals herself as a basically 19th-century invention, more linked to the male interpretations of historic witches [...] than to age-old village traditions', 'self-proclaimed' and 'city-based.' Willem de Blécourt, p. 150.

6 Gabriel Troc, 'Exorcism şi vindecare în Biserica Ortodoxă', *Caietele Tranziţiei,* 2. 3 (Cluj–Napoca: 1998).

nia, the underlying pattern of today's witchcraft accusations continues to be decidedly rural-traditional.

If neo-paganism can be described as an amalgamate of various forms of new (religious) spiritualties, accessed individually in the name of personal evolution and spiritual growth, the rural-traditional witchcraft discourse represents a type of diagnosis reserved only for times of extreme duress, when all the other explanatory systems have failed to offer viable solutions. Entering this type of discourse does not represent, for the actors, a time for spiritual enlightenment or for gaining a deeper meaning of life. It represents a state of all-consuming war best synthesized, following Willem de Blécourt, as 'misfortune ascribed to other human beings'[7] based not on a facile mechanism of delegating aggression (like scapegoating) but on the fundamental belief that evil both exists and resides in *this* world. Accessing a neo-pagan religion is a matter of personal choice and the result of a selection operated into the many fields of spiritual paths available at any time out there in our contemporary society. It must have been the success the neo-pagan, urban-invented traditions which gradually emerged in the post-1950s Western world[8] that prompted Jean-Pierre Olivier de Sardan to declare that magic was becoming 'a fashionable counter-culture.'[9] In contrast, entering a witchcraft discourse does not play out as a fashionable choice or an informed spiritual decision, nor is it an individual quest. Dictated by stringent need rather than choice, the witchcraft diagnosis stems from a preexistent traditional code of interpreting unhappiness that is community based and usually accessed through the suggestions made by a third-party incidental diagnostician. In short, entering a witchcraft discourse represents a

7 De Blécourt, p. 151.

8 Willem de Blécourt and Owen Davis, 'Introduction: Witchcraft continued', in *Witchcraft continued. Popular magic in modern Europe*, ed. by Willem de Blécourt and Owen Davis (Manchester and New York: Manchester University Press, 2004), 1–13, p. 1.

9 Jean-Pierre Olivier de Sardan, 'The exoticing of magic from Durkheim to postmodern anthropology', *Critique of Anthropology*, 12. 1 (1992), pp. 5–25, ‹http://coa.sagepub.com› [accesed November *17th*, 2007], p. 14.

period of marked crisis in someone's life, one that s/he is most eager to solve (heal) and then leave behind.

The pragmatics of traditional rural witchcraft in Europe is mainly based on what Liiceanu[10] called a 'favorability transfer': a vital force set in motion through magical forces, resulting in a winning and a losing side. Economic prosperity, marital success, beauty, and health are all considered forms of vital 'surplus,' susceptible of causing envy and vulnerable to attempts of hijacking through spells and charms. The witchcraft discourse of contemporary Romania follows these same general lines, with one significant variation: The rather pragmatic 'surplus' stake seems to have lost its relevance, considered less and less a reason for a presumed witchcraft attack. Instead, the actors point to feelings: The suspected magical aggressors are supposedly motivated by pure hate or vengefulness rather than greed, with nothing else to gain from the spell except personal satisfaction out of causing unhappiness. This variation may reflect the modern recontextualization of the witchcraft discourse within urban settings, as well as a marked simplification of the 'aggressor' pole under the influence of the Orthodox religious discourse.

However, the (re)invention of spiritual traditions[11] such as neopaganism, the recontextualization of rural magic in urban settings, and the reimposition of the Orthodox Church on the public scene (at least in Romania, Bulgaria and Russia) after the demise of communism are all examples of the reenchantment of the world. As Richard Jenkins argued, 'The imperialism of formal-rational logics and processes has been, and necessarily still is, subverted and undermined by a diverse array of oppositional (re)enchantments.'[12]

10 Aurora Liiceanu, *Povestea unei vrăjitoare* (Bucureşti: Editura ALL, 1996), p. 81.

11 Eric Hobsbawm discusses these modern traditions not as purely fictional cultural 'inventions' but as ritual reinterpretations and reappropriations that create the effect of perennial values in the historical context of rapid social changes. 'Introduction: Inventing Traditions', *The Invention of Tradition*, ed. by Eric Hobsbawm and T. Ranger (Cambridge University Press, 1983), 1–14.

12 Richard Jenkins, 'Disenchantment, Enchantment and Re-Enchantment: Max Weber at the Millennium', *Max Weber Studies*, 1 (2000), 11–32,

Neither the scope and effectiveness of rationalization nor the decline of established Christian religion in the Western world can be denied. But these processes seem to have opened a path for pluralistic forms of reenchantments rather than proving to be dead ends for any forms of spirituality. Whether we talk about urban-based neo-paganism or reinterpreted rural witchcraft discourse, we have to acknowledge beliefs in magic in contemporary Europe as expressions of 'epistemological pluralism,'[13] not as the erosion of the authority of science. We do live in a secularized world in which the scientific discourse remains the dominant paradigm and rationalistic pragmatism defines the everyday province of meaning.

Researching the Witchcraft Discourse

This study is based on ethnographic material from field researches that I undertook in parts of Northern Transylvania[14] between 2005 and 2009. The fieldwork material is mainly discursive—that is, it takes the form of *discourses* about witchcraft, victims, sorcerers, and spells. Therefore, the material substantiating this study consists mainly of narratives: memories, opinions, stories and happenings, suspicions and accusations, gossip and rumors, recommended remedies, and steps to be followed. It was supplemented by information gleaned through visiting professional fortune tellers, often as a client, and attending religious services dedicated to healing interventions. The field material revolves around the victims' perspectives. Consequently, my theoretical approach is focused on the view of the *accuser* rather than the *accused*. Although the red thread of this book is a spatially localized case study examining one contemporary form of witchcraft discourse, my aim is to open up and contextualize the data by encompassing, whenever possible,

‹http://maxweberstudies.org/kcfinder/upload/files/MWSJournal/1.1pdfs/1.1%2011-32.pdf› [accessed October 12th, 2014], p. 12.

13 Richard Jenkins, p. 17.

14 Râşca village (Cluj County, Apuseni Mountains); Reteag, Giugeşti and Dumitra villages (Bistriţa-Năsăud County); Deta (Timiş County); and the towns of Bistriţa, Baia-Mare and Cluj-Napoca of Romania.

relevant comparative European material of both contemporary and historical characters.

On the basis of the Romanian research material, the following chapters of this study will address four main questions:

- How does a witchcraft situation appear in someone's life? On what premise does it evolve from a pale suspicion unto an assumed situation that has to be dealt with? What are the reasons for assuming that an abnormality in someone's life situation can only be explained through the witchcraft discourse?
- Who are the main actors, and what specific roles do they play, interplay, and exchange within the witchcraft situation development plot?
- What are the current healing therapies, or unwitchments, available in the investigated regions of Romania? To what extent do they seem to work for the involved actors?
- One of my research findings is that the position of the therapist seems to be exclusively held by religious specialists, monks, and priests belonging to the Orthodox denomination. What does this exclusiveness tell us about the complex magic and religion relation in a contemporary European society? The particular form of mutual relations between magic and religion in contemporary Eastern Europe, as well as the intermingled sources historically shaping the magic–religious discourses, can offer crucial insights into socially contextualized cultural strategies of dealing with unhappiness.

The overall presentation of my fieldwork material regarding the experiences of being bewitched as a collection of narratives initially concerned me; in anthropology, collecting words (through interviews) is always seconded by recording facts (through the participant observation). However, Jeanne Favret-Saada also experienced this: 'In the field, (...) all I came across was language. During the long months, all I could find were words.'[15] Only few, if any, elements within the witchcraft discourse can be accepted as clear-cut empirical facts. For instance, a researcher cannot document the palpability, the factuality of the effects caused by a casting of a spell, such as they are lived by the presupposed victim and his/her family. As an outsider to the witchcraft discourse and a representative of the scientific frame of thought, all the researcher can docu-

15 Favret-Saada, p. 25.

ment are the accounts of the events, the actors' cause–effect interpretations specific to the logic of the witchcraft discourse, and the explicative larger 'mythology' surrounding any concrete story. What on the outside may present itself as a plot with specific actors and a narrative structure takes the form of a dramatic sequence of emotionally marked events for the insider, ever to last as a fragment of personal history. Perceiving the episodes of witchcraft as *words* rather than *facts* does not make them any less 'real.' They are real because they form a part of people's lives, and they inform their decisions and their general vision upon the world.

Willem de Blécourt and Owen Davis define the witchcraft discourse as 'a shorthand note denoting the whole complex of thinking and acting in terms of witchcraft.'[16] As it stands, this discourse revolves around a complex relationship between three actors: the accuser (the victim); the therapist (the unwitcher); and the magical aggressor. However, in the field, this is not exactly what the researcher of witchcraft typically encounters.

Rather than accessing the classic triangle (victim, aggressor, and therapist) or rectangle (the victim and his therapist, pitted against the aggressor and the witch), the researcher of witchcraft will always have direct involvement with only one of the two poles—because they are mutually exclusive. As Dominique Camus realized,[17] although they are part of the same drama, an aggressor and a victim, as well as their respective therapists, belong to two different types of discourses. Galina Lindquist's anthropological research in present-day Russia[18] focuses on the relation between the magi and the client; Jeanne Favret-Saada's ground-breaking fieldwork in Bocage (France) was based on the victim–unwitcher couple, as the only pole clearly identifiable in witchcraft situations. Dominique Camus' research in contemporary rural France documents both poles: the couple of the victim and the unwitcher; as well as that of the ag-

16 Willem de Blécourt and Owen Davis, p. 3.

17 Dominique Camus, p. 10 and 218.

18 Galina Lindquist, *Conjuring Hope. Healing and Magic in contemporary Russia* (New York, Oxford: Berghahn Books, 2009).

gressor, who is the client of the provider of sorcery expertise. However, he took them as independent, unrelated entities, each with its own interpretative discourse and stories. The researcher cannot access the accuser and the accused simultaneously because that would mean a direct link between the two, following the accusation, in the form of the accused publicly accepting the position of aggressor. Naturally, that never seems to happen. Usually, naming the aggressor plays a crucial part in the victim's own drama, as a process of initial cathartic naming of the source of evil contaminating his/her life, which enables the person to move on to the ritualistic aspect of the unwitchment. It is a verbalization process that has little to do with the accused. When and if at all confronted, the latter can only deny: not only his/her involvement but also the belief in witchcraft altogether.[19]

In the context of my research, similar to that by Jeanne Favret-Saada, the only pole I could clearly identify in the contemporary Romanian cases was that of the victim: the annunciator (or incidental diagnostician), the professional diagnostician (mostly diviners), and the unwitcher (predominantly Orthodox clergy). While I was able to map most of the diviners and the religious therapists operating in the area, I never found any indication of active specialized magical aggressors offering corresponding services. It seems like the only magical specialists active now are the diviners, and it must be noted that their participation into the witchcraft discourse is marginal and minimal (confirming or placing the diagnosis of bewitchment for affected clients). There are virtually no lay unwitchers, no village witches,[20] and no magic practitioners similar to the

19 Jeanne Favret-Saada showed that the presupposed magical aggressors respond by obstinate silence to such accusations or by pretending to not believe in spells and the like, p. 32.

20 Aurora Liiceanu portraits in *Povestea unei vrăjitoare (The Story of a Witch)* one of the last well-known village witches active in Vadu Izei (Maramureş, northen Transylvania) in the 1970s. My own research indicates the fact that, up until the 1970s and 1980s, people in need were often resorting to lay unwitchers or skilled women (in dealing with *those things*), while now they exclusively appeal to Orthodox clergy.

contemporary *magi* figures practicing in Russia as described by Galina Lindquist.[21] Yet, despite the contemporary lack of public magic practitioners to whom people might ascribe wrongdoings to, or to whom they might even appeal when wanting to cause harm to somebody else, the witchcraft discourse persists and gets to play, from time to time, a part in people's lives in today's Transylvania. Why that is so, how exactly the process works, and what this tell us about collective strategies of dealing with unhappiness are all questions that shape the aims of this study.

Writing about Contemporary Witchcraft

Writing about European witchcraft discourses is no easy task. The vast specialized literature available is mostly historical in scope. It is as if it has been decided that this is a matter of the past, best placed in the framework of premodern or early modern times of backwardness and superstition, at a time when the light of reason and science had not yet triumphed against the shadows of ignorance. To talk about witchcraft of today comes across as a peculiar endeavor that should be located in some exotic, outer-European context: If witchcraft cannot be confined to the mysterious times of the past, then it should at least be located on some distant, non-European setting, whose distance from modern Western thought allows us to view it as nothing more than a delightful cultural curiosity. But magic and witchcraft have always existed in Europe. And the discourse did not end in the West with the end of witch trials and persecutions, nor did it end in the East with modernization, urbanization, Communism, or post-Communism.

---

21 The magi in contemporary Russia are urban magical practice specialists and charismatic individuals assisting their clients in a wide variety of circumstances whose common denominator is a life crisis. The sources of the contemporary Russian magic discourse are incredibly varied, combining to create a unique phenomenon: folk medicine, local rural traditions of healing, and folk magic mixed in late Soviet and post-communist times with Western New Age definitions of bioenergetic fields, studies of the paranormal, and other established non-Russian complementary therapies. See Galina Lindquist, pp. 30–40.

From the point of view of any modern national meta-discourse, this is not the type of research to present a favorable image of a nation, as it carries the risk of portraying the 'primitive within' as the rule rather than the exception. Especially for the countries of Eastern Europe, post-communist or not, Greek Orthodox or not, these type of researches can carry the risk of furthering a general perception that equates this region with the darker, less-developed *other* side of the 'European' coin.

For the actors involved in, or aware of, witchcraft situations in real-life scenarios, this is not 'folklore' to be researched. Especially in post-communist countries, the effects of the communist discourse in shaping the 'folklore' field (including national dress, local dances, songs, and material artifacts) are ever-lasting and part of the common public perceptions. More importantly, this is not informative 'knowledge' to be accessed through casual inquiries but *praxis* as equipment for living. The experience of being bewitched always illustrates a deep crisis situation in the victim's life. This aspect makes it a delicate, nearly taboo, topic for discussion: having been bewitched is always part of the very personal, not representative–collective part of life. At the same time, because witchcraft is generally condemned as retrograde, superstitious, and backward from the position of the dominant positivist–rationalist discourse, the actor is often painfully aware of the disadvantageous, marginalizing effects of a diagnosis of bewitchment. This type of experience is thus inherently isolating and ends up taking the form of a suspended, bracketed story through the years—difficult to research in the absence of a more personal approach.

Between this 'institutional snake' and this 'dragon from the *other*'s territory,'[22] the social science researcher seems to be the only one who addresses the magic subject (as well as the adjacent, nar-

22 Marianne Mesnil illustrates, through this metaphoric image, the relation between the researcher functioning as a representative of the dominant rationalist scientific discourse and the actors directly engaged in the systems of practices and beliefs that the former sets to study. Marianne Mesnil, *Etnologul, între şarpe şi balaur*/Marianne Mesnil şi Assia Popova – *Eseuri de mitologie balcanică* (Bucureşti: Paideia, 1997), p. 13.

rower field of witchcraft) as traditions in a dynamic sense, as a common repertoire of meanings and guidelines, as long-practiced collective solutions answering to actors' needs in difficult life moments.

Whether we consider the witchcraft discourse as a cultural code; a 'province of meaning' (Alfred Schutz) counterbalancing everyday life or a particular trans-generational vision upon the world that a contemporary individual can access when in need, its ultimate value is empowering: a cultural strategic tool that can assist with fighting off adversity in one's life. It has to be taken into consideration as one of those phenomena that cannot be dismissed as 'survivors' from a begone era but as cultural facts that prove to be so neccessary that they get to be continuously reinterpreted and reintegrated into the daily lives of contemporary people. At least for the Romanian case, I can safely argue that the traditional witchcraft discouse is far from demise. The very fact that it adapts to the context of a modern (yet still changing) society means it retains its fundamental value as a functional repertoire of both meanings and means designed to confront unhapiness.

Chapter 1: Difficult Life Situations and Witchcraft

In this chapter, I will describe four main types of difficult life situations that often lead to a witchcraft attack diagnosis, as documented during my 2005–2008 anthropological field research in Northern Transylvania, Romania. The structure of this chapter is dictated by the results of my ethnographic material.

I found the following four types of life situations to be the most common to trigger witchcraft interventions:

1. delay of marriage;
2. unhappy marriage or problematic love relationship;
3. inexplicable illness, 'mal de vivre'; and
4. *Mana* and fertility transfer.

The first three types of witchcraft scenarios are still very frequent in contemporary Romania and constitute the main material of my research. The fourth described here, the *mana* and fertility transfer, is probably the most successful and long-lasting witchcraft scenario across all of Europe. As a type, this is the epitome of traditional European witchcraft. All the others are basically variations on the theme of 'misfortune ascribed to other human beings.'[23] The fertility/vitality transfer is also the predominant type of witchcraft situation in the rural areas of contemporary France, as described in the French anthropological and ethnological literature referenced here.[24] However, in today's Romania, it is the least frequently applied.

---

23 Willem de Blécourt, 'The Witch, her Victim, the Unwitcher and the Researcher: the continued existence of traditional witchcraft', *Witchcraft and Magic in Europe. The Twentieth Century,* ed. by Bengt Ankarloo and Stuart Clark (University of Pennsylvania Press, 1999), 141–219, p. 151.

24 Jeanne Favret-Saada, *Les mots, la mort, les sorts* (Paris: Gallimard, 1977); Dominique Camus, *Puteri şi practici vrăjitoreşti. Anchetă asupra practicilor actuale de vrăjitorie* (Iaşi: Polirom, 2003); Owen Davies, 'Witchcraft accusations in France, 1850–1990', *Witchcraft Continued. Popular Magic in Modern Europe,* ed. by Willem de Blécourt & Owen Davies (Manchester and New York: Manchester University Press, 2004); André Julliard, 'Urgia Sorţilor. Vrăjitoria zilelor noastre în Franţa', *Magia şi vrăjitoria în Europa, din Evul*

In the case of rural France, for instance, the accelerated changes of French society due to the industrialization and urbanization of the late 19th and 20th centuries only seemed to have reinforced the witchcraft discourse, in particular the fertility transfer scenario. As shown by Owen Davies,[25] this has a lot to do with the tensions created through changes within the French society between a new national identity and preexisting regional identities, between the rural traditional and modern urbanity. The self-definition as 'paysans' (Engl.> *peasants*) is assumed by country people as a badge of honor, expressing their resistance to these social changes; a part of the values associated with this way of life is the belief in witchcraft and magic.

In the case of contemporary Romania, witchcraft and magic have less to do with the rural way of life and its associated values but more with the fundamental ability of this discourse to offer explanations for unhappiness and the means to fight it. For this reason, it has migrated from villages to cities, where it can hold an equal explanatory value to other, more sanctioned discourses. The only one that could not migrate simply because it does not make much sense in an urban setting is precisely the fertility transfer scenario, which is mainly linked to agricultural concerns such as fecundity, milk mana, and crop production. The other types—delay of marriage; unhappy marriage or problematic love relationship; and unexplainable illness, 'mal de vivre'—are all, in contrast, types of difficult situations likely to be encountered by people from cities and villages.

The final reading of a situation as a witchcraft attack is not always, as I will further show, a simple matter of drawing a conclusion based on the level of duress experienced in someone's life at a certain time. Sometimes a witchcraft crisis is steeply announced by forms of brusque, violent outbursts (abrupt illness, sudden physical pain, and aggressive altercations in the family), and specific symptoms immediately alerting the people involved that something

---

Mediu până astăzi, ed. by Robert Muchembled (Bucureşti: Humanitas, 1997), pp. 274–326.

25 Owen Davies, 'Witchcraft accusations in France, 1850–1990', pp. 107–132.

strange is going on. At other times, there is even less time to deliberate and doubt: The actors instantly assume they are in the presence of a witchcraft situation when they find physical object-spells (usually a collection of specific substances wrapped in paper) inside their domestic perimeter. But, no matter how transparent the symptoms or how clear the physical signs announcing the presence of a witchcraft situation, the entrance into the witchcraft discourse is never a matter of a simple leap from 'the world of daily life' into an alternative sphere of meaning.[26] It represents a liminal moment during which the actor has to stop, ponder, and recollect: s/he has to reorganize both memory and identity in order to step on the path opened by the witchcraft diagnosis, which is at that point perceived to be the only one left to offer the promise of resolution.

1.1 Witchcraft Situations and Reasons for Entering the Witchcraft Discourse

How does an episode of witchcraft appear in someone's life? On what premises does a difficult time in someone's life evolve from a nameless affliction to the suspicion of witchcraft and then further into a situation assumed as a real witchcraft attack by the actors? On the basis of her research in rural France (Bocage region) in the 1970s, Jeanne Favret-Saada[27] outlined the necessary conditions for a difficult life episode to be marked as witchcraft:

- Only misfortunes repeated over time and variable in form qualify for a witchcraft diagnosis;

---

26 Alfred Schutz defines the world of daily life as the world 'which the wide-awake, grown-up man who acts in it and upon it amidst his fellow-men experiences with the natural attitude as a reality.' That is the paramount reality of day-to-day living. But, every person intermittently lives also in other finite provinces of meaning, such as the world of dreams, the world of art, the world of religious experience; they all come with cognitive styles and accents of reality different from the world of daily life. Alfred Schutz, 'On Multiple Realities', *Philosophy and Phenomenological Research*, 5 (1945), pp. 533–576, ‹http://www.marxists.org/reference/subject/philosophy/works/ge/schuetz.htm› [accessed 10 March 2014]

27 Jeanne Favret-Saada, pp. 22–24.

- A third party delivers the diagnosis of bewitchment based on a previous, similar experience;
- The victim consults a medical doctor, a priest, and a magical therapist, in that order, following the order of discourse. The witchcraft discourse is only accepted after the possibilities offered by positivist and religious discourses are exhausted.

Although this scheme is relevant to the overall discussion in this book, it must be remembered that witchcraft and sorcery 40 years ago in Bocage (France) or any Romanian village are necessarily different from what is found in today's complex, heterogeneous, multivoiced society. Moreover, today the Roman Catholic Church and Protestant denominations take very different approaches to witchcraft than the Eastern Orthodox Church. The Orthodox doctrine, which is the predominant Christian confession in Romania, fully participates in witchcraft discourse, acknowledges the existence of witchcraft as a specific form of evil in the real world, and actually offers the main therapeutic means of unwitching today. This means that, in contrast to Favret-Saada's scheme, in Northern Transylvania the unwitcher is not the one resorted to after a priest has been consulted, simply because the only legitimate unwitcher nowadays *is* the Orthodox priest himself. Nevertheless, Jeanne Favret-Saada's conceptualization remains useful in this context because it draws attention to the annunciator (the actor first naming a difficult situation as a possible occurrence of witchcraft) as the main figure triggering the entrance into the witchcraft discourse. In addition, the conditions outlined by Favret-Saada highlight the fact that a witchcraft diagnosis is not a random choice of the afflicted actor but something assumed with due gravity and only when two conditions are met: the crisis extends well beyond any limit of acceptable life difficulty and temporal duration; and the manifestations of the crisis vary, one misfortune being replaced by or added to another, variations that cannot be explained through the more acceptable scientific or religious discourses.

I will now go through the most typical situations encountered during my fieldwork, which may be explained by actors through a witchcraft diagnosis. With these, I hope to illustrate: the physiognomies of the social relations reflected by a witchcraft crisis; normative ideals of 'wellness'; current conceptions about the extent of insidious evil able to infiltrate someone's life; and the way in that witchcraft scenarios, just like any other social discourse, can change and become more or less relevant depending on narrative changes within the larger cultural context.

Delay of Marriage

In Romanian society today, being single or uncommitted after the age of 25 years or thereabouts is still a serious issue, especially for young women. Mothers and grandmothers sometimes seem to be more concerned than the young women in question themselves, and they are usually the ones who call for action. There is an acutely perceived social pressure about being married (and thus socially respectable and legitimate), which illustrates very well the persistence of old patriarchal structures and values linked to historical, agropastoral type of society, and culture.

The 'it goes without saying'[28] assumption operating here is that for a young, healthy, gainfully employed woman who comes from a good family and wants to be married *'it's not normal'* not to be. As expressed by Galina Lindquist in the context of contemporary Russian society: 'A woman, especially, who has never married is likely to be tacitly pitied and considered flawed and incomplete. Parents who fail to see their children (especially daughters) married may consider this as their major defeat in life.' Being married is an essential legitimation of the social persona in any society where the personal and familial ties are the only fully functional, valid, and

---

28 Jean-Pierre Olivier de Sardan calls this colloquialism the basic system of representations existent in every given society: 'the warp and woof of those actions, discourses, actions and interpretations which are an integral part of daily life; those symbols and meanings which are undefined yet tacitly accepted by everyone, and which are at the same time not subject to interpretation because they are overshadowed by the trivial actions and fundamental interactions of daily life,' in 'The exoticing of magic from Durkheim to postmodern anthropology', *Critique of Anthropology*, 12 (1992), 5–25 ‹http://coa.sagepub.com› [accessed November 7, 2007], pp. 10–11.

safety networks.[29] In Russia, similar to Romania, one of the first targets of the Soviet state was to eliminate the patriarchal family structure and ties, aiming to replace it with an aggregate of homogeneous citizens loyal only to the state and the socialist order. In both Russia and Romania, that social project failed as soon as this ideology clashed with real-life conditions, and faced with serious scarcity of resources, people had to find other ways to survive. Familial ties, as well as any type of common interest ties, became the main route of access to resources, such as extra food, access to jobs, housing, and better healthcare. Crudely put, the communist–socialist regime's social project in both countries, which aimed to completely pulverize the old traditional familial values, only managed to reinforce them. This is one reason why they are still so pertinent today, even long after the demise of the communist regime. The 'being married' theme is to be judged today not only in terms of patriarchally conceived personal identity (legitimizing a young woman through the familial name of her husband's family) but also in terms of belonging to more than one support network able to assist her in daily life. For the parents, to have their daughter or son married means to finally see them *safe*, not simply (supposedly) happy and socially accomplished.

The issue of competition on the marital market can translate into unhappiness in the actors' love life or even into the impossibility to settle through marriage into a long-term, stable love relationship. Such types of difficulties strongly motivate young women to look for an answer, along with their mothers or other close relatives. The first stop on the route to resolution is, in most cases, a fortune-teller's card spread diagnosis.

When the client is a young lady, a standard divination session always contains a compulsory card spread toward the end of the session called 'on the fate' (Rom.> *pe soartă*). For all unmarried women, the phrase '*to have fate*' means to have inscribed in their destiny the clear chance at getting married one day, like a predesti-

29 Galina Lindquist, *Conjuring Hope. Healing and Magic in contemporary Russia* (New York, Oxford: Berghahn Books, 2009), p. 57.

nation, presented by the diviner along with some elements of the predestined partner mythology. This fate spread is executed regardless of the client's manifested interest in the subject and so will take place regardless of whether the client specifically asked for it or not. Compared to any other issues that could interest a young woman (career, money, and health), a card divination session for this type of client predominantly stresses the aspects pertaining to: love life, relationships, marriage, reproductive health, and having children.

Determining whether or not a client 'has fate' proves to be a generic endeavor, in the end: for most young women, the destiny of getting married is confirmed through this card spread. Therefore, the 'fate reading' cannot offer an answer for a case in which the client, despite this positive opening in her destiny, is not yet married. In the context of a divination session, this contradiction between the predestination of getting married (confirmed through the card spread) and the reality of the opposite situation can only be explained through a witchcraft diagnosis. More than providing a name for a difficult situation, this diagnosis points to the malevolent intervention of other people, motivated by envy, competition, or revenge. The subtextual statement at play here is that the only thing able to block a bright, clear, well-deserved destiny of getting married is exterior evil in human form. In Russia, the diagnosis given by the magi for a similar situation is 'the crown of celibacy,' defined by them as a 'spoiling' of the individual's bio-energetic field caused by some immoral deeds or crimes committed by the victim's ancestors in the past.[30] It, thus, functions more according to the logic of kinship sin, but equally alleviates the afflicted person of any direct responsibility for their marital situation.

In the Bistrița-Năsăud county of Romania, there is one priest from a small village who has an extended regional reputation for solving marital deadlocks. People lengthily cite numerous cases of young women (teachers, civil clerks, and doctors) who sought his help for addressing this issue from all over the region and, by following the recommended rituals, they spectacularly got married in one

30 Galina Lindquist, p. 58.

year or less from complying with the steps of the ritual. The process is usually based on the generic idea of bridal destiny blockage, which is to be released by means of the religious acts and can, therefore, vary in complexity according to the diagnosis' particular gravity. The lightest form of this diagnosis can be a mere momentary quandary, in which case, the religious ritual works as a catalyst triggering the desired sequence of events leading to marriage. Being bewitched is at the other end of the scale, a severe and very serious diagnosis—comparable to a chronic, life-threatening condition in a medical context.

The gravity of any case of a magically bound marriage (Rom.> '*cununiile legate*') can be illustrated by the fact that it has the power to block the marital destiny of the targeted individual indefinitely; or, even more extreme, it can kill its target. In the village of Mocod,[31] in Bistrița-Năsăud, the case of a medical nurse who found it impossible to get married had been inexplicable to the local community for a long time, given her highly rated personal qualities and good familial provenance. The mystery was solved when an elderly woman asked her to come see her on her death bed, only to confess that she had magically bound the nurse's marital destiny in favor of her own daughter, less endowed with desirable qualities. Following the dying woman's indications, the nurse went on to unbind a 'thread of the dead' (Rom.> *ață de la mort*, used to bind the deceased's legs in the coffin) from some thorn bushes on a barren field near the village. The old lady finally died at peace, and the nurse reportedly was married shortly after.

In a case from Dumitra,[32] also in Bistrița-Năsăud, one of my informants' sisters tragically died very young, at only 21 years. The local community and the afflicted family explained this terrible occurrence as the result of the malevolent magical intervention by the mother of the young woman's love rival. The sudden, rapidly aggra-

---

[31] Fieldwork information, summer of 2008. The episode reportedly took place only a few years earlier, 2005 or 2006.

[32] Fieldwork information, summer of 2007. The tragic event unfolded at the beginning of 1980s.

vating, and strange illness could not meet a coherent medical diagnosis at that time. All the supplementary ritual interventions—consulting Orthodox monks and going through religious unwitchments; visiting lay unwitchers; and undergoing magic rituals—proved equally fruitless. In the local collective reading of the situation, the evil spell proved stronger than any type of cure, thus pushing the victim toward her ultimately fatal destiny.

The fatal outcome of such a case illustrates the highly acerbic character of marital competition. In particular, in rural areas, it is sometimes treated as life-and-death war. A spell directly connected to the binding of marriage that can potentially have a fatal effect is called *'de orândă'* in Romanian. In a localized and archaic parlance, this term signifies a spell meant to hijack or break someone else's rightfully earned marital position. In practice, the spell aims at killing an already married woman so that its beneficiary can take her place by marrying the widower. The suspicion of such a case arises especially when: the presupposed victim suddenly falls ill, afflicted by an unexplained affection, and dies quickly; the widower remarries after a short while; the woman who replaces the first wife is not, from the point of view of the local community, a partner of equal social status and is known as a 'woman who knows how to handle those things' (Rom. > *femeie ce ştie a face*). The extreme lethal effect of these type of spells is assigned to the fact that they ultimately belong to the larger category 'of/from the dead' spells (Rom> *vrăji de la mort*), the most feared kind of sorcery, considered in today's explanatory mythology to be the only one that is potentially unbreakable.

It is easy to observe then how the suspicion of witchcraft spread within a rural community can be sufficient to discredit a person and their family. In time, if various unexplained events can be linked to such a person or family by the local community and read as facts proving their witchcraft wrongdoings, the suspicion becomes an irrevocable social stigma.

Q.: How would you know who are the people who ... you know, it's better to stay away from?
A.: Well, you know because you hear about it around, you listen to people talking. Now, if the mother knows how to handle those things, they say the daughter knows too, you know? And that's a thing to consider. At any rate, one has to stay away from those ... those evil doers.' (Rodica, woman, age 53, Râşca village)

For this reason, making an unfounded witchcraft accusation can function as a social strategy to disrepute others. For instance, in a case from Reteag (Bistriţa-Năsăud, North Transylvania, 2007–2008), one local nursery teacher started to invest a lot of time and effort in disseminating the accusation that a woman from a certain family threw spells and magically bound the marriage chances of her neighbors' daughters in favor of her family's own eligible young women. This spreading of rumors seemed transparently linked to an ownership dilemma: the nursery teacher and her husband were living, at the time of my research, in an old woman's house, to whom they were related to as godchildren.[33] Clearly, the right of ownership of the house, in the case of old lady's demise, fell on the biological family of the latter: the very family accused of witchcraft. Godchildren have no right of inheritance and would find themselves with no place to live unless the lady's will explicitly states otherwise. Therefore, the accusation strategy can function as a way of gathering public support from the local community, particularly from the pre-

[33] The godchildren–godparent relation still functions in contemporary Romania as a type of *spiritual* kingship (named as such and differentiated from consanguinity and affinity by H. H. Stahl, 'Rudenie spirituală din năşie la Drăguş', *Sociologie românească*, vol.1, no. 7–9, (1936), Bucureşti). Through both or either of two of the Holy Mysteries, baptism and marriage, the Godparents become lifelong responsible for the child's or the couple's spiritual well-being. Unregulated (and thus nonexistent) from a legal point of view, the institution of godparent kinship was, nonetheless, always highly functional and based on a specific set of mutual rights and obligations, going well beyond the strictly canonical indications of the Church. Dejan Dimitrijevic-Rufu offers an illustrative description of the spiritual guardian angel and social integrator roles played by the godparent, in his study 'Rites de passage, identité ethnique, identité nationale. Le cas d'une communauté roumaine de Serbie', *Terrain*, n° 22, p. 119–134, ‹http://terrain.revues.org/3092› [accessed July the 2th, 2007]

supposed victims' families, which in the end can lead to public, if tacit, disparagement of the accused family and, more importantly, to the elderly lady's decision to disinherit her biological family in favor of her godchildren.

Gossip has been widely discussed in anthropological literature either as an institution of social control (usually among peers)[34] or as a form of deflected protest[35] in social contexts where status differences do not allow more room for direct expressions of antagonism. For instance, Staley Brandes shows how the folkloristic narratives pursued by the villagers from Spain, Brittany, or Portugal create the image of the hypocritical, oversexed, and greedy priest, thus undermining the clerical status by gossip and slander.[36] In the context of gossip as a social value maintaining control among peers, as discussed by Regina Dionisopoulos-Mass, the aspect relevant to the Reteag case is the fact that it highlights what exactly is considered a social deviation. However untrue, believed, or not entirely believed by members of the local community, the accusations spread by the nursery teacher point to the fact that witchcraft is a form of disreputable deviance. And, from the point of view of knowledge as equipment for living, such accusations cannot be simply muted, overlooked, or ignored.

Unhappy Marriage, Problematic Love Relationship

A connected yet different situation occurs when the parents of one part of a couple (in many cases the man's parents[37]) reach the

---

34 Regina Dionisopoulos-Mass, 'The Evil Eye and Bewitchment in a Peasant Village', *The Evil Eye*, ed. by Clarence Maloney (New York: Columbia University Press, 1976), pp. 42–62, p. 53.

35 Stanley Brandes, 'Conclusion: Reflections on the Study of Religious Orthodoxy and Popular Faith in Europe', in *Religious Orthodoxy and Popular Faith in European Society*, ed. by Ellen Badone (Princeton, New Jersey: Princeton University Press, 1990), pp. 185–200, p. 197.

36 Stanley Brandes, p. 189.

37 During my fieldwork, all the cases that I encountered where the parents were accusing the other part of operating love binding rituals (love sorcery) were the man's parents. That has to do with the perceived distribution of roles in a love-related witchcraft scenario, following the social dynamics of

conclusion that the marriage is ill-suited enough as to suggest that their son or daughter has been spell-bound. Such a suspicion comes to the fore when the partner under scrutiny does not reach certain standards (social or educational level, economic status, or family descent). Other aggravating aspects can contribute to a confirmation of the existence of a witchcraft situation, such as: the relationship between the partners is difficult, violent, and awkward; pecuniary interests are evident in the intentions of the other family; and the supposedly bewitched young person would not give up the problematic marriage relation despite advice to do so from family and friends.

It is generally believed that one obvious sign of a marriage that is forced through spells, i.e., where one of the partners is magically bound to the other, is the fact that conflicts arise between the spouses immediately after their marriage. The hallmark of such a situation is the fact that the relationship will not hold in the long run.

> *'I'm telling you, since he got married, my Adi has a bizarre behaviour. I tell him sometimes: honestly, Adi, it's like somebody washed your brains. He's completely out there... The animosity between them started no more than two months after getting married. And the priest remembered that G. (the bride) refused to drink the wine during the marriage religious service, he said she was the first one, in his experience, who did something like that*[38]*. So, he held a special religious service a month after they got married. On his own initiative, just because of the wine incident (he told me about that last time we met). And immediately they stopped getting along, completely, until they got divorced.' (Ițu, woman, age 66, Bistrița)*

---

the traditional rural society: The women are the ones who have to get married, and they are the ones who actively compete over suitors. In this competition, especially when magic is involved, men supposedly play the part of innocent, blind victims.

38 Some people believe that a bride's refusal to drink the blessed wine during the marriage religious ceremony is the clearest, irrefutable proof that she has actually spell-bound her partner. With all the obvious risk of self-exposure through such a public refusal, the potential price to pay by the presupposed magical binder if drinking that wine would have been the highest: her death. (Fieldwork information, Bistrița, Reteag: 2008; Năsăud: 2006).

'I didn't have a choice ... I had to let Aurel marry that woman. Because he had eyes only for her. Nine years they stayed together, and then—finished. It's true that I did my best for him to find another, to not take that one. He was a beautiful boy, but he destroyed himself with that one, our ex daughter-in-law. She destroyed him. I went about it one way, while they [the daughter in law and her parents] went about it the other way[39]. *(...) But it never lasts. The partner won't stay in the end with the one who binds. That's the way it is. They do it then, but afterwards it won't work anymore ... It doesn't last, it un-binds in time'. (Mărioara, woman, age 62, Reteag village)*

Laura Stark's research on witchcraft and sorcery in late 19th- and early 20th-centuries Finland also revealed this motif of forced marriage through spells. Ensnaring a husband through love magic (by feeding him food or drink in which the unmarried woman placed her own bodily fluids, for instance) was considered an illegitimate type of sorcery in Finnish rural life, and it gave rise to a number of narratives exploring the rightful consequences that await the magic-user after the marriage. In one such story, the man was fed magic substances and the couple got married, but 'almost immediately after the marriage the feeling of closeness ended and in its place came the former feeling of disgust and revulsion.'[40] With divorce hardly an option at the beginning of the 20th century, the only way out of such a situation as depicted in the folkloric Finnish narratives were: suicide or insanity of the husband or attempted murder of the wife. Ultimately, the listeners were warned that the women resorting to magic did reach their purpose (getting married); but they also condemned themselves and their partners to lifelong, bitter unhappiness.

---

39 The expression 'going about it one way' meant, in this context, that my informant sought the help from Orthodox religious rituals, while being convinced that the in-laws, at the opposite end of the scale, were dwelling into sorcery rituals—with or without professional help. Therefore, this is also a statement about moral standpoints: she did the *right* thing, while the others were doing the *wrong* things. This polarity is supposed to confirm whose side was the rightful one.

40 Laura Stark, 'Narrative and the social dynamics of magical harm in late nineteenth- and early twentieth-century Finland', *Witchcraft Continued. Popular Magic in Modern Europe*, pp. 69–88, p. 85.

In the case of contemporary Romania, the ones who go forth to remedy the situation are often the parents, frequently against the wishes or even without the knowledge of their son or daughter. The ultimate purpose of the magical–religious therapeutic intervention is to break up the couple, regardless of whether or not they are married already. In the context of the patriarchal values that are still persistent in Romania, divorce remains a social practice discouraged for men and women alike. Gail Kligman's research from 1978 in Ieud, Maramureş (Northern Transylvania) showed how, with the communist regime in full force, the villagers 'attributed the high natality and the absence of divorce to the tenacity of religious and secular tradition.'[41] Divorce in rural areas is still rare to this day, whereas the national divorce/marriage ratio for 2010 stood at 28%.[42] Such statistics, as much as they can illustrate contemporary practice, can do little to illuminate the dominant discourses behind them, and one of those is the perception of divorce as an individual's failure, the suggestion that, if she or he could not last in a marriage, there must be 'something wrong' with that person.

This can serve to demonstrate how serious a case must be before parents would think of assuming it to be the outcome of a witchcraft situation. The witchcraft discourse actually surpasses the value of marriage and even the parent's fear to condemn their son/daughter to the still enduring social stigma of divorce.

Inexplicable Illnesses, 'Mal de Vivre'

Another life situation that is often diagnosed as the result of a witchcraft attack is that of prolonged illnesses and misfortunes, frequently combined with anxiety and depression. Although the medical discourse often can explain the mechanism of singular diseases,

41 Gail Kligman, *The Wedding of the Dead. Ritual, Poetics and Popular Culture in Transylvania* (Berkeley, Los Angeles, and London: University of California Press, 1988), p. 26.

42 The divorce to marriage ratio is the number of divorces to the number of marriages in a given year (the ratio of the crude divorce rate to the crude marriage rate). ‹http://en.wikipedia.org/wiki/Divorce_demography› [accessed April 7, 2015]

it cannot explain the recurrence of many illnesses nor the variation in form of the symptoms. By contrast, a diagnosis of a sorcery intervention can explain both the recurrences and the form variations.

Even in our modern society, an illness is perceived to be fundamentally irrational. On an individual level, when it becomes personal and concrete, an illness is something that should not have happened: 'For the ordinary layman disease is not a rational mechanistic process of bacterial infection but a "thing," a sort of pervading mysterious essence that strikes you out of the blue. (...) Even the expression "to be taken ill" suggests such an infestation of evil presences.'[43]

Knowledge of its physical causes is not able to eradicate the fundamental irrationality of a disease as it is perceived by the afflicted individuals and those close to them. Grafted on this subjective sensitivity, this irrationality of an illness can turn into the irrationality of a malefic witchcraft intervention since they share the same feeling of an arbitrary, undeserved evil attacking from the exterior. However, an illness situation evolves into the suspicion of witchcraft only when the diagnosis is sustained by cumulative, aggravating factors: the medical diagnosis proves uncertain and contradictory; some symptoms disappear only to be replaced by others; the state of suffering is aggravated by other misfortunes and adversities (death in the family, loss of employment, financial difficulties, etc.). In the end, only the witchcraft diagnosis can make some sense out of such a disconcerting state marked by chaotic situations, intense emotional stress, fear, loss of control, and the feeling of a generalized evil contaminating one's life.

> *'You wouldn't believe how much my Luci's behaviour changes the minute we cross the border ... (...) I'm telling you, the moment we get into the car at home and until we get to the border, he's like a crazy person: anything annoys him, he shouts, then his chest hurts (you know, his heart condition). Once we cross the border, everything changes completely; he is the most polite, warmest, most attentive human being. Sometimes I can't believe my*

---

43 E. R. Leach, 'Primitive Magic and Modern Medicine', *Health Education Journal*, 7 (1949), 162–170, ‹http://hej.sagepub.com› [accessed October 27, 2007], p. 167.

eyes, the transformation. And the same coming back home: all is well until we cross the border back. (...) And the way he is at home, everyday: when it's not the heart, it's the kidneys, or the liver; everything he tries is cursed, he went bankrupt twice; and he always shouts and curses, at me and the girls... I know he can be different, I've seen it with my own eyes ... when travelling outside of the country. That's why I think they [his relatives from another town] have put a spell on him, to kill him or drive him mad, so that he wouldn't claim the inheritance. In this rhythm, they will succeed too, because he continues to refuse to see a priest. It's been more than 4 years now, of hell and suffering ...' (Rodi, woman, age 59, Bistrița)

'I think it was last year sometimes when M., the neighbour, came to see me and said to me: "You know what, Maria? There is only one possible explanation for this, for all of this: that somebody did some spells to harm you. Let me know if you intend to do something about it, I know a priest who can help." I'm not the one to be interested in these types of ideas, never was interested in these old wives tales. And yet ... after all this time, after all this pain, after it never ending, it suddenly occurred to me there might be something true... or possible, in this idea. M. said it's the only thing that can account for everything, for every year in the hospital, for very new illness, for me never feeling well, for fighting so much with him... for all, really. The only explanation is that N.'s ex [her partner's ex-wife] did some spells to harm me. After a while, I felt it's a possibility. And I went along with the unwitching.' (Maria, woman, age 56, Bistrița)

This is the type of an extremely difficult situation explained as a witchcraft intervention that fits best Favret-Saada's description mentioned at the beginning of this chapter: a long crisis, unsolvable by the means of the positivist or religious discourse, cumulative, and continuously changing in form. More often than not, it takes the intervention of a third-party annunciator to name this crisis as a possible effect of witchcraft, like in the above-mentioned example of Maria. At the individual level, the finding of a name for a previously unexplained and seemingly unsolvable period of duress is an incredibly liberating moment for the afflicted actor. From there on, she/he can actively concentrate on what to do rather than helplessly wait for the next blind blow.

As for the reasons why someone would commit magical aggressions, possible explanations include: pure envy, revenge, and unfair competition on the marital market. Some even believe that certain people are irrevocably destined to be evil:

> *The priest told me this: there are evildoers in this world. I didn't understand, as long as I never hurt somebody. But he said there are evildoers, God left them like this ... to hurt other people. They can't help themselves, they can't do otherwise. (Rodica, woman, age 53, Râşca village).*

But as soon as a diagnosis is established and a potential aggressor identified, the reasons behind the witchcraft attack become irrelevant. The only concern for the victim is to undertake the long process of religious and/or magical therapy, promising to restore her/his normal life.

Identifying the aggressor and deducing the reasons for the intended forms of harm have always played an essential role in the traditional witchcraft discourse, everywhere in Europe. In contemporary Romania, it is strongly discouraged under the influence of religious Orthodox discourse. Just like the aggression involved in throwing back an evil spell (the hallmark of a laic unwitching process), meditating upon an aggressor's reasons can induce negative feelings within the victim that are contrary to Christian morality and could interfere with the purifying purpose of the therapeutic religious ritual.

Milk Mana and Fertility Transfer

Mana is a word of Melanesian origin that entered the language of classical anthropology at the end of 19th century through Robert Codrington's work of 1891 and quickly evolved into a key concept. The author (a missionary) defined mana as 'a force altogether distinct from physical power, which acts in all kinds of ways for good and evil, and which it is of the greatest advantage to possess or control.'[44] This concept was initially seen by classical anthropology as specific to outer-European societies. One notion often employed by anthropologists of that period to make *mana* more comprehensible to a European academic public was *energy* but defined as of a su-

---

44 Robert Codrington, The Melanesians: Studies in Their Anthropology and Folklore (Oxford: Clarendon Press, 1891), p. 118.

pernatural, impersonal kind: a potency-related force, transmissible, and contagious. Although manifesting itself through any imaginable inanimate object or being (from peculiarly shaped stones to animals, from living individuals to ghosts), mana was an impersonal principle distinct and independent from any such exterior vehicles.

In Romanian traditional rural culture, *mana* is a magical category describing, similar to the classical anthropology's key concept, potency-related, impersonal, natural forces such as fertility and fecundity which can be lost, stolen, protected, and transferred. However, the difference between this mana of a European rural context and the one researched by 19th-century anthropology in 'exotic' settings is that the former has a limited coverage: Romanian mana would never be linked by peasants to inanimate objects, wild animals, or human beings (alive or ghosts). As pointed out by Gheorghe Pavelescu, 'a being is a mana carrier only if that being is useful to humans.'[45] Therefore, this particular notion of mana privileges and is limited to the immediate points of interest of human subsistence, i.e., vegetal and animal lives sustaining a rural economy. This Romanian mana category is first and foremost linked to milk production, but it is equally important to defend, maintain, or supplement the crops' mana through magic means. As such, it can be included in what George M. Foster described as the concept of 'limited good,' crucial to the understanding of any traditional European peasant world view:

'By "Image of Limited Good" I mean that broad areas of peasant behaviour are patterned in such a fashion as to suggest that peasants view their social, economic, and natural universes—their total environment—as one in which all of the desired things in life such as land, wealth, health, friendship and love, manliness and honour, respect and status, power and influence, security and safety, *exist in*

45 Gheorghe Pavelescu, *Magia la români: Studii şi cercetări despre magie, descântece şi mană* (Bucureşti: Minerva, 1998), p. 273. [My translation]

finite quantity and *are always in short supply,* as far as the peasant is concerned.'[46]

The *mana,* as a staple term in Romanian for the mysterious forces behind more concrete manifestations of fertility, fecundity, and abundance, is conceived as occurring in nature in limited quantity only; therefore, the only way to supplement one's own allotment is at the expense of someone else's allotment. Given the harsh realities of rural life—marked by scarce resources, where long hours of hard physical work produce just enough to keep the household going—the level of agricultural production in traditional rural societies usually aimed at day-to-day subsistence. Surplus in any form was rare, always noted in the community, and met with envy or suspicion. Envy meant that the better-off person made herself/himself a potential target to the evil eye or sorcery attacks—which is why it was considered wise to try and hide or at least not publicly flaunt, economic success. If somebody all of a sudden started to do well, the other members of the local community would suppose that this was only possible through an increase of luck. And given the notion of limited good, this could only occur through the hijacking of someone else's prosperity and good fortune.

Households, as the minimal and only production cell in a traditional rural economy, were constantly in a state of competition with one another over the resources available to them. As noted by Laura Stark for the case of late 19th-century to early 20th-century Finland,[47] this meant that neighboring farm households were often engaged in sorcery wars with one another. This constant suspicion of one's neighbor was in fact one of the marks of traditional rural witchcraft all over Europe: a neighbor is not close enough to truly be part of the inner circle (not a family member) but close-by and thus provided with physical access by geographic vicinity; neighbors also have the best reasons to commit magical aggressions in order to

46 George M. Foster, 'Peasant Society and the Image of Limited Good', *American Anthropologist,* 67 (1965), p. 296.

47 Laura Stark, 'Narrative and the social dynamics of magical harm in late nineteenth- and early twentieth-century Finland', p. 71.

steal prosperity and increase their own. Add to this the frequent conflicts between neighboring families (border and land disputes), and we can easily understand why the first one suspected in any witchcraft situation was the geographic neighbor.

Jeanne Favret-Saada's field research in Western France between 1969 and 1971 shows how in the French case witchcraft attacks were often targeted at the leader of an agricultural unit, i.e., the male head of the household. Even when those who suffer the effects of such a magical aggression are the wife and/or the children, the one it is ultimately aimed at is the man.[48] This centripetal 'escalation policy'[49] is based on the relation established between the body of the targeted man and all those elements affected *in his stead* (his wife, his children, his animals, his tools, and his mechanical means of production). Distinctively different from the Cartesian self, defined as separated from all the exterior attributes of this self, the bewitched's self is constituted by himself plus his possessions, the entire social and spatial ensemble attached to his name. The potential victim's vital force (or bioeconomical potential) is directly proportional to this social body placed in his possession. Furthermore, from a topological point of view, this vital force is invested in a space: Every familial head owns one clearly delimitated spatial territory where he and his possessions reside. The consequence of this distribution of visible space and invisible vital force is that there is no *vacant* vital space: 'There is a vital space completely occupied by domains, each carrying the name of their possessors.'[50] In this topology of space and correspondent bioeconomical potentials, one can economically achieve only as much as one's own space and possessions allow. The witch is the only one imagined as not playing by these rules of direct proportionality to possessions. Motivated by jealousy, the magical aggressor tries to steal as much vital force as possible from the victim in order to significantly increase her/his

---

48 Jeanne Favret-Saada, p. 333.

49 Jeanne Favret-Saada, p. 334.

50 Jeanne Favret-Saada, *Deadly Words. Witchcraft in the Bocage* (Cambridge: Cambridge University Press, 2010), p. 197.

own bioconomic potential. This is a classic case of what Liiceanu[51] called 'favourability transfer' (already mentioned in the **Introduction**): vital force is set in motion through magical force, resulting in a winning side and a losing side. A significant gain in this scenario can only be achieved through the hijacking of vital force belonging to another name in favor to one's own name and possession.

During my research in Northern Transylvania, I have encountered such transfers of favorability through magic means in two significant forms.

The first of those is the binding of marriage of a young woman, as discussed earlier. This type of witchcraft situation represents a transfer of favorability only when it not only victimizes the intended target but also affords a gain on the side of the aggressor: Another young woman, less naturally endowed or less lucky, suddenly acquires success and more opportunities of marriage. The same magical transfer, in an extreme form, can be identified with the '*de orândă*' (>Rom.) spells, through which the potential beneficiary (spinster, widow, or widower) tries to gain a marital place that is already occupied by the person targeted and, thus, can be obtained only through killing that person.

The second form in which the favorability transfer most often occurred is intimately linked to the milk mana theft complex, an ever-present magical threat against which people still take magical precautions today, even when they explicitly state their objectivist reservations. For instance, they draw a cross on the right hip of a cow with some milk, which marks the end of every evening's milking time in Râşca village. Another precautionary gesture consist in furtively throwing some salt into the milk before selling it in order to prevent the mana from leaving one's household.[52] Nevertheless, on

---

51 Aurora Liiceanu, *Povestea unei vrăjitoare* (Bucureşti: Editura ALL, 1996), p. 81.

52 Field information, Mocod, 2008, Bistrița-Năsăud County. The salt is marked out in the Romanian Ethnology as a substance symbolically standing in for the mana principle of every household, directly linked to the desired abundance. Antoaneta Olteanu, *Şcoala de şolomonie. Divinație şi vrăjitorie în context comparat* (Bucureşti: Paideia, 1999), p. 357.

the whole, milk transfer through magical theft scenarios seems to be in steep decline due to the social and economic transformations of rural areas.

In contemporary Romania, 54% of the total population live in cities while 46%[53] reside in rural areas. The whole way of life of those whose livelihoods are still based on the rural-agricultural mode of production is once again changing. The final outcome of various successive reforms that have been implemented over the past years is difficult to anticipate. Insufficient subventions, the lack of effective state support, and the contradicting character of governmental policies, all seem to warrant a rather pessimist outlook for the directly interested rural actors. There are other factors that exacerbate the situation: natural disasters (draughts and flooding) compromised the harvests of many past years; new standards, and regulations dictated by the EU membership of 2007 (whose logic tends to get lost on the sinuous path from the local authorities to the individual producer); the abandoning of villages by the youths' migration to urban areas within Romania or abroad: all these factors add up to a picture of a changing world that is reshaping the very basis of its ways of life.

In the absence of relevant statistics on this subject, it can prove quite tricky to pinpoint what exactly people in the countryside do live off. Also, the disparities in the economic profile and status between different regions are quite significant. Therefore, the few observations from my own fieldwork can only serve as general guidelines, and their validity may be rather limited to the northern part of Transylvania.

Having a household that can produce some of the necessary foods needed to sustain family members might be seen as an advantage. Historically, during the food-deprived periods of the communist regime, this has been the (only) great advantage of rural

---

53 *Rezultate definitive ale Recensământului Populației și al Locuințelor (caracteristici demografice ale populației) – 2011*, (Institutul Național de Statistică, 2011), ‹http://www.recensamantromania.ro/wp-content/uploads/2013/07/REZULTATE-DEFINITIVE-RPL_2011.pdf› [accessed December 2014], p. 1.

people compared to urban inhabitants. The collectivization allowed every family to keep and cultivate their own garden, more or less the same size they work on today; so, they managed to have most of the products that became virtually absent, or strictly rationed, in all the big cities after 1980: eggs, milk and milk-related produce, fruit, vegetables, and so on.

In rural areas, a regular cash income is not something easily obtainable in every household—in contrast to urban spaces. This is because the people in rural areas have fewer opportunities for regular employment than people in the cities—one of the reasons why young people continue rural–to-urban migration, within Romania and into foreign countries. Probably, the most commonly expressed regret that I came across in my research was that, for better or for worse, during the communist regime, the villagers were being employed, either at the collective farms or at various factories in the area (long since bankrupt or disbanded); whereas, now, employment opportunities are rare. Rural households can consist of three generations or have the grandparents living in another houses in the same courtyard with their married children and grandchildren, with at least one adult earning a stable income as an employee at the local school, the nursery, the grocery shop, the bar, the City Hall, or similar places, while the grandparents chip in with their pensions. Regardless of their personal work obligations, all adults work around the clock in the family household: They cultivate small plots of land usually adjacent to the house, where they grow local crops (potatoes, seasonal vegetables, and corn, which is mostly fed to the animals) and fruit trees; they mow the grass in the summer so they have hay to feed the livestock during the cold season; they keep cows for milk and chickens for eggs, pigs for meat, sometimes even horses for transport, all of which require constant care. Sometimes, the rural household can make some money out of selling surplus produce, either locally or to various companies collecting for processing and redistribution. However, this seems to happen less and less, as the legislation of the past few years set out to regulate this sector is often criticized as imprecise, unreliable, or simply inapplicable by the affected actors. With or without the extra income from selling extra produce, the cash income of rural households is, more often than not, quite small.

Needless to say, the rural world of today's Romania is no longer the same prewar agricultural-traditional society that was primarily based on patriarchal values and an economy of household subsistence; nor is it the rural milieu of the communist regime, where the peasant-workers were laboring the fields of the state-owned collective farms or commuted daily to work in the cities' factories. On the other hand, it is also not, or at least not yet, set up like modern farming businesses—either as large-scale, highly mechanized farms or as small-scale, family-oriented farming enterprises aiming both at income flow and sustainability. The rural northern Transylvania of today retains something of both historical local models and, at the same time, manifests an aspiration toward Western-inspired models of agricultural production.

During the summer of 2008, I had the opportunity to document the staging of an apotropaic (defensive and protective) ritual dedicated to the prevention of mana transfer by the family who lived next door to the family I was staying with in Reteag (Bistrița-Năsăud County). The reason for the ritual was that the family's cow had had a calf. In order to magically secure the new born, the cow, and its milk at one of the most vulnerable moments (as moments of passage are usually considered to be), they entwined three iron chains and placed the resulting hurdle on the stable's threshold. Neither the cow nor the calf was allowed to leave the magically protected stable for about a week. No stranger to the household (i.e., nobody apart from the resident family) was allowed to enter the courtyard or the house. Supplementary restrictions aimed at further preventing the possibility of mana transfer through loss or theft: no object or substance could leave (e.g., as a borrowing) and nothing could enter the household (as a gift).

This particular ritual has to be placed in the larger context of milk theft or milk transfer.[54] Arnold van Gennep[55] documented the existence of this ritual in Russia, usually carried out in spring when the cattle were first taken out of the stables to pasture. Aurora Liiceanu[56] and Gheorghe Pavelescu[57] confirm the same ritual staging in both Maramureş and the Apuseni Mountains in Romania. Whether a chain or a bar, one essential element used in all these rituals is the apotropaic function of iron—one of the best known and most commonly employed magically defensive substances. Another element is the specific function of the threshold, which illustrates the liminality principle perfectly. The evil to be warded off or prevented through this type of apotropaic ritual varies: premeditated attacks from mana thieves (witches); involuntary loss of mana through magical transfer; or the effect of the evil eye.

The family who performed this ritual in above-mentioned case depends mainly on income from agricultural production. The main sources of income of the household are their small state pensions, the animals they keep (cows, pigs, and poultry), small-scale potatoes, vegetables, and fruit trees cropping, and the occasional paid labor outside the household with their horse wagon. The household of this family is part of a larger context of the village's progressive structural changes. Some of the neighboring houses, inherited or bought, are being modernized by city-folks and transformed into comfortable holiday or pension retreat homes. The insidious confrontation between two very different ways of life can be best illustrated by the fact that these neighbors actively encourage those families whose income is based on an agricultural subsistence to just let it go: to sell at least some of the animals they keep in order to reduce their work volume and be able to enjoy the modern pleas-

54 For a comparative reading of this magic scenario in Eastern Europe: Marianne Mesnil, 'L'Europe des Aires Culturelles', *Premier atelier européen sur la culture orale européene* (Strasbourg: Conseil de l`Europe, 1990), pp. 206–217.

55 Arnold Van Gennep, *Riturile de trecere* (Iaşi: Polirom, 1996), p. 158.

56 Aurora Liiceanu, p.42.

57 Gheorghe Pavelescu, p. 58.

ures of leisure and holiday. It goes without saying that most of the neighbors disapproved of the above-mentioned ritual and considered it something retrograde, better suited to the distant, ignorant past than our modern time.

Intuitively, the fertility transfer theme should retain its cultural relevance in an agricultural context where the productivity of livestock and crops remains an essential day-to-day preoccupation of the household. As the above-mentioned research in rural France showed, this is particularly the case when agricultural productivity is still linked to traditional modes of production and, highly significant, the connected values are converted into terms of regional identity, marking a form of opposition to industrialization, urbanization, and standardization imposed by the creation of the French nation. And such is also the case for rural contemporary Transylvania or at least for the part where agricultural production is still relying on the quasi-traditional, minimal household-orientated mode of production. However, the part of a rural identity assumed as a badge of honor by the rural actors is less applicable to Transylvania. Similar to the English case pointed out by Owen Davies, where '*peasant* has long been used as a derogatory term denoting a backward, lowly, subservient agricultural labourer,'[58] in Romania, the corresponding term (Rom.> *ţăran*) carries a negative connotation; so much so, in fact, that it functions rarely as a self-describing term and more as an insult in daily parlance.

Be that as it may, the implicit values carried by any term cannot directly shed light on the reasons behind the decline of mana preoccupations in a rural-agricultural context, especially when within larger social context witchcraft scenarios still function as a valid explanatory discourse and the other three types described earlier (delayed marriage; unhappy marriage or problematic love relationship; and inexplicable illness, 'mal de vivre') are only being reinforced through common practice.

One crucial insight into this context is provided by the argument presented by Susan Hoyle, who discusses the decline of witchcraft

---

58 Owen Davies, p. 121.

beliefs in mid-Victorian times. She identifies as the major cause of this decline not the expected success of scientific attitudes but the rise in popularity of a new type of narrative: the detective story. As the argument goes, the witchcraft discourse is a narrative, a way of connecting events and facts into a coherent story line according to specific criteria of plausibility. But so are all the other explanatory narrative schemes available out there at any given time in a multi-voiced society: They all are ways of converting selected events into connected story line sequences governed by the causality principle. As Hoyle suggests, the matter might not be how well (i.e., scientifically correct) these narratives respond to human life dilemmas but how *fashionably* they do so: 'There is increasing evidence that the advance of science and scientific attitudes makes little difference to what we believe. (...) What people believe does change, that much is clear, but why is far less so. I suggest that it has something to do with fashions in stories and story-telling. If it is a good story, then people believe it until a better story comes along; what is good and what is better is the moot point.'[59] If the case in point for Hoyle is the decline of the witchcraft discourse's whole narrative scheme for the English society once new, forensic stories gained popularity during the 19th century, the case of contemporary northern Transylvania is that of the progressive decline of only one of the local witchcraft discourse's main four themes, i.e., the milk and mana transfer. Interestingly, the more successful counternarrative usually referred to in my informants' accounts is that of the veterinarian.

> *'Q: How did you know your cow's milk has been [magically] stolen?*
> *A: Well, you saw that the cow suddenly had sore udders, and wouldn't stay to be milked ... and also the milk would be blue, thin and very little. That's when we were saying that somebody must've stolen her milk. Nowadays they put some ointments on, give it some jabs, the vet comes and sees ... Back then, we didn't have those. We only knew of 'bozgoane' [physical object-spells]. But now there are drugs and medicine and stuff like that. Well,*

59 Susan Hoyle, 'The witch and the detective: mid-Victorian stories and beliefs', *Witchcraft Continued. Popular Magic in Modern Europe*, pp. 3–68, p. 64.

after all, people don't even keep cows the way they used to... (Măriuța, woman, age 77, Giurgești village)

The veterinarian's narrative is now the one usually called upon to explain the diminishing quantity or quality of the milk provided by the family cow. It does so by providing medical explanations and remedies that are trusted to work better than the witchcraft diagnosis and the corresponding remedies. The vet's skills and tools (the syringe, the jabs, and the ointments) contribute to the staging of a more convincing healing story line than the bygone cunning woman, her herbs, and her incantations. The belief invested in the healing potential is essentially the same, only the main characters and the story supported by them have changed.

However, by decline of the transfer of favorability scenario, I do not mean demise. As Ioan Pop-Curşeu's observations from 2008 in Geoagiu de Sus (Apuseni Mountains) prove,[60] it only took a seemingly harder to explain situation for the mana transfer through witchcraft scenario to be accessed again. Several families from the center of that village complained that their cows stopped giving milk as richly as expected and that it was thin and spoiled too quickly. They accused a local woman known for her magical abilities to steal the milk's mana and suspected her of working the spells together with her son. The situation reportedly improved only after one of the supposed victims managed to steal a grape from the suspected woman's courtyard: Apparently, the milk is expected to bounce back after the afflicted actor steals something from the suspected aggressor. In the Apuseni region, as is usually the case for mountain areas, people rely more on livestock than on field work. If they maintain this as the main occupation and source of income, then it is safe to suppose that the witchcraft scenario of the mana transfer will continue to be relevant for all situations that the local veterinary might be unable to explain.

There is one more aspect to emphasize: this transfer of favorability theme of the witchcraft discourse is the only one out of the four

60 Ioan Pop-Curşeu, *Magie şi vrăjitorie în cultura română* (Iaşi: Polirom, 2013), p. 341.

discussed here that cannot migrate to urban milieus. The other three are witchcraft scenarios that I was able to document in cities and villages equally. They hold a general relevance in the Romanian society of today because they are versatile and can thus answer life crises, unhappiness, and difficult situations of teachers, public officials, lawyers, peasants, workers, pensioners, or students—of any actor who has some sort of personal exposure to the witchcraft discourse. By contrast, the mana transfer could not hold any relevance in any other context than the rural agricultural life because it is so intimately linked to the specific concerns of agricultural livelihood. Its occasional revival or complete disappearance will depend entirely on the direction the changes of rural life in Romania take, whereas the other themes will likely continue to be applicable regardless of the particular social context. It is also important to stress that, as long as we talk about those types of witchcraft that ascribe misfortune to other human beings, it does hardly matter what particular theme one deals with, nor does the analytical distinction of urban/rural carry much weight: It is the European rural-traditional witchcraft scenario that is at work here. The fact that it has migrated from rural life and adapted to city life in Romania points to the potential of the witchcraft discourse to explain and solve unhappiness, whereas socially it has a lot to do with the transformations that followed the demise of the communist regime. I will discuss this more in the fourth chapter of this book, **Magic and Religion.**

1.2 Symptoms, Signs, and Signals of a Witchcraft Situation

The concrete circumstances facilitating the entrance into the witchcraft discourse can be sudden or temporally extended. What both these cases have in common is the fact that they function as a psychological threshold and a temporal milestone, marking the moment when the actor draws the line and, from there on, enters the witchcraft discourse as bewitched.

Some of the most common symptoms suggesting a diagnosis of bewitchment are: physical pain, inexplicable sudden illness, altercations in the family, and any other types of violence characterized by sudden, brutal breakouts, and acute manifestations.

'G.'s mother used to come to visit, and she stayed for hours on end. Every time after her leaving, these horrible head and back pains would start right away ... I was feeling so sick every time, that I just can't describe. I can't describe that pain. Rodica [the neighbour] was absolutely terrified.' (Ițu, woman, age 66, Bistrița)

'I was visiting an aunt of mine one time, on Epiphany. Nothing wrong, I was jolly, healthy, happy ... normal, for the 27 years I was then. And on my way to her I just dropped in the middle of the road and couldn't walk anymore. A stabbing pain here, in the gut, paralysed me. My mum and my sister in law carried me on their arms to our destination. Afterwards, the doctors from Timişoara did all kinds of tests on me, kept me in the hospital and did everything they could think of on me, but nothing, no diagnosis or cure was found. And I was dying! Finally, I found a cunning woman in Timişoara who managed to turn it around.'[61] (Mārioara, woman, age 62, Reteag village).

'I'm telling you, for a very long time, every Christmas and Easter there was scandal in our house. The old woman [the mother of my informant's son-in-law] did something[62] to ensure there's always a row in the house, so that her son can act as the master. They always lived with the impression that we didn't really accept him. I mean, such a roistering, that all the neighbours were overhearing it—to die of shame. Never ever was any scandal or shameful things of the sort in our house before ... Now, thank God, all is good and peaceful, but that only happened after the old woman's death'. (Floricuța, woman, age 63, Dumitra village).

Such signals of acute intensity hinting at a suspicious situation are typologically opposed (though they can in practice also be juxtaposed) to another way of recognizing the presence of an anomaly: the retrospective evaluation. When the victim traces events backward from a milestone moment, unconnected events can suddenly appear to be both linked and suspicious. They may include a de-

---

61 'To turn it around' means to retrace the steps of the spell backward in order to neutralize it to the point of returning to the initial state, previous to the imbalance caused by installation of the evil spell. More often than not, this process was complemented with the redirecting of the spell back to its original sender by the laic unwitcher.

62 That is, she threw a spell.

layed marriage, unfulfilled desires, multiple inexplicable misfortunes, and so on. As Edmund Leach observed, 'the diagnosis of sorcery is normally retrospective—a kind of symptom analysis.'[63]

In both approaches, the moment of diagnosis involves the recollection and analysis of all previous episodes that generated suspicions. It also provides the motivation for following a set of actions in the future. The suspicion of bewitchment does not arise from the moment of crisis alone but requires the identification of previous 'evidence.' This evidence consists mainly of bad relationships and problematic incidents or conflicts with relatives, neighbors, or acquaintances. There is also the particular situation of a community's general suspicion regarding a particular individual, considered skilled or prone to witchcraft interests and activities, with which the presupposed victim remembers having direct contact in the recent past. The bottom-line is that any witchcraft diagnosis is also the starting point of the long process of retrospectively reinterpreting happenings, discussions, and interactions as parts (signs) of the bewitchment.

There is a set of very direct and visible 'signs' in the presence of which the actors instantaneously assume the fact that they are entering a witchcraft situation. The relatively unitary term naming them, in Northern Transylvania, is '*bozgoane*/*blozgoane*' (>Rom.), meaning thrown, tangible, physical spells.

These are signs in the sense highlighted by Victor Turner[64]: unlike a symbol, which is 'the best possible expression of relatively *unknown* fact, a fact, however, which is none the less recognized or postulated as existing,' a sign represents 'an analogous or abbreviated expression of a *known* thing.' Thrown charms are easily recognizable as such, especially in rural communities, because they are limited to a single referent through cultural convention. *Bozgoane* usually consist of a collection of substances and things (feathers,

63 E.R. Leach, p. 163.

64 Victor Turner, following Carl Jung's distinction between 'sign' and 'symbol', in *The Forrest of Symbols. Aspects of Ndembu Ritual* (Ithaca: Cornell University Press, 1976), p. 26.

hair, ash, horseradish, nails, dirt from unclean ravines, etc.) wrapped in paper.[65] Common belief has it that they should never be too closely examined: One ought to avoid touching them in order to avoid direct contamination. In Reteag, special attention is paid to dead frogs or coal found in one's path. The former is considered to be commonly employed in spells, and the latter could easily be not proper coal but the residues of burnt substances during a sorcery ritual. The identification and the subsequent diagnosis of such thrown charms are irrevocable if they are found inside the domestic perimeter (under the bed, under the TV stand, on the roof corner) or anywhere within its exterior border (near the gate, near the house's door, under the threshold, on the alley, or anywhere in the garden). Through extension, any suspect and out-of-place object can present itself as a potentially evil spell-carrier object: a fancy evening dress found on a hay heap; a chicken egg recovered from the exterior corner of the roof; even a horseshoe in the middle of the road.

That is why the inhabitants of Râşca refrain from touching or picking up any strangely placed objects they occasionally find lying in their path. For this specific local rule of conduct, both I and my colleague Iulia Hossu proved insufficiently prepared by our previous theoretical ethnological readings. While taking a stroll together with Măriuța (woman, age 44, farmer), one of our informants during our first research in Râşca (2005), my colleague asked whether people in the village put lost horseshoes one would occasionally find lying around on their stables for good luck. We had formed the idea from ethnological literature that horseshoes would always be associated with good luck in European, and especially Romanian, rural culture. The question was met with sudden, tense silence on part of our friend; she scrutinized us with suspicion before answering with another question, seemingly unrelated: Where and when exactly did Iulia see such an object? Iulia was made to answer a precise, quick

65 In Dumitra, such a ball of paper discovered in the living room corner had written on it the name of the beneficiary of the thrown spell, whereas in Giurgeşti, a similar paper was inscribed with the name of the intended victim.

line of questioning through which, we later realized, Măriuța was trying to find out who might be a potential magical aggressor or a witchcraft victim (i.e., the person in front of whose house said horseshoe had been placed) and how long ago this was (i.e., whether the threat was still present). So, while we had assumed universal cultural values as they are usually presented within ethnological literature, Măriuța translated the information into the local code of witchcraft, with no point of intersection to our own code.

When found on neutral ground, away from any direct addressee, any out-of-place object is usually interpreted as *'bozgoană'* and evokes the danger of attaching itself to the first passer-by foolish enough to touch it—according to the belief that any thrown spell *has to cling to somebody*. At the same time, it visually evokes the obscure, gratuitous, and, above all, indiscriminating threat of pure evil in this world.

In all the cases I documented throughout my research in present-day Romania, the spell is transmitted through a concrete medium: thrown charms (*bozgoane*). The physicality of the malefic spell-carrier object suggests that having a concrete transfer agent for the aggressive intention is an absolutely indispensable condition for the spell to travel and to clinch to its victim.

If the afflicted actor cannot recall any contact with a potential *bozgoană* in the near past, the attention shifts toward other possibilities of transfer. Spells can also operate through ingestion or physical touch. Such potential vehicles of transmitting evil spell are usually identified retrospectively and do not sustain a synchronous decoding like proper *bozgoane*-signs. They can take many forms: the flowers or the chocolate given as a present by a guest[66] (the presupposed magical aggressor); anything to eat or drink, already contaminated[67]; the traditional plum brandy and cake consumed at a wedding,[68] and so on. The spell is caught like a contagious disease through direct points of contact with its addressee—in a very similar

66 Fieldwork information, Bistrița, 2008.

67 Fieldwork information, Râşca, Cluj County, 2006.

68 Fieldwork information, Dumitra, Bistrița-Năsăud County, 2008.

manner to the way we imagine germs and bacteria to work. The concreteness and physicality of the transmitting vehicle (touched, steeped on, and ingested) does, however, not take away from the fact that magical force is a compulsory quality required from the presumed attacker. As **Chapter 2** of this book will show, any spell (or a spell-carrier object) means absolutely nothing without the *grace* (Rom.> *har*), a type of supersensible power common to both magical and religious specialists.

Hence, the degree of certainty when identifying an object as a sign of a witchcraft situation can vary. Most often, the importance of an object within a witchcraft affair becomes transparent only through recollection: a seemingly inconspicuous ingested, touched, or stepped on element can prove to be the very agent of infestation. Sometimes the mere placement, the strangeness of finding a certain object in a certain place can raise the suspicion.

At other times, there is no uncertainty: the actors instantly assume they are forcibly part of a witchcraft situation as intended recipients of the spell. Such is the case when proper *'bozgoane'* are discovered inside the household perimeter or when a rag doll pierced with a wooden stake is found near the house gate.[69] Such a direct confrontation with an object read as a thrown spell amounts to an instant entrance into the witchcraft discourse, particularly when the finder's whole life context of late can certify this diagnosis through the presence of various misfortunes, proving the fact that the spell had already clinched. This acknowledgment forces immediate action.

The Pink Dress

It was in October, about 15 years ago in the village Râşca in the Apuseni Mountains. Rodica was preparing to throw some hay from the barn loft in order to feed the cows, as she did every morning. Once she climbed the hayloft, she suddenly spotted, to her amazement, a pink evening dress sitting on top of the hay. It was a very

---

69 Field information from Tiha village, Bistriţa-Năsăud County, 2008. This episode took place in 1986.

fancy dress, made out of crepe, and decorated with white lace and ornate buttons. As she was staring at it, not knowing what to do or think, her husband Gheorghiță came along to join her. They took the dress down and examined it, without touching it directly—only with the hayfork. After a while of looking at it and discussing it, Rodica wanted to put the dress on fire. But Gheorghiță did not agree. He insisted they take it with the fork and dump it in the little stream of water marking the boundary to their neighbor.[70]

On the next morning, Rodica was still deeply bothered by the incident. She had some purchases to make and went to the dairy shop. When she saw that there were no other customers, she decided to speak to the dairy lady about what happened. As it turned out, she knew more about it than Rodica had hoped: Apparently, the dress belonged to Mariana, a woman living couple of houses down from the shop. Mariana had complained about a valuable pink evening dress gone missing from her home at some point during the Pentecost holiday—how come Rodica had not heard anything about it, she added?

Although apprehensive, Rodica needed some sort of explanation; so, she decided to go straight to Mariana and ask her. Mariana was home that morning and invited Rodica in. Her fist reaction after hearing Rodica's story was to confront her: '*Now you talk to me straight, Rodica. Now you tell me: are you the one who took my dress from my home?*' Deeply resentful of this accusation, Rodica denied. Then, the two women set off to see the dress and talk to Rodica's husband Gheorghiță, as a direct witness to the dress' discovery. Mariana immediately recognized the pink dress as hers, listened again to the story, but was still expecting a resolution in the form of the two spouses admitting to theft. When that did not happen, she took the dress and left home. Both she and the couple, far from hav-

70 In the region, it is believed that torching a potential *bozgoană* would only unleash its destructive magical charge. Putting it on water, on the other hand, is believed to neutralize its malefic power. Women are the ones usually credited with possessing knowledge of this kind. In this case, the man was more aware of the conventions of handling such a dangerous object.

ing set the record straight, remained resentful and distrustful of each other.

After another sleepless night, Rodica set off in the early morning to consult a priest from another village, about 15 km from Râşca. She had never been there, nor had ever consulted that priest before, but he had a reputation for being able to offer answers and solutions to strange, complex situations—just like the one Rodica was dealing with then. She reached the priest's house around 7.30 a.m., hoping that he was awake. Seeing a light in the front room, she mustered up all her courage and started to knock at the door. She immediately stopped when the priest shouted from the room: '*Have you got no soul? I'm only a human too, why do you people keep bothering me so early?*' So, she waited in silence for a while, fearful and intimidated. When he was ready, the priest opened the front door and ceremoniously invited Rodica in. She briefly told her story and asked him to shed some light on the mysterious apparition of the pink dress in her hay.

The first thing the priest did was to confirm he actually knew about the affair but in a rather unexpected way: Apparently not long after the dress' disappearance, Mariana's husband had come to see this same priest about it. He brought along some staple of wood as payment for the priest, with the request that the latter would hold future masses and prayers designed to identify the thief.[71] The priest told Rodica about all this in order to see her reaction: in all likelihood, there was a chance that she was the thief he was trying to smoke out through ritual interventions. Her guilt or innocence was to be established there and then: He stepped into the next

71 As suggested by Gheorge Pavelescu and Éva Pócs' research in Transylvania, the Orthodox priest gets to play the part of village witch in some rural communities. One of his abilities is to identify and punish thieves when hired to do so, through the means of religious ritual: He can conduct a curse-mass or recite prayers to punish the guilty (reading the Psalter) in conjunction with the afflicted family's fasting. Gheorghe Pavelescu, p. 48; Éva Pócs, 'Curse, *maleficium*, divination: witchcraft on the borderline of religion and magic', *Witchcraft Continued. Popular Magic in Modern Europe*, pp. 174–190.

room, put the liturgical garments on and then invited Rodica to join him. The room, smaller than the first one, was filled with religious icons, books, and candles, suggesting that it was often used as a space for prayer. Following the standard protocol for such situations, Rodica kneeled and the priest lifted his priestly stole, placing it above her head.[72] He started to read and recite a set of prayers, most of them following the structure of a curse rather than grace. If Rodica had been the thief, she was expected to shake, sweat, and collapse under the weight of the ritual: The truly guilty are not supposed to resist the power of priestly maledictions. But, Rodica did not budge and showed no sign whatsoever of being affected. Therefore, at the end of the ritual, the priest asked her to rise and congratulated her: It was clearly established now that she was not the culprit. But then, who was? And to what avail?

The priest was unable to answer those questions. In his view, the most likely scenario was this: Somebody had stolen the pink dress from Mariana's home, either as simple theft or as a potential physical agent to be used in directly targeted sorcery rituals.[73] The priest's own rituals aiming at unmasking the thief, effectively working as a curse, must have brought a lot of distress and misfortune into the thief's life (just as they were meant to), leaving that person with no other choice but to get rid of the object through which this rightful punishment was finding its way. So, he or she must have chucked the dress randomly in the first convenient place.

However welcome it was to Rodica, this explanation did not go a long way with view of dissipating the tensions created by the incident between Rodica's and Mariana's families. On the contrary:

72 Kneeling in front of the priest is also the physical position required for confession in the Orthodox Church.

73 A maleficent spell is believed to work best when it incorporates something with direct connection to the target's body, a category ranging from bodily fluids, hair or nails, to clothing, jewelry, and anything worn or touched by the potential victim. This follows the contiguity principle in magic: 'the identification of a part with the whole.' The part stands for the complete object, and the separation in no way disturbs the contiguity. Marcell Mauss, *A General Theory of Magic* (London and New York: Routledge, 2001), p. 79.

'From thereon, we kind of kept ... a grudge, a suspicion, one to another. We kept our distance and our mutual distrust to this day.' These conclusive words were uttered by Rodica with a hint of regret. But, as regrettable as it is, the situation seems nonetheless unavoidable. Once the faintest hint of a witchcraft suspicion finds its way in between two families, there is hardly any way to regain trust.

From the very moment she saw the dress on top of her hayloft, Rodica read it as a potential *bozgoană*, as a physical sign showing that she is in the presence of some unnatural, witchcraft-linked occurrence. Although the pink evening dress was far from the form of a conventional *bozgoană* (the collection of substances mentioned earlier), it was read as one due to the strangeness of its placement and the complete mystery as to its provenance. Even when the latter conundrum was elucidated and the ownership of the dress clearly established, the affair was far from closure. At this point, by establishing contact with the other party, what came into play was the examination of Mariana's 'real' intentions. For Gheorghiță, Rodica's husband, the pink dress was equally a *bozgoană* at this point as much as it was at the beginning, because he maintained the conviction that Mariana's family had purposely chucked this magically charged dangerous object on their property with the clear intention to harm them.

For Mariana and her family, what first came as a rather common, although disruptive and troubling, act of theft from their residence became a witchcraft threat once they realized the occurrence is not completely elucidated by the rational explanation of a theft: For instance, the room with the dress also contained other even more expensive valuables, but nothing else was missing. A dress, on the other hand, is something that a person wears in close contact with the body—therefore, representing the perfect medium for a sorcery ritual intended to harm the owner. From then on, the pink dress was read as a potential *bozgoană* in Mariana's family as well, and they started to act accordingly by enlisting the help of the priest.

Why would they continue to think that Rodica and her family are the real culprits, given Rodica's actions and the priest's testing ritual that, supposedly, confirmed Rodica's innocence? Why would Gheorghiță think Mariana's family had purposely thrown the dress on their property in order to harm them? None of these suppositions made perfect logical sense when examined in the context of the happenings, and the families had never had, prior to this incident, any kind of conflict that would justify this mutual tension (they are not geographic neighbors). But, the answer to the *why* question has little to do with rational logic, as it belongs to witchcraft situation type of logic: simply put, they could not afford not to. They could not afford to not be suspicious because, when dealing with the force of true evil underlying all potential witchcraft situations, it has to be met with the appropriate constructive paranoia.[74] Once they interpreted (at their respective moments) the pink dress as a potential *bozgoană*, both families started to think and act in terms of witchcraft[75] not because something had happened to sustain the discourse, but because witchcraft is not the kind of possibility to be casually dismissed without the appropriate mentality and protective measures.

1.3 Entering the Witchcraft Discourse

To name a situation as 'witchcraft' means to set in place a defensive mechanism meant to preserve one's mental health and interior coherence. This can only happen at the meeting point between the specific explanatory categories available in any given society for mis-

74 Jared Diamond describes constructive paranoia, an attitude perhaps more common to the traditional societies than to our own contemporary westernized world, as a mindset able to identify any potential danger in one's specific environment, followed by precise steps taken by individuals to minimize the risks. Jared Diamond, *The World Until Yesterday. What Can We Learn from Traditional Societies* (Penguin Books, 2013), pp. 243–275. As strategic, preemptive wisdom, such a constructive paranoia proves to be an attitude paramount in the witchcraft situations I have so far described. It is, however, far less relevant for other types of life situations.

75 Willem de Blécourt and Owen Davies, 'Introduction: Witchcraft continued', *Witchcraft Continued. Popular Magic in Modern Europe*, pp. 1–13, p. 3.

fortune and the individual interior path to reconfigure memory. As a consequence, accessing a witchcraft discourse can only happen in a society that still maintains this particular explanatory frame as a valid form of interpreting unhappiness—however marginalized, competing, or unvalued this may be from the standpoint of the more dominant perspectives of science and/or religion. Also, engaging in such a discourse is not a matter of simple personal choice like a momentary whim. It is a laborious interior process based on complex strategies of reorganizing memory with an apotropaic finality: 'a way of preserving the past while keeping it at a distance.'[76]

Social Discourse and Personal Choice

Witchcraft situations represent only a tiny fraction of the wider, more complex field of magic. Characterized by heterogeneity, the contemporary magic's domain can be thought of as one aspect of popular culture.

In today's world, this 'popular culture' has to be understood as *popularis*[77] or, simply put, the culture belonging to people. Throughout the 19th and the 20th centuries, the national ethnologies of the European continent, particularly those of Central and Eastern Europe, maintained 'popular culture' as a core concept exclusively limited to the cultural artifacts of the traditional peasant rural milieus, i.e., as 'folklore.' Contemporarily defined popular culture stands for 'both "folk" or "popular" beliefs, practices and objects rooted in local traditions as well as "mass" beliefs, practices, and objects generated from political and commercial centres.'[78] Also, today's popular culture can be regarded as the hallmark of an ever-changing fluid soci-

76 Kathleen Marks, *Toni Morrison's Beloved and the Apotropaic Imagination* (Columbia: University of Missouri Press, 2002), pp. 51–52.

77 John Storey, *Inventing Popular Culture. From Folklore to Globalization* (Blackwell Publishing Ltd, 2003), p. XII.

78 Chandra Mukerji and Michael Schudson, 'Popular Culture', *Annual Review of Sociology,* 12 (1986), pp. 47–66, ‹http://www.jstor.org/stable/2083194› [accessed April 2010], p. 48.

ety, as the everyday expression[79] of shared values, practices, and knowledge. This everyday orality, the fluid medium of a continuous exchange of ideas between most diverse sources, is fundamentally syncretic[80]: from local to national, from regional to global, from books to movies, from philosophical ideas to music, from traditional crafts to mass production—ideas and goods circulate, mingle, and generate further creations.

The witchcraft discourses are part of this oral culture, circulated at the level of everyday living and disseminated through mass media. Despite the aura of mystery and secret surrounding them, these explanatory strategies can be accessed at any time, by anyone, when needing to make sense of situations of intense existential crisis. In those European social contexts where witchcraft discourses are still functional, they belong to 'culture' in its wider sense of 'equipment for living':

'That culture (language, art, science, law, religion, marriage, politics, merriment, common sense—the whole kit and caboodle) consists not of bodiless ideas suspended in impalpable mental states, delicate motions of the soul and spirit, but of what the American action theorist, social critic, and all-round man of letters Kenneth Burke [1941] has called "equipment for living," equipment that is substantial, at hand, usable, and used, ought not by now to be so difficult a notion.'[81]

Together with art, science, religion, or common sense, the explanatory discourses of magic in general and witchcraft in particular provide substantial and instrumental tools able to assist the contemporary individual in the process of living. The witchcraft dis-

79 Jocelyne Bonnet, 'Les allocutions des presidents', *Premier atelier européen sur la culture orale européene* (Strasbuorg: Conseil de l'Europe, 1990), p. 35.

80 Marianne Mesnil, *Etnologul, între şarpe şi balaur*/Marianne Mesnil and Assia Popova – *Eseuri de mitologie balcanică* (Bucureşti: Paideia, 1997), p. 35.

81 Clifford Geertz, 'Shifting Aims, Moving Targets: On the Anthropology of Religion', *Journal of the Royal Anthropological Institute* (11, 2005), pp. 1–15, ‹http://onlinelibrary.wiley.com/doi/10.1111/j.1467-9655.2005.00223.x/epdf› [accessed March 2015], p. 6.

course as one of the valid explanatory categories for unhappiness in a particular social or cultural context points to something more than a mere process of cultural survival[82]; it shows that it represents a *cultural fact* so necessary that it gets to be continuously reinterpreted and readapted into the lives of contemporary human beings.

The crises confronted under the witchcraft label start as an extended period of duress without a name, not fitting into any of the established (and socially accepted) categories of distress in the contemporary world: medical emergencies; depression; economic hardship; or, in a religious reading, a trial sent by God to test the faithful. Even in a European society that still includes witchcraft as an explanatory category for unhappiness, it is never the one first chosen because the actors tend to respect the order of discourse.[83] They always defer their unhappiness to the voices of authority established by the powerful institutional agents such as the educational system, the church, and the medical council.[84] Only when, and if, the explanations offered by these voices of authority prove insufficient, the witchcraft discourse comes to the fore.

This does not necessarily mean that the other discourses are abandoned altogether. As observed by André Julliard,[85] turning to a witchcraft explanation does not mean, from a pragmatic perspective, to turn away from the medical care or the comfort of religious belief, for the simple reason that, in everyday life, magic is not necessarily lived as contradicting religious and scientific principles and values.

82 The term 'survival,' which is subtextually deprecatory, implies the idea of a linear, mechanical cultural survival where the complex social-cultural context fades away, while the feeling of fear and insecurity prevails. Usually linked to 'superstition,' it functions as opposite to the less negative term 'belief,' which is supposedly anchored in a fully functional social context and a complex mythological horizon.

83 As expressed by Jeanne Favret-Saada in the context of her research in rural France, the people from Bocage know, as opposed to Evans-Pritchard's Azande, that there are other explanations possible apart from witchcraft, p. 34.

84 Favret-Saada, p. 34.

85 André Julliard, 'Urgia Sorților. Vrăjitoria zilelor noastre în Franța', p. 279.

In cases of illness, following empirical prescriptions (pharmaceutical drugs and hospitalization) can occur simultaneous to the following of magical–religious actions if the illness and its causes are not sufficiently elucidated by empirical explanations. In other words, the actors accepting a witchcraft discourse might have entered this particular explanatory frame last, but that does not mean that they definitively leave all the others for good. They come back to the other approaches at various times, depending on the situation,

In this light, the witchcraft discourse appears to be nothing more and nothing less than a survival strategy: When confronted with overwhelming unhappiness or even the ultimate threat of the end of one's physical existence, people tend to use *all and whatever they can* in order to fight back and save themselves. Analytical distinctions, precrisis allegiances, or even moral standpoints, all tend to lose ground in favor of the ultimate pragmatic purpose: solving the crisis, getting better, and restoring the day-to-day normal existence.

The Apotropaic Dimension of Witchcraft Situations: Ritual Gestures and Interior Memory

The word *apotropaic* means today, especially in the social sciences, 'intended to ward off evil.'[86] As a type of rite or ritual gesture, it usually describes magical–religious actions meant to prevent future misfortunes according to specific cultural scenarios about *what* and *when* is to be considered a potential threat. Generally speaking, an apotropaic act is a preventive strategy (*ante-facto*), distinctive from other *post-facto* ritual actions meant to remedy an already installed evil occurrence (such as exorcism, for instance).

The word itself has ancient Greek roots, combining the prefix *apo-* meaning (distancing) from, and the noun *tropos, -ou,* meaning turning away.[87] Through convention, the resulting word is understood as 'turning away from evil' or 'warding off evil.' It is worth not-

---

86 Kathleen Marks, p. 6.

87 The online Oxford Dictionary defines apotropaic (adj.) as 'supposedly having the power to avert evil influences or bad luck', from Greek *apotropaios* 'averting evil,' ‹http://www.oxforddictionaries.com/definition/english/apotropaic›.

ing that the very idea of evil, engrained in today's understanding of the term, is actually missing from its etymological construction. The reason why the apotropaic is today a name for turning away specifically from *evil* has to do with two different social and temporal contexts. The first is its emergence in ancient Greek culture, where *apotropos* designated a relation of adversity with supernatural evil through the aversion rites dedicated, as Hellen Harrison first showed,[88] to keeping at bay deities from the underworld. The second context is offered through the term's adoption in modern social sciences as an operational concept designating the particular set of gestures, rituals, individual psychological attitudes, or material devices (such as amulets and talismans) meant to prevent and to protect from harm.

In the particular context of the witchcraft discourse, the relevance of apotropaic strategies can be identified on two distinct levels, each one with its own approach.

The most striking of these is the ritual level, when actors previously involved in witchcraft situations employ various strategies specifically targeting the possibility of falling victim to an evil spell in the future.[89]

One less-obvious strategy represents an individual psychological dimension: the subjective interior relation with one's memory. This protective aspect, common to all actors placed within a witchcraft situation scenario, describes the initial moment of acknowledging and entering the discourse. The key moment of accepting the diagnosis that one has been bewitched is based on a process of

88 'It is clear then that Greek religion contained two diverse, even opposite, factors: on the one hand the element of *service* (*theraipeia*) and, on the other, the element of *aversion* (*apotropē*). The rites of *service* were connected by ancient tradition with the Olympians, or as they are sometimes called the Ouranians: the rites of *aversion* with ghosts, heroes, underworld divinities. The rites of service were of a cheerful and rational character, the rites of aversion gloomy and tending to superstition.' Jane Ellen Harrison, *Prolegomena to the study of Greek religion* (Cambridge: Cambridge University Press, 1903), p. 10.

89 I will discuss this type of apotropaic in the 3rd Chapter, **Therapeutic interventions.**

rememory, defined by Paul Ricoeur[90] as an overlap between the cognitive dimension of memory (the acknowledgment accompanying a successful remembrance) and its pragmatic dimension (rememory as effort and labor similar to action). The rememory, as an active and often tense process, is intimately linked to the narrative function. Through verbal expression, 're-memory takes the course of narration.'[91] It is the story we tell to ourselves when looking to make sense out of a sequence of past events, meant to bring us one step closer to closure.

Much like a detective trying to put together clues and pieces of a puzzling crime, we build that story in a quest to identify relevant elements and eliminate those that have no significance within the plot. For example, a set of previously irrelevant details become suddenly indicative and, in the particular context of witchcraft accusations, highly suspicious: successive unannounced home visits; ingesting or drinking something offered by the potential aggressor; a casual handshake. The coherent narrative has to be able to highlight those and eliminate other details that have no bearing on the desired meaning sustaining the witchcraft diagnosis. That is precisely the point of articulating the apotropaic dimension of the remembrance process placed in the service of a witchcraft discourse. The following subchapter will focus on the rememory strategy employed by the afflicted actor when entering a witchcraft discourse, aiming to highlight the (self) protective function of this interior process.

Building the Narrative

Any kind of event, in order to make sense, starts with a story. To make sense out of something means to put order within the memories in such a way that, through successive selections, the resulting explanatory narrative is able to retrospectively sustain an effect of wholeness.

---

90 Paul Ricoeur, *Memoria, Istoria, Uitarea* (Timişoara: Amarcord, 2001), pp. 75–76.

91 Paul Ricoeur, p. 158. [My translation].

Any explanations we offer to ourselves take the form of an interior discourse following retrospective rearrangements of facts and images. This process of interior putting in order is very much akin to the structure of narrative function and, as a consequence, answers to the principles of narrative selection. The plot, as the essential unit that transforms a nameless sequence of events into a coherent story, ties together in a tight unit initially heterogeneous, even discrepant elements, such as: circumstances, characters, interactions, random facts, intended or unintended results,[92] and so on. The selective function works here as the ability to strategically remember and conveniently forget: We can always tell a story differently; we can suppress or displace important accentuations that can alter the final meaning; we can reconfigure the main actors and the general plot lines differently.[93] Therefore, the process of rememory as an interior discourse can be, just like any story, manipulated (some would argue that it always is). And it is in this ability to conceal some avenues of a story while highlighting others where its apotropaic dimension resides. Through selective forgetting and strategic reminding, we protect ourselves from the trauma and from all the underworldly (subconscious) forces threatening to divide our psyche. After all, as Ricouer put it: What would a memory that cannot forget be, if not something monstrous?[94]

Going back to the witchcraft discourse, constructing a personal narrative able to retrospectively sustain a witchcraft diagnosis is not something completely up to the actor. Apart from the interior apotropaic strategies, we have to take into account the general themes imposed by the witchcraft discourse genre. In cases where the potential victim is confronted with this type of discourse for the first time and, consequently, does not have all necessary knowledge to come up with a coherent narrative, all the other involved actors (the annunciator; the diviner; the therapist) contribute in the step-by-

92 Paul Ricoeur, *De la text la acțiune* (Cluj–Napoca: Editura Echinox, 1999), pp. 15 and 21.

93 Paul Ricoeur, *Memoria, Istoria, Uitarea,* p. 540.

94 Paul Ricoeur, p. 501.

step clarification and guidance. The essential themes to be elucidated always are:

the Who: 'Is there, by any chance, someone who would want to hurt you?'[95] Within the historical, rural traditional witchcraft discourse, this moment was something more than simply making a supposition regarding a plausible culprit. As research shows,[96] in many parts of Europe it was believed that a witch can actually, whether forced or willingly, lift her own curse and cure her own *maleficia*; therefore, identifying the magical aggressor was the first and most promising chance the victim had at healing. In contemporary Romania, identifying the aggressor is the first step of building the narrative (giving a name to the cause of evil) and a very important moment for the victim's interior discourse. But, as previously shown, it tends to play less of a role within the following, more concrete phases of a witchcraft situation.

the How: Here are examined all the direct or intermediated contacts between the potential victim and the supposed aggressor and the ways through which the evil spell could have been transmitted: physical touch, ingestion, etc.

the When: When did the first signs that something is completely off first start?

In particular, if the When and the How can be correlated, and the When proves to be immediately posterior to the How, the discourse about a malevolent magical intervention can be sustained. Any other supplementary detail can only, at this point, reinforce the story without significantly altering the core.

Therefore, elaborating this discourse comes as a dialog between the afflicted actor (her/his pain and distress) and elements of the exterior explicative apparatus, where the annunciator, the diviner, and the therapist initially play the part of guides and translators.

95 Jeanne Favret- Saada, p. 24. [My translation].

96 Willem de Blécourt, 'Boiling chickens and burning cats: witchcraft in the Western Netherlands', *Witchcraft Continued. Popular Magic in Modern Europe*, p. 94; Willem de Blécourt, 'Witch Doctors, Soothsayers and Priests. On Cunning Folk in European Historiography and tradition', *Social History*, vol. 19, no. 3 (1994), pp. 285–303, ‹http://www.jstor.org/stable/4286217› [accessed October 2014], p. 298.

is undergoing an unwitchment ritual. This secrecy has always been the dominant sentiment marking magic's entire domain. Within the witchcraft discourse, and from the point of view of the afflicted actor, it has the specific function of isolating the actor to such a degree that the potential aggressor has no way of knowing that his/her actions are being counteracted and, therefore, cannot readapt the attack strategy. The same secrecy is part of any personalized Orthodox religious ritual: much like the confession, what happens between the priest and the faithful, what they discuss, what the priest recommends, asks, and does is to remain solely between the two of them and God. Only when the specific ritual requires further involvement from other actors, needed to help out with particular ritual steps (such as holding specific fasting on specific days), the number of those knowing about it is likely to increase.

But the actors undergoing an unwitching therapy do not give up this secrecy once the ritual period is over and they can get on with their lives. From there on, they will talk with caution, if indeed at all, about the experience. The first reason is that they are all too happy to leave such a painful period of their lives completely behind; not to think about it, and not to speak about it out loud is the easiest way to move away from the trauma. The second reason is the fact that, in our complex contemporary society, all actors accessing a witchcraft diagnosis know very well where the social rating of that particular discourse lies. They might not personally feel ashamed for resorting to it, but they would definitely prefer to avoid being judged by others (branded as superstitious and retrograde) by simply not talking about it. Hence, what started as ritually advised silence tends to continue as social cautioned, lifelong silence.

To conclude, entering the witchcraft discourse by naming a previously nameless suffering and the consequent rememory strategy of building a support narrative is a temporally suspended interior moment during which the actor stops to retrospectively make order within his/her own perceptions. The apotropaic finality of this process is unmistakable: It protects the psychic coherence of the actor by giving a quasi-familiar face to a previously generic evil deeply affecting his/her life. At the same time, this interior reflexive–defensive process is the one triggering the shift from being a victim (the passive pole) to becoming an actor seeking to regain the control of his/her own existence. Having a name for the particular evil confronted means having, at last, the appropriate weapons and strategies to deal with unhappiness, accessible through the witchcraft diagnosis. Therefore, entering the witchcraft discourse through the apotropaic strategies of rememory can be seen as a *tropos*: a return, a turning away, and a figure of speech (metaphor) for a process of readjusting the memory in order to preserve the coherence of the self.

Chapter 2: The Actors in Witchcraft Situations

This chapter will describe the main actors of a witchcraft situation. Through an assessment of the differences between the distribution of roles within traditional-rural witchcraft discourse all across Europe and that of today's Romania specifically, we will be able to highlight significant changes in the discourse. These are important because they reflect a process of readjustment of the general lines of the discourse to a complex, Westernized, contemporary, cultural, social, and economic context. The same process of adapting elements of the witchcraft discourse to a society different from the standard, traditional-rural model will be once again discussed for the case of rural contemporary France. These evolutions matter greatly because they show how, through various readjustments, the generic lines of the witchcraft model (and mainly the ascribing of misfortunes to another human being), far from decline, continue to be relevant in several European social and regional contexts of today.

We have seen in the previous chapter how one of the main themes of the witchcraft discourse, the *mana* and fertility transfer, is on a descendant path in terms of popularity, less and less accessed in today's Northern Transylvania. At the same time, the three other situations that can call for a witchcraft diagnosis (delay of marriage; unhappy marriage or problematic love relationship; and unexplainable illness, general and temporally extended 'mal de vivre') maintain their relevance. The witchcraft discourse is changing, along with the people, their cultural ideas, narrative preferences, social practices, and social structures. If in today's Romania the bewitching of crops is no longer a valid scenario and the bewitching of milk-producing cows is less and less applied, research in northwestern rural France shows how not only livestock but also the agricultural mechanical tools of production, even cars, fax machines, fridges, and so forth can be bewitched.[100] Therefore, the discourse can change as to integrate inanimate elements specific to the most modern conditions of living. Or, in Italy, if the evil eye is feared in the countryside for the damage it can do to animals and crops, it is feared in towns for it can cause a young person to fail an examination.[101] The overall explanation employed for a suffered misfortune can be the same, whereas the life domain it is directed toward can change, reflecting the variations between social environments (rural versus urban) and the everyday preoccupations determined by those (agricultural productivity versus acquiring social status and social capital).

Such adaptations and changes of the discourse can equally be documented at the actors' level. In today's Romania, the most poignant element is the fact that the priests and monks of Orthodox denomination, the dominant religious confession in the country, seem to exclusively hold the position of the unwitcher, in contrast to both the historical local data (suggesting that a good proportion of laic unwitchers were activating until 20 or 30 years ago) and to the situation in most Protestant and Catholic countries, where the clergy are no longer directly participating in witchcraft situations.

This transformation reflects the Romanian Orthodox Church's gradual, but ultimately successful, process of reinstatement as a pole of authority on the Romanian public scene after the fall of Communism in 1989. This reinstatement process and its social consequences will be discussed in more detail in the fourth chapter of this book, **Magic and Religion.** Here, it will suffice to say that the fact that the clergy is occupying the therapist position of a witchcraft situation not only reflects a successful religious monopole but also generates other sets of changes. It is transplanting the religious moral implications inside the core of the unwitching ritual (discour-

---

100 Owen Davies, 'Witchcraft accusations in France, 1850–1990', *Witchcraft Continued. Popular Magic in Modern Europe*, ed. by Willem de Blécourt & Owen Davies (Manchester & New York: Manchester University Press, 2004), pp. 107–132, p. 128.

101 Lola Romanucci-Ross, *One Hundred Towers. An Italian Odyssey of Cultural Survival* (New York: Bergin & Garvey, 1991), p. 140.

aging victim's feelings of anger or entitlement to revenge) and has a direct effect at the aggressor pole. It is not yet a complete depersonalization,[102] but it is most certainly a blurring of the image of the magical aggressor within the witchcraft discourse of today's Romania. It could not go any other way; as a mere mental representation that the victim is encouraged by the religious discourse to attach a name to but at the same time warned to avoid digging deeper, the aggressor functions simply as an opening line to the interior narrative sustaining the witchcraft diagnosis of the victim. But, it is seldom a factor in later stages of the healing process.

The French case comes with its own very interesting developments and adaptations of the discourse in terms of roles and actors. The most remarkable one is what Willem de Blécourt described as 'a gendering of witchcraft that so far seems to have been unique in the European context'[103]: Although European witchcraft is and has always been predominantly feminine, the documented rural French witchcraft has a higher proportion of men implicated in the discourse than women. For instance, Dominique Camus' research in Rennes and Dinan during the 1980s gave him access to a total of 18 magic specialists (unwitchers and sorcerers), 14 of which were men.[104] Similar to this gender distribution, as shown in the previous chapter, the ultimate target of the magical attack is usually the man[105]—the head of the family; the chief of an agricultural exploitation; the source of the vital force fueling the domain comprised under his name.

---

102 Witchcraft can become depersonalized when the human cause of bewitchment disappears from view. Such a process can well point toward a gradual weakening, followed by the disappearance of the discourse. Willem de Blécourt, 'The Witch, her Victim, the Unwitcher and the Researcher: the continued existence of traditional witchcraft', *Witchcraft and Magic in Europe. The Twentieth Century*, ed. by Bengt Ankarloo and Stuart Clark (University of Pennsylvania Press, 1999), pp. 141–219, pp. 215–216.

103 Willem de Blécourt, p. 216.

104 Dominique Camus, *Puteri şi practici vrăjitoreşti. Anchetă asupra practicilor actuale de vrăjitorie* (Iaşi: Polirom, 2003), p. 21.

105 Jeanne Favret-Saada, *Les mots, la mort, les sorts* (Paris: Gallimard, 1977), p. 333.

All of these examples show how the general lines of the traditional witchcraft discourse can be adapted to new standards of living, new social milieus, and new preoccupations. Cars and livestock can be bewitched, men can be targeted more than women, and a reinstated religious discourse can not only participate in the witchcraft discourse but even create a monopole at one of its poles. The witchcraft drama can unfold in new settings, with different actors and modern symptoms. But, it is still the old witchcraft scenario of the traditional kind as long as it maintains the core statement regarding the ascription of unhappiness to the malefic actions of other people.

2.1 The Witchcraft Discourse: General Lines and Specific Actors

In its most basic form, bewitchment designates a conflictual relationship between two actors: a magical aggressor (the witch or sorcerer) and the targeted individual (the sufferer or victim). This type of relation is possible through the manipulation of magical force, set in motion by means of proper actions (rituals, spells, and charms). The two actors presumably share the same set of beliefs, which sustains access to the same symbolic code. With this approach, we are not too far from Marcel Mauss, who posited that the system of magic consisted of three main elements: actions (rites), agents (e.g., the magician), and representations (ideas and beliefs corresponding to the magical actions).[106]

Investigating an episode of witchcraft as part of real life requires a very different approach. The experience of being bewitched is initiated and concluded by the person who perceives themselves as the victim or sufferer of a magical aggression. The victim is, therefore, the main actor. He or she may engage with a number of other actors:

- close relatives and friends who might be involved in the situation;
- someone who makes the diagnosis of bewitchment;

[106] Marcel Mauss, *Esquisse d'une théorie générale de la magie* (Paris: Quadrige/P.U.F., 1991), p. 10.

- an intermediary (for instance, a professional fortune teller); and
- therapists (in contemporary Romania, mostly Orthodox priests or monks).

These categories are not fixed, but interrelated and overlapping.

The magical aggressor is notably absent from this scheme. Although the existence of someone occupying this pole is a prerequisite, s/he never actively engages in a crisis situation but appears only as a discursive referent.[107] Nevertheless, the presupposed aggressor is a named, living individual. Identifying the aggressor, placing her/him on spatial and temporal maps, and tracing the suspicions to a person rather than an undifferentiated evil are key steps in the victim's transformation from a passive to an active subject.

The impossibility of directly associating an aggressor with a bewitched–unwitcher couple does not simply mean that the former does not exist. As already mentioned in the **Introduction**, Dominique Camus' research in northwestern rural France in the 1980s gave him access to professional unwitchers and their clients, as well as to some professional magical aggressors (or sorcerers) and their clients (the beneficiaries of a magical aggression committed against somebody else, at their request). That was a very interesting addition to Jeanne Favret-Saada's research undertaken about 15 years earlier in roughly the same area, when she determined that no person in the area of Bocage presented him/herself as a professional sorcerer,[108] as opposed to the relative notoriety of unwitchers; therefore, her approach was built exclusively around the victim unwitcher couple.

That is precisely the case of my own research in northern Transylvania: I never found any indication of active specialized magical aggressors, nor have I met more than one person hinting at ever being tempted to harm somebody else through magical means. My own explanation was that people in the region simply take their religious devotion and the Orthodox religious ethics far too seriously to

[107] The same absence has been documented by Jeanne Favret-Saada during her research in rural France. Jeanne Favret-Saada, p. 32.

[108] Jeanne Favret-Saada, p. 50.

risk eternal damnation: witchcraft, sorcery, and even wishing harm to somebody else are themes continuously addressed during church sermons, prayers, and rituals. Always wishing for the best, even for one's enemies, is the recommended moral attitude within the religious discourse.

But, there are anthropologists[109] who think that, just because a researcher does not find them, it does not automatically mean that magical aggressors do not exist at all other than as the crucial reference in the victim's discourse.

The first relevant line of argument here stresses the fact that potential aggressors, even more so than unwitchers or victims, are operating under the rule of strict secrecy that governs all domains of magic. This is even more the case because they are situated on the amoral side of the ethical border of the witchcraft discourse.

Let us take this step by step. From the position of the dominant positivist, scientific discourse, both religion and magic are irrational and superstitious; from the position of the religious discourse, all magic (including divination) is immoral and sinful because it goes against the divine plan, trying to force a human agenda against that of the higher powers; from the inside of the magic discourse, divination, unwitching, apotropaic (defense and protection), and healing magic are valued as morally sound, while bewitching is seen as criminal and deviant. Therefore, the moral value of an act of witchcraft is judged according to the intentions of harm against another person comprised in the magical act: bewitching out of hate, envy, jealousy, revenge, greed, or lust (to name only some of the emotions routinely associated with committing a magical aggression), in order to torture, steal from and cause depletion, impede judgment, or even kill—all these are negative intentions associated with acting through the magical force. It is easy to see, then, how a supposed professional magical aggressor would have more reasons than most to

[109] Willem de Blécourt shows that authors such as Richard Jenkins (when writing about Ireland), Dömötör Tekla (Hungary) or Carmelo Lison Tolosana (Spain) have little doubts regarding the existence of people dwelling into sorcery rituals in real life. Willem de Blécourt, p. 188.

keep their activities secret, and their clients to forever deny that they would ever resort to such a despicably low level. The supposition that magical aggressors are virtually invisible due to paranoid secrecy but not at all inexistent seems to be supported by Dominique Camus' research results, too.

Another factor to consider is the regional difference[110] or, better yet, the continuous variations within the witchcraft discourse. As long as the witchcraft discourse is alive and valid, it will change in time, while displaying remarkable differences between regions. Such discrepancies are to be observed even between the smallest neighboring territorial units, not to mention county-sized units or larger historical territorial units. If, in Transylvania, for instance, my research shows that the only legitimate active unwitchers today are exclusively members of the Orthodox clergy, it also shows that the two laic unwitchers I was able to map are active in two other historic regions: one in Banat and the other one in Moldavia. Also, thanks to mass media, the ambiguous contemporary popularity of self-proclaimed witches from the capital of Bucharest (the historical region of Wallachia) can be a common topic of discussion at any time in Transylvania as well. Although such characters are perceived as charlatans in everyday life and as frauds when compared to proper systems of the witchcraft discourse, the very fact that they exist suggests that the witchcraft discourse of Wallachia can only be something entirely different nowadays when compared to the Transylvanian or the Moldavian one. Therefore, generalizations can be tricky. This caution is particularly relevant when discussing the witchcraft discourse specific to contemporary Europe: the bigger the territory, the more attention needs to be paid to the fine balance between the localized traits and the bigger picture, i.e., the essential characteristics that define any contemporary witchcraft discourse and its social meaning and functions.

110 'The more a researcher participates in the witchcraft discourse, the more unique its local manifestations seem to become', Willem de Blécourt, p. 219. However, no historically modern or contemporary region is an isolated island: elements of local discourse travel geographically, along with people.

The third element pertaining to the existence or nonexistence of aggressors (people who do resort to magic or magic specialists in order to cause harm) lies with one quality intrinsic to any discourse in general, namely ostention: 'the acting out of traditional narratives—what one folklorist describes as the dramatic extension of legend complexes into real life.'[111] In general, narratives, rumors, legends, or dominant explicative scenarios are judged in relation to their referential function, i.e., their relation to reality and the extent of their ability to mirror reality. As the saying goes, every legend contains a grain of truth. But, discourses not only rephrase and mirror reality; they are also able to generate facts in real life. People can be inspired by stories and can try and recreate the stories they liked in their own lives. Likewise, the big narratives carrying social functions that are present in every society and regulate what is and what is not possible in terms of life projects restrict what people can choose to be and do. Given the virtual invisibility of magical aggressors during my research in northern Transylvania, the amount of discursive material I was able to collect—about who they might be, why they might act, their predestination, and the punishment themes—is impressively sizable. My first thought was that this quantity was simply illustrating a matter of compensation: the less real witches to point to, the more stories to tell about possible ones. Also, the archaic folkloric tradition still plays a big role as a source to draw from when needing to explain the unexplainable. One incident that I will discuss further (in the subchapter '**And yet, who are the magical aggressors?**' of this section) poses the question whether such narratives can actually inspire action in real life: an employee from Dumitra school did some spells to prevent her husband from leaving her but, after not succeeding, she tried again, this time aiming to cause an illness to her love rival. The explanatory narratives in Transylvania pertaining to witches and their trade tools always car-

[111] Stephen Mitchell, 'A case of witchcraft assault in early nineteenth-century as ostensive action', *Witchcraft continued. Popular magic in modern Europe*, ed. by Willem de Blécourt and Owen Davis (Manchester and New York: Manchester University Press, 2004), pp. 14–28, p. 21.

ry very rich details; it is easy to suppose that one can be inspired to act based only on this apparently generic, in fact surprisingly factual discursive material, and the eventual gaps in the information (what exactly to use for the spell, when, where, etc.) can be easily filled in with some further enquiries. Therefore, the concept of ostensive action can be helpful in highlighting the possibility that, when witches are no longer identifiable as such in the field, the magical aggressor pole is kept relevant through narratives; and, who knows, the same narratives might inspire people to secretly act as witches—enriching the narrative even further.

But with or without the witches being actors within a witchcraft situation, what is important in any given region at any given historical time is the perfect parallelism, with no points of contact, between the victim's pole and the aggressor's pole. As pointed out in the **Introduction**, Dominique Camus' most illuminating formulation stresses that 'one cannot simultaneously understand the bewitched and the bewitcher. Although part of the same general drama, they do not belong to the same discourse, each of them having their own interpretation of events that does not bear contradiction.'[112] Even though he was able to document both unwitchers/victims and sorcerers/ill-wishers, he was unable to establish any sort of direct rapport between the two parties. In the research reality, the theoretical triangle (victim, aggressor, and therapist) or rectangle (the victim and his therapist, pitted against the aggressor and sorcerer) functions simply as poles, with the other present only as the imagined discourse reference. They refer to each other, but they do not have a type of connection in real life that would be able to support the supposed bewitched–bewitcher report.

In the case of my own research, similar to that by Jeanne Favret-Saada, the only pole to speak of was the one clustered around the victim. In the following pages, I am going to describe and analyze the actors and the specific roles they play, interplay, and exchange within a witchcraft situation.

---

112 Dominique Camus, p. 218. [My translation].

2.2 Roles and Actors

Afflicted Actors

A vast network of actors (diagnosticians, intermediaries, and therapists) participate in various interactions, occupy specific positions at certain moments, and exchange roles at others. The central component of this dynamic picture is the actor assuming a diagnosis of being bewitched, initially placed at the victim pole. The discursive, factual, and ritual interactions with the other key actors transform the victim from a passive sufferer of magical aggression into an active agent. The aimed finality of all unwitching ritual actions is to regain a state of normality.

One common prejudice is that members of complex societies who appeal to magic and sorcery are representative of the superstitious 'primitive within.' However, the people I met during my field research are neither undereducated nor (semi-)illiterate; they come from cities as well as villages and include intellectuals, public officials, peasants, and workers. The complexity of the reality in the field makes it impossible to adopt simplified, standard, categorical portraits.

Some concrete data might help illustrate this point. During the four years of my research (2005–2009), I traveled between 10 localities, 3 of which were cities, 2 were smaller towns, and 5 were villages. I interviewed and revisited 31 key informants, without including a hard to estimate number of informal or less-structured discussions on correlative topics with various people. The completely reconstructed witchcraft situations that I am basing my approach on stand at a number of 12. There were only two informants that went through witchcraft situations more than once in their lives (two times each). But, many more of them acted as annunciators, or as informed advisors, for witchcraft situations affecting their family and friends based on their personal previous direct experience.

There is a clear predominance of women actors upholding the witchcraft discourse in today's Romania. Of the 31 key informants, only 3 were men. One of them, although he was the apparent direct target of a witchcraft attack, remained profoundly skeptical and accepted to discuss the incident only like a funny anecdote rather than a serious threat; in the end, it was his mother who went forth to address the potential situation. Another one was directly involved in a witchcraft situation affecting his sister. He, therefore, remained profoundly convinced of the discourse's validity and continued to employ various apotropaic strategies to prevent falling victim to an evil spell in the future. The third man I interviewed took part in a witchcraft situation targeting his family. He never doubted the explanatory discourse, but it was mostly his wife who took the steps necessary to solve the situation. More often than not, even when they believe in witchcraft and consider themselves involved or affected, men tend to leave the practical part to women, as they consider them more knowledgeable on the matter.

The age of my informants ranged from 27 to 78 years. The 25–35 years age group was mostly represented by feminine actors dealing with the impossibility of getting married. The more mature age groups consisted of women concerned about their daughters', sons', granddaughters', and grandsons' marital well-being (either as delayed marriage or as problematic love relationship). Also, the unexplainable illness, general and temporally extended 'mal de vivre' theme, was common with the more mature age groups, especially the 45–65 yeas category, and quite uncommon for younger women.

The educational level of my informants ranged vastly from a very basic to PhD level. Most of them were at least high school graduates, if not BA graduates. In terms of occupation, they were: peasants, farmers, teachers (ranging from nursery teachers to intermediate school teachers, and one headmaster), business people, accountants, diviners, pensioners, public clerks, factory workers, etc. Many of them have lived in more than one locality throughout their lives, and most of them travel frequently anyway, either for their jobs or for family interests. Even the actors from apparently remote mountain villages are connected to the 'world at large' through both the mass media (radios, TVs, even Internet) and good transport links to neighboring cities or smaller towns.

I am insisting on these aspects because, when discussing contemporary witchcraft discourse, an implicit assumption links the persistence of this explanatory frame to actors from remote regions or isolated villages, characterized by semi-illiteracy, a 'traditional' (backwarded) mentality, poverty, and ignorance. A good example in this respect is a study about Franconian magic,[113] which starts by describing the region as rural, secluded, adhering to Catholicism, poor, bypassed by the progress of the rest of the German society, etc., traits that might explain the persistence of ancient customs (including the belief in witchcraft). This is implying that the only way to rationally explain the belief in witchcraft in Europe in contemporary times can only be backwardness, lack of education, precarious economic conditions, and geographic seclusion of the people still employing that particular discourse—traits usually associated with the historical Dark Ages or outer-European 'primitive' populations. Or, in Jeanne Favret-Saada's rather acidic terms expressing her discontent with the way that both ethnological studies and journalism treated witchcraft beliefs in the Bocage region of her research: 'How convenient that there should be a district full of idiots, where the whole realm of the imaginary can be held in.'[114]

The witchcraft discourse that Jeanne Favret-Saada researched in the northwestern part of France is rural on two levels: as a social context, it is mainly employed in the countryside (mostly villages and small towns); and as type of witchcraft discourse, it is rural insofar as it evolves around the core delegation of unhappiness to the maleficent intervention of other people. Today's witchcraft discourse in Romania is rural only with regard to the latter point, i.e., only as a type of ascribing misfortune to the magic aggression secretly committed by someone else. In terms of the social context, as shown by the previous discussion, it is equally found in villages and cities.

---

[113] Franconian Switzerland is a province of Central Germany. Hans Sebald, 'Franconian Witchcraft: The Demise of a Folk Magic', *Anthropological Quarterly*, 3 (July 1980), pp. 173–187, ‹http://www.jstor.org/stable/3317824› [accessed October 12, 2014]

[114] Jeanne Favret-Saada, *Deadly Words. Witchcraft in the Bocage* (Cambridge: Cambridge University Press, 2010), p. 4.

This particular aspect highlights a rather surprising permeability and social mobility of the discourse, which is no longer limited to the countryside in Romania.

This social permeability of the witchcraft discourse of today's Romania has a lot to do with the historical reshaping of social categories and social milieus, particularly under the communist regime. The gradually forced urbanization and industrialization engineered by the communist regime after its installment at the end of Second World War resulted in massive rural-to-urban migrations, where former peasants, housed in newly built block of flats, were to become the new workers and city dwellers needed so direly by the communist order. In fact, these habitations often became 'vertical villages,'[115] maintaining a quasi-rural way of life, a rural mentality, and modes of interpersonal relations. To this day, there is a certain social mobility between rural and urban milieus in Romania that might continue to sustain the circulation of the witchcraft explanatory discourse.

Another factor is the post-communist influence of the Orthodox religion in Romanian society, which accepts magical aggression as a valid diagnosis for unhappiness. As a post-1989 development, Romanian society turned from the former official atheist ideology of the communist state to being a European country with one of the highest rates of practiced religion. As one statistical research published in 2010 shows, 93% of Romanians believe in God, 53% go to mass at least once a month, and 73% practice prayer at least once a week.[116] Therefore, an urban inhabitant can have just as much access to the explanatory frame of the witchcraft discourse as a rural inhabitant, either through the direct or indirect ties to the rural milieu (familial provenance, neighbors, and friends) or through the Orthodox day-to-day religious practice. As my research shows, the witchcraft discourse might be a diagnosis of interest in times of

115 Gabriel Troc, '«După blocuri» sau despre starea actuală a cartierelor muncitoreşti', *Idea. Artă şi Societate*, pp. 15–16 (Cluj Napoca: 2003), ‹http://idea.ro/revista/?q=ro/node/40&articol=184› [accessed February 1, 2006]

116 *STISOC 2010: Raport de Cercetare - Publicul şi Ştiinţa* (Bucureşti: 2010), ‹http://www.stisoc.ro› [accessed July, 2011], pp. 51–52.

hardship even for city people with minimal ties to the countryside and diminished interest in religious activities, as long as two conditions are met: The time of duress experienced by the actor is exceeding any conventional explanation, eludes resolution, changes in form, and starts taking its toll on the emotional well-being of the person affected; and a third-party annunciator's timely intervention offers, through this diagnosis, both a name (a structural context) and a set of possible means to solve the crisis.

The 'Incidental Diagnostician'

As Jeanne Favret-Saada's research in rural France shows, there is usually an annunciator,[117] someone who triggers the entrance into a witchcraft-oriented discourse by naming the abnormal situation as such. I call this person an 'incidental diagnostician.' S/he is always close to the victim and can 'read the signs' because s/he is a survivor or witness of a similar bewitchment. S/he usually remains involved as an informed advisor, drawing on previous experience and knowledge of the actions necessary to counteract the bewitchment.

The annunciator is usually someone who is part of the main actor's support network. As shown in the first chapter, much like in Russia, surviving in Romania during the communist regime required quite a strategic approach in terms of knowing how to rely on already existent networks (one's own family, plus the family of the spouse) and how to further the network through establishing rapports with valuable contacts, acquaintances, 'relations.' The foundation of this safety net was, as shown by Galina Lindquist in the context of Soviet Russia, friendship. Friendship as a value grounding the communist (and, indeed, post-communist) safety social networks is not simply a matter of reciprocal sympathy, based on two individuals' common set of interests, tastes, etc. It is a social contract marked by reciprocal obligations, so much so that 'commitments to friends came before all other social commitments, certainly

[117] Jeanne Favret-Saada, *Les mots, la mort, les sorts* (Paris: Gallimard, 1977), p. 82.

well before those to the State and its ideology.'[118] That is because such a friend was the person to rely on during the communist regime, particularly in the 1980s when food was scarce. And one way to obtain it was to have a contact at the local state groceries shop able to set aside some goods and resell them to family and friends. In response to such a service, one would offer whatever help was available for him/her to give: assistance with by-passing bureaucracy in administration, favoring one's son during school examinations, obtaining some extra diesel fuel from one's workplace as a mechanic, etc. In short, this is the way the famous secondary economy of the socialist states worked:

'Since the centre would not supply what people needed, they struggled to do so themselves, developing in the process a huge repertoire of strategies for obtaining consumer goods and services. This strategies, called the second or informal economy, spanned a wide range from the quasi-legal to the definitely illegal.'[119]

Such networks, based on this particular type of mutual interest friendship, are still quite functional today in post-communist Romania—and, as Galina Lindquist's study shows, in Russia as well. It is not a matter of access to food or a basic means of survival any more but a matter of social connections and access to services. If one needs a better workplace, the easiest way to find one is through this support network. If one needs to change an expired ID, one will find a contact within the local police center able to assist with the speeding-up of the process. Big or small, the favors to be obtained through 'relations' (the personal contacts, the friends, and their contacts) are the day-to-day exercise of by-passing the requirements of a distrusted bureaucratic State and those of the recently established capitalist (dis)order.

All this is only to highlight why the annunciator is actually taken seriously in a crisis situation and why this actor is entitled to voice

---

118 Galina Lindquist, *Conjuring Hope. Healing and Magic in contemporary Russia* (New York, Oxford: Berghahn Books, 2009), p. 209.

119 Katherine Verdery, *What Was Socialism, and What Comes Next?* (Princeton University Press: 1996), p. 27.

an opinion. Seldom part of one's close family, the incidental diagnostician is usually a neighbor, a friend, a 'relation'. From a Western perspective, one could say that what this person does is 'meddling' into the private affairs of a family in a vulnerable moment of suffering while the standard attitude should really be to back off and participate only if and when invited. And yet, the annunciator is entitled to intervene based on his or her belonging to the same safety network as the afflicted family; put more simply, on the factual and moral basis of having offered valuable informal services in the past. What surprised me in some of the cases of my research was the fact that this annunciator was often not even liked, as a person, by the afflicted actor and the close family. Nevertheless, s/he was always trusted. Their voice was heard and further shaped the discourse of the affliction not on the basis of an emotional affinity but on that of the functional long-term sharing of day-to-day challenges.

The incidental diagnostician's most essential contribution is to formulate the bewitchment diagnosis at the crucial point where the victim has already exhausted the explanatory schemes of other, more prestigious discourses. For the afflicted actor, added to the stress of a difficult situation is the lack of knowledge what it actually is and how to fight it. The annunciator is the one who, through naming the situation, facilitates the entrance into the witchcraft discourse. S/he also assists with building the narrative, deducing together with the main actor what past sequences (of events, encounters, conflicts, and interactions) prove relevant and sustain the diagnosis. Therefore, his/her role can be first described as the utterer of the liminal call able to transform a chaotic painful situation, no longer resembling the day-to-day normal living, into a named crisis that can possibly be healed. Second, the role of the annunciator is to assist the victim with building the retrospective narrative of being bewitched, therefore, acting as a guide and a translator between the main actor and the explanatory discourse. Third, from a social point of view, the incidental diagnostician acts as a link in the 'chain of transmission'[120] of the witchcraft discourse and has the crucial role of perpetuating the discourse.

But, as long as this actor does not have the authority or competence to confirm a diagnosis of witchcraft, s/he has to be at least theoretically dissociated from the 'professional diagnostician' (the fortune teller and/or priest).

The Fortune Teller

Visiting a fortune teller is not a compulsory step involved in any (as of yet) unexplained crisis situation, but I documented the presence of this actor in most of the investigated situations. The fortune teller normally occupies the place of an intermediary in witchcraft situations. All of the diviners I encountered or heard of in the investigated northern Transylvanian region were women; therefore, I shall refer to them using feminine terms from here on.

A crucial point of the democratization of information, namely the oral and everyday fluidity of knowledge circulated within popular culture, is constituted by mass media access. In contemporary Romania, information pertaining to the magic discourse casually obtained through public television, radio broadcasts, and newspapers and magazines is frequently cited within the witchcraft discourse:

> *'Didn't you see? Nowadays, they even promote them on TV. They even rate them, who's the biggest ... who's the biggest witch. Not here, but over there, in the South.' (Mărioara, woman, age 62, Reteag village)*

Even so, the route of identifying and appealing to magic specialists remains predominantly the interpersonal one. None of my informants or respondents ever seemed to have resorted to the self-proclaimed Wallachian witches, fortune tellers, or astrologers offering their services through mass media channels. The common conception of those who publicly *expose* themselves through the means of modern market promotion is that they are charlatans. The reason for that is that authentic and capable magic professionals are those who supposedly know how to protect themselves through secrecy;

120 Willem de Blécourt, p. 215.

they can be identified, and then accessed, only through personal recommendations and word of mouth. Similar to the cases described by Jeanne Favret-Saada from Bocage, where the unwitchers promoting themselves through adverts in local newspapers were seen by the locals as 'scandalous characters, aberrant in relation to the system,'[121] the genuine diviners of contemporary Transylvania are not supposed to need publicity and their clientele, relatively stable, slowly increases simply through social proximity.

Nevertheless, the impact of information circulation is significant: Most of today's magical specialists cannot limit themselves to the more or less traditional elements of their practice. Hence, a card-reading session can be supplemented by the practitioner with astrological interpretations, and the coffee-reading session might be enriched with bioenergetic or naturist notions. No matter how well established through their specific techniques, these clandestine professionals understand and fully assume the necessity to stay competitive by gathering more knowledge and diversifying the product they offer.

Traditional rural divination techniques, such as divination in wax, with a pail (Rom.: *ciubăr*),[122] with corn beans (Rom.: *datul în bobi*), or in flour, have almost disappeared. They have been replaced by more modern divination techniques, namely divination with playing cards, coffee divination, and Gypsy Tarot (with a 36-card deck), which I found were dominant in both rural and urban areas. Classical Tarot (with a 78-card deck) and astrology are gaining in popularity but remain exclusively urban techniques.

It is of little consequence for a client consulting a diviner what her particular competence is, whether she 'sees' in coffee, playing

[121] Jeanne Favret-Saada, p. 62. [My translation].

[122] Divination with a pail ('*datul in ciubăr*') is a traditional form of rural divination based on the magical numbers seven and nine. It consists of seven or nine girls, younger than seven or nine years of age (to ensure sexual purity), who 'read' the answer to a question in water in a pail. Complicated and variable in form, it has not been practiced in twenty or thirty years but is remembered by locals in Dipşa, Piatra-Fântânele, and Tiha villages (Bistriţa-Năsăud County).

cards, Tarot cards, and Gipsy Tarot and whether she's an astrologer or a clairvoyant working with visions. The thing that matters the most for a client appealing to a diviner's skills is to obtain guidance, clarifications, or even possible solutions for unfulfilled wishes (getting married; being more financially successful; or getting a better job) or forms of destiny blockage (the suspicion of being bewitched, cursed, or the annihilating force of a suspected past kinship sin).

Professional fortune tellers are active in both urban and rural areas of today's Romania. By 'professional fortune teller,' I mean individuals who either earn the main part of their income or at least significantly supplement their income through this activity. The term 'professional,' in this context, has more to do with their specialized competence than with a status as a self-employed freelancer. Because divination is not legally regulated in Romania, from a legal point of view, it represents an illegal means of gaining profits.

Given the tendency toward (relative) anonymity of individuals, as well as the specialization and delegation of services dynamic defining urban milieus, urban diviners are usually perceived simply as mere fortune tellers (not possible witches) who work like professionals in almost any other field. Rural fortune tellers, on the other hand, can be so prominent (even 'famous' on a regional level) that they can alert a community's suspicion, i.e., local villagers often think of them as possible witches. The situation in rural areas is intensified by the tendency to believe that anything related to magic (including divination) is malefic. It is rooted in the basic dichotomies of religious discourse, which have been reinforced considerably post-1989 through the successful public reinstatement of the Orthodox Church in Romanian society. This perception is also related to the not yet forgotten rural-traditional model of the bygone village witch.

> *'There is a diviner in Cepari village. She has loads of cars parked in front of her house, daily. They come to see her from all over the place, even foreigners from quite afar. Sometimes, there are so many clients that their cars block the street ... I've never been to see her, myself. Why, because she says she reads in cards, she foretells with cards, but people in the village don't think so ... No, everybody is convinced that she's a skilled one, one who knows how to*

throw a spell on somebody. Even the local priest, he accepts her confession in the church and lets her come for liturgy, but he refuses to give her the sacraments. They can do that, you know; and that's like a penitence for one's sin. So, she must have great sins to atone for.' Silvia (woman, age 34, Năsăud)

For the professionals of magic in today's Romania, the line separating the two moral attitudes of magic (the benign, helpful side versus the malefic, aggressive side) is quite clear, and whichever side is initially chosen by the practitioner is the one she will have to stick to all the way:

'I read in coffee, as you very well know. I also might read the Psalter at midnight, offer some religious advice and tell my clients who could help them further. But I don't always get what people expect of me ... Not two weeks ago, one woman came and, at the end of the session, asked whether I could do some spells to keep her boy together with the girl he likes, as she would be most suitable for him. She even said we wouldn't harm anybody, as we would only help love to flourish. Hear that. Like, forcing somebody's free will is not harming anybody. Really. They don't get it, they simply don't get it: you can't be close to them both, God and the evil one, at the same time. Just as one cannot be in two places at the same time, so too us, the skillfull ones, cannot fight on two fronts. Who says they can, they lie. You have to choose from the very beginning whose side you're on, who you work with: the good, or the evil.' (Liudmila, woman, age 49, diviner, Cluj-Napoca)

However, for the public and potential clients, things are not always so straightforward. Divination has always been perceived as the simpler, quasi-benign side of the magical practice, slightly less condemned and more tolerated than other magic practices. In the past, it was often employed not by diviners limited to this one trade (like those of today) but by professionals of magic looking to diagnose, answer, and then solve a client's dire situation. Such, for example, is the case of Madame Flora described by Jeanne Favret-Saada[123] in 1972 in France. Madame Flora was basically an unwitcher; her complicated card divination sessions were looking to diagnose the bewitchment, help identify the aggressor, and offer hope. But, her more important work, that of unwitching, followed

123 Josée Contreras et Jeanne Favret-Saada, 'Ah ! La féline, la sale voisine... ', *Terrain – L'incroyable et ses preuves*, 14 (1990), pp. 20–31, ‹http://terrain.revues.org/document2968.html› [accessed October 2006].

immediately after the divination sessions; the latter functioned as an introduction to the larger ritual implications of the witchcraft situation. That is also the case for one of the two laic unwitchers I was able to map during my research. She was from the historical region of Moldavia. Presenting herself initially as a simple diviner, her more extended magical knowledge came through as soon as she identified a potential witchcraft situation that she felt she could help with. This is representative of the bottom line: people imagine these specialists of the magic domain as too tempted by what this field could offer beyond the simple foretelling. Magical knowledge is not intellectual knowledge. It is a weapon and a serious existential advantage; these diviners clearly have 'the grace' or 'the force' to dwell into its domain; so, how could they not give in to temptation? Why would they stop at the line bordering the divination's domain and not seek more power?

> *'I'm sure most of them know more than they show or pretend to know. Only God knows what they can really do, besides this fortune telling front ...' (Lenuța, woman, age 28, Dumitra village)*

Trying to establish a clear-cut divination practice is a real difficulty for any practitioner, even those in the cities. The rural-traditional model of a magic specialist capable of all and everything that this field has to offer, using divination only as a frontispiece, was in the minds of the villagers always linked to a 'double moral personality'[124]; this model still carries a lot of weight in people's perceptions. However, the new Westernized model of a diviner running her practice as a business, provider of a uniquely specialized service, is the one toward which my diviner informants for the most part aspired to, within the limits imposed by the lack of legislation supporting such businesses.

Coming back to the role of the fortune teller in the witchcraft discourse, the answer presented to the client at the end of the divination sequence establishes the part she plays in this process.

---

124 Gheorghe Pavelescu, *Magia la români: Studii şi cercetări despre magie, descântece şi mană* (Bucureşti: Minerva, 1998), p. 76. [My translation].

First, the fortune teller can be *the diagnostician* of an episode of witchcraft. She can trigger the entrance into the witchcraft discourse much as the incidental diagnostician can, assuming the client has not previously considered her/his unsatisfactory situation in terms of witchcraft. The fortune teller's additional contribution lies in the fact that her giving a name to the client's difficult situation comes as an assessment that bears no contradiction rather than a suggestion—after all, she is a specialist. If the client already believes that her/his suffering may be due to witchcraft, she intervenes as a professional diagnostician. Her specific techniques are employed in order to confirm, or sometimes contest, such a possibility. Mrs Gabor (woman, age 73, Deta, Timiş County), a diviner relying mostly on Gipsy Tarot, has two successive modalities of diagnosis able to establish whether or not the client might be bewitched[125] even before laying the cards on the table. If one is bewitched, or even the unaware bearer of a kinship sin, then the eyes are cloudy, the gaze is unfocused; that is why Mrs Gabor first scrutinizes her visitors with acuity. The second proceeding is to ask the client to hold a set of religious beads (rosary) in her/his left hand, before asking them to cut the cards: if the hand is shaky or the client starts to sweat and shiver, then there most certainly are evil spells to consider.

Second, the fortune teller is the *intermediary* in most of the diagnosed episodes of witchcraft. Once the diagnosis of witchcraft has been suggested or confirmed, the fortune teller recommends the next steps and, thus, ceases to be professionally involved. Without exception, I found that these next steps follow Orthodox religious rituals and involve clergy or monks. Usually, the recommendations followed precise 'clinical pathways': certain monasteries for particular types of problems and certain other priests or monks for others. This may seem paradoxical considering that the Orthodox Church is officially vehemently opposed to professional fortune telling and considers frequenting a diviner a serious sin. Nonetheless, fortune tellers gain credibility through their strategic use of religious termi-

[125] Field information, Deta (Timiş County), August 2007.

nology, their doctrinal competence, and their recommendation of certain prayers, fasts, icons, and amulets.

Third, a fortune teller prolongs her/his involvement by acting as a *therapist*. With few exceptions, this particular role is one of the past. Nowadays, this position is normally occupied by an Orthodox priest or monk. At this point, some clarifications on the rural magic specialists of the past in Romania are in order.

The Traditional Unwitcher and Magical Healers

In Romania, the lay therapist in a witchcraft case is called '*dezlegătoare*'. In magical contexts, the verb '*a dezlega*' denotes the magical unbinding (i.e., undoing) of the evil spell causing the magical aggression. Normally, the ritual of retracing the steps to undo the evil aggression is accompanied by its redirection back toward the aggressor. Such actions are meant not only to 'return the favor' and balance out the effects of a spell but are also meant to hurt, punish, and cause havoc in the aggressor's life to a degree that outbalances the aggression. In Jeanne Favret-Saada and Josée Contreras' terms, the unwitcher, similar to the sorcerer, is a possessor of abnormal force, which is beneficial for his/her clients but definitely malefic[126] when turned against the magical aggressor. It is easy to see, then, how the actions of a laic unwitcher can be qualified as equally aggressive and damaging. Redeemed as moral and justified only from the point of view of the victim, these actions aim to provoke effects as deadly as possible into the life of the presupposed magical aggressor. That is why the theoretical dichotomy between good and evil magic (*dezlegătoare* vs. *sorceress*) does not function as such a clear-cut distinction for people in everyday life: It is assumed that anyone who knows how to undo an evil spell must also know how to cast it. Also, the generic historical rural model of the village witch in Romania was that of an individual (mostly women, sometimes men) able to successfully work, through magical means, in both ways. Resorted to by some people as unwitcher, sometimes so-

---

126 Josée Contreras et Jeanne Favret-Saada, 'Ah ! La féline, la sale voisine... ', p. 21.

licited as a sorcerer/sorceress, such a character was always perceived as morally ambiguous. Aurora Liiceanu's ethnographic research describing Anuța (one of the last renowned village witches of the northern Transylvania region, who died in 1977) shows that her moral standpoint in a witchcraft situation was more or less coincidental with that of her client: 'She only knew the truth of the client, who offered her a version sustaining that they were the victim of somebody else's actions.'[127] Hence, it is safer to suppose that to be an unwitcher rather than a sorcerer/sorceress was more of a situational matter, depending on the client's interpretation of what needed fixing in their lives, and less a matter of moral scruples on the part of the magic specialist.

A related term to that of *dezlegătoare* (unwitcher), theoretically distinct but rarely dissociated in practice, is the Romanian *descântătoare* (a healing specialist). *Descântecul* can be defined as a form of magical incantation accompanied by precise ritual gestures and the use of specific substances or objects, mostly employed in the fighting off of illnesses. Because of its poetic richness and archaic language, *descântecul* was one of the folkloric species most studied in Romanian ethnology, though mainly as a form of poetry rather than the complex ritual it really was. The fact that *descântecul* was mostly versified facilitated its inclusion under the category of folk poetry instead of that of magical healing. Every *descântec* was dedicated to a unique affection; therefore, it was always a '*descântec* for': migraines, arthritis, tuberculosis, tonsillitis, ulcer, skin abscesses, wall eye, insomnia, the evil eye, etc. These affections come under the form of a vast morphology including, but not limited to, specific illnesses we would today file under medical conditions, which back in the day were instead closely linked to traditional perceptions of illness as something supernatural: God's punishment, supernatural spirits, or the occult evil doings of enemies.[128] The

---

127 Aurora Liiceanu, *Povestea unei vrăjitoare* (Bucureşti: Editura ALL, 1996), p. 68. [My translation]

128 I. Aurel Candrea, *Folclorul medical român comparat. Privire generală. Medicina magică* (Iaşi: Polirom, 1999), p. 331.

names of these affections are, similarly to the general language of *descântece*, of an archaic parlance that always requires translation into the conventional medical names they have today. The only way of obtaining the knowledge of such a ritual incantation was to 'steal' it (learning it by heart through direct observation) while the expert was performing it.[129]

This Romanian category of magical healing through incantation is similar, in many respects, to the still current French *Le secret* (>Engl. 'the Secret'), described as a gestural ritual with incantations dedicated to a unique purpose.[130] Knowing one such a *secret* does not mean that the performer is perceived as a professional healer[131]; that would require far vaster knowledge and abnormal force. *Le secret* needs to be passed on before death, similar to the case shortly described by Sabina Magliocco for Sardinia in 2001.[132] Her informant was taught how to cure warts using a specific incantation passed on by his grandfather before he passed away. To recite the words of such an incantation without the context of a proper healing ritual means, for both the Sardinian *meikina* (medicine) and the Romanian *descântec,* the instant loss of one's power to heal that specific affliction. In practice, the individuals who possessed the knowledge of *descântece* were mostly women, though not necessarily witches, who knew a small number of such ritual healing incantations dedicated to curing an equal number of physical affections. Gheorghe Pavelescu's interwar research in the Apuseni Mountains of Transylvania, carried out in 1940, registered a total number of 200 *descântece* in 41 villages from 60 informants.[133] The number of informants knowing more than the standard two or three *descântece*, namely 6, 8, 9, or even 13 incantations, was extremely

129 Gheorghe Pavelescu, p. 74; Aurel Candrea, p. 332.

130 Dominique Camus, p. 29.

131 Jeanne Favret-Saada, *Les mots, la mort, les sorts,* p. 85.

132 Sabina Magliocco, 'Witchcraft, healing and vernacular magic in Italy', *Witchcraft Continued. Popular Magic in Modern Europe,* ed. by Willem de Blécourt & Owen Davies (Manchester & New York: Manchester University Press, 2004), pp. 151–173, p. 151.

133 Gheorghe Pavelescu, pp. 180–183.

low (only 5 informants of 60); so, it is safe to suppose that these were actually magic specialists.

The absence of these magic specialists today, both laic unwitchers and magical healers using incantations, is commonly explained by a generational shift. What is more, people generally assume that their specialized functions have been taken over by Orthodox clergy:

> *'Nowadays, there's no one left to use the incantations ... All the old women who knew them are dead. Now we only go to the priest to bless.' (Māriuţa, woman, age 77, Giugeşti village).*

As mentioned before, I was able to document the existence of only two active lay unwitching therapists at the exterior edges of the investigated region, one in Timiş County and other in Suceava County. Both of them are located in different historical regions than Transylvania, the Banat and Northern Moldavia. And, with the exception of a commonly known, religious form of a *descântec* dedicated to curing the evil eye,[134] the age of the magical healing incantations is also gone. But, when I appealed to collective memory, people remembered that many more such specialists (laic unwitchers or magical healers) were active until roughly 20 or 30 years ago. Some personal examples offered by my informants can help illustrate this point.

Mārioara (woman, age 62, Reteag) appealed, in 1976, to a renowned unwitcher (woman) who was active then in Timişoara. Roughly at the same time, Floricuţa (woman, age 63, Dumitra village) contacted an unwitcher (woman) from Agrieş (Bistriţa-Năsăud County), and then, for another problem, she went to see a famous unwitcher (man) from Sălişte (Maramureş County) in the 1980s. Another woman who performed healings through magic incantations (*descântătoare*) solved a young girl's hopeless medical case through weeks of ritual interventions in Dumitra during the 1980s. In Giurgeşti, the best-known local unwitcher (there were several women who knew how to heal through magical incantations, but this one was the only one able to undo a spell) maintained an am-

[134] To be discussed in Chapter 3: **Therapeutic Interventions**.

biguous regional fame until she died, at the beginning of 1990s. The same informants appeal today, in case of need, to Orthodox priests and monks, according to the specific set of issues they want to address.

The Orthodox Priest or Monk

The fact that it is members of the Orthodox clergy who occupy the position of magic therapist in witchcraft situations is by no means new. Nor is this, historically speaking, a phenomenon exclusive to Orthodox Christianity. Priests were acting as unwitchers particularly within Catholicism,[135] where this fluctuating phenomenon was highly dependent on the exact historical period and region discussed and on the particular relations between the canonical religion and localized popular religion.

Of equal importance when discussing the phenomenon of priests as unwitchers is the more general popular usage of insignia of the catholic church (such as holy water, blessed salt, or images of saints), not as means of spiritual edification but as sources of magical power (particularly as apotropaic and healing devices) or as tangible countermagic.[136] Representatives of the catholic church in late 16th-century Italy condemned such popular practices of 'putting familiar Christian devices to purposes not approved by the Church,'[137] just as Sardinian priests of modern times 'often frowned upon (and continue to disparage)'[138] a popular religiosity that com-

135 De Blécourt gives a short account of the unwitchings and exorcisms by Catholic clergy at various times in European history in 'Witch Doctors, Soothsayers and Priests: On Cunning Folk in European Historiography and Tradition', *Social History* 19, no. 3 (1994), pp. 285–303, pp. 299–300.

136 Willem de Blécourt, 'The Witch, her Victim, the Unwitcher and the Researcher: the continued existence of traditional witchcraft', *Witchcraft and Magic in Europe. The Twentieth Century,* ed. by Bengt Ankarloo and Stuart Clark (University of Pennsylvania Press, 1999), pp. 141–219, p. 185.

137 Marry O'Neil, 'Magical Healing, Love Magic and the Inquisition in Late Sixteenth-century Modena', *Inquisition and Society in Early Modern Europe*, ed. by Stephen Haliczer (London, Sydney: Croom Helm, 1987), pp. 88–114, p. 91.

138 Sabina Magliocco, 'Witchcraft, healing and vernacular magic in Italy', *Witchcraft Continued. Popular Magic in Modern Europe*, p. 157.

bines popular saints' cult celebrations with folk healing and ecstatic states.

For centuries, the Catholic church had the difficult task of fighting against, negotiating with, introducing innovations to, and accepting transformative elements from a popular religiosity best described as 'religion as practiced'[139] or, in Sabina Magliocco's terms,[140] 'vernacular' magic and religious rural culture from all across Europe. But, Catholic priests and monks always were and still are (just like their Orthodox counterparts), more than the representatives of their Church's voice of authority. They were also social actors, parts of specific communities, and invested with particular roles within those communities. Therefore, they had to be 'sensitive to demands from their congregation'[141] and respond to concrete, as well as spiritual, needs. As Jeanne Favret-Saada's research in France shows, the local Catholic priest can be perceived, in the community, as a 'minor unwitcher'[142] due to the fact that he is the depositary of blessed salt and holy water. But, the Church regional officials at the time of her research (1970s) were already openly discouraging such superstitious attitudes on the part of the faithful, as well as the priests' direct intervention in witchcraft situations. In the long series of reforms that marked Catholicism, the Second Vatican Council of 1966[143] decided for a fresh approach destined to make the Catholic religion more relevant to a globalized, modern society and, thus, relinquished superstitious, retrograde attitudes and practices; the priest, in this context, is to act exclusively as a teacher of his community, not as an unofficial medicine man.

---

139 Ellen Badone, 'Introduction', *Religious Orthodoxy and Popular Faith in European Society*, ed. by Ellen Badone (Princeton, New Jersey: Princeton University Press, 1990), pp. 3–23, p. 6.

140 Sabina Magliocco, p. 152.

141 Willem de Blécourt, 'Witch Doctors, Soothsayers and Priests: On Cunning Folk in European Historiography and Tradition', p. 300.

142 Jeanne Favret-Saada, *Les mots, la mort, les sorts*, p. 23.

143 More about the changes brought within the Catholic religious practice by the Second Vatican Council, in Ruth Behar, 'The Struggle for the Church: Popular Anticlericalism and Religiosity in post-Franco Spain', *Religious Orthodoxy and Popular Faith in European Society*, pp. 76–112.

On the other hand, Orthodox Christianity has always been, especially as practiced in rural areas, of a certain 'laxity'[144] when tolerating elements foreign to a more strict reading of Christian dogma. As shown by Iveta Todorova-Pirgova in the case of contemporary Bulgaria, the accepted dichotomies applied in daily life by Orthodox communities have little to do with an opposition of *pagan* versus *Christian* and more with '*virtuous=in the name of God* versus *evil=in the name of the devil.*'[145]

Discussing the case of Christian Orthodox religion in Greece, Charles Stuart argues that there is a *genetic* relationship between Orthodoxy and local rural culture. Centuries of interaction and mutual accommodations have resulted in an indigenous tradition (visible to this day) that might surprise outsiders through the uncanny similarity between rural magical rituals and the central rituals of the Church: 'Ultimately the matter comes down, not to *who* is performing the ritual, but to what the Church declares. Such declarations can take time to be pronounced, and may later be reversed.'[146] The Orthodox Church's dogmatic enlightenment of its followers, and the fighting off of their superstitions, are doctrinal attitudes as valid today as they were in the past within all the Eastern Orthodox national churches. Nevertheless, as the case of the Evil Eye Prayer shows, it is not uncommon for a principle that is fought off at a certain historical point in time to become acceptable at another. For example, for centuries, the Orthodox Church did its best to discourage the Evil Eye explanatory mythology by heavily relying on theological arguments ascribed to several Fathers of the Church (partic-

144 Gabriel Troc, 'Exorcism şi vindecare în Biserica Ortodoxă', *Caietele Tranziţiei*, 2.3 (Cluj–Napoca, 1998).

145 Iveta Todorova-Pirgova, 'Witches and Priests in the Bulgarian village: Past and Present', in *Demons, Spirits, Witches*, Vol. 3: Witchcraft Mythologies and Persecutions, ed. by Gábor Klaniczay and Éva Pócs (Budapest, New York: Central European University Press, 2008), pp. 283–294, p. 287.

146 Charles Stewart, 'Magic and Orthodoxy', *Greek Magic. Ancient, Medieval and Modern*, ed. by J.C.B. Petropoulos (New York: Routledge, 2008), pp. 87–94, p. 93.

ularly Basil, John Chrysostom, Jerome, and Tertullian[147]); yet, sometime after the 17th century, the Orthodox ecclesiastic authorities incorporated a special prayer against the evil eye into the Small Prayerbook (*Mikron Evkhologion*).[148] This is not a unique example of the Orthodox Church ending up discreetly incorporating those elements that it could not abolish. But, it is still more correct to say that its general historical attitude was one of tacit tolerance rather than downright acceptance.

A good example of such a case in Romania was offered by Ştefania Cristescu-Golopenţia's interwar field research in Drăguş (Făgăraş, Southern Transylvania). She was surprised to observe how in the day-to-day existence of the people in the region religion and magic harmoniously blended into one another. The similarity between the religious and the magical rites (based on the same genetic relationship between Orthodoxy and local village culture as discussed by Stewart for the case of Greece) meant that, in Drăguş, people had little interest in distinguishing between religion and magic in everyday life. The reason for this conciliatory attitude was the fact that religion was not lived, by the people of Drăguş (Făgăraş), as a dogma; 'it was lived as an old custom'[149] in the way they were taught to practice it by their forefathers.

Working on the same time period as Ştefania Cristescu-Golopenţia's study, Gheorghe Pavelescu documented a clear overlap of functions between lay unwitchers and Orthodox priests in the Apuseni Mountains[150] (1939–1940). But, what back then seemed to be a peaceful coexistence tends today to take the form of exclusiveness. In Romania, the Orthodox Church plays a most direct and an essential role *within* the witchcraft discourse. There are specific religious rituals dedicated to dealing with this type of situation, usually

147 Matthew W. Dickie, 'The Fathers of the Church and the Evil Eye', *Byzantine Magic*, ed. by Henry Maguire (Washington, DC.: Dumbarton Oaks, 1995), pp. 9–34.

148 Charles Stewart, p. 90.

149 Ştefania Cristescu-Golopenţia, *Gospodăria şi credinţele magice ale femeilor din Drăguş (Făgăraş)*, (Bucureşti: Paideia, 2002), p. 52. [My translation].

150 Gheorghe Pavelescu, pp. 48–49.

described with the same term as the corresponding magical ritual (Rom.> *dezlegări*), while members of the clergy play, in this equation, the part of the therapist.

Jeanne Favret-Saada's account of the step-by-step development of an episode of witchcraft in Bocage (see above, **Chapter 1: Situations**) holds that the magical therapist is consulted only after the medical doctor and priest. But, in modern Romania, medical treatments (prescribed pharmaceuticals and hospitalization) can be pursued alongside magical and religious options. This is especially the case when the illness and/or its causes are not sufficiently elucidated by empirical explanations.

Like fortune tellers, clergy and monastics can play several roles:

First, they can take the role of the *professional diagnostician*. Not all members of the clergy are open to the possibility of naming or encouraging a diagnosis of witchcraft, but unsurprisingly the most-frequented Orthodox priests in crisis situations are those who do. The divination technique known as 'The Opening of the Book' (Rom.> '*deschiderea cărții*') is specifically associated with the priesthood, although the Romanian Orthodox church had repeatedly condemned it as a major sin, in both the past and the present. The practice was recorded in 1810–1811 and, together with the popular frequenting of magical healers (*descântătoare*), condemned by one of the most prominent figures of the Transylvanian Age of Enlightenment, Petru Maior.[151] But, it was, undoubtedly, far older. I. Aurel Candrea's book on medical folklore from 1944 reproduced two versions of this custom.[152] In one of them, the Orthodox priest opens 'the Book' (the Bible) after holding a specific religious ritual for the healing of a bedridden, ill person with the explicit purpose of assessing the chances of survival. If the book opens where the font was red, it means hope: the suffering person was going to recover. If the book opens where the text was typed in black, then there was no

151 Valer Simion Cosma, 'Preotul, tămăduirea și cartea în lumea țărănească a secolului al XIX-lea', *Conferințele de vară de la Telciu* (ed. a II-a), edited by Valer Simion Cosma and Edit Szegedi (Cluj Napoca: Eikon, 2014), pp. 97–112, p. 103.

152 I. Aurel Candrea, *Folclorul medical român comparat*, p. 245.

hope left, and s/he was going to die. The significance of this magical–religious divination technique has to be linked to the historical value of the Bible in any rural traditional European society, as 'The Book *par excellence*,'[153] as the ultimate depositary of licit sacred knowledge. The manipulation of the Bible for divination techniques has never been limited to clergy; as mentioned before, one of my informants visited a famous unwitcher (man) from Sălişte (Maramureş County) in the 1980s, whose preferred method of diagnosis was the Opening of the Book. And yet, as the sacerdotal 'handler of the sacred books,'[154] the Orthodox priest and monk remains credited with the ability of best deciphering the secret knowledge transmitted through the Sacred Book divination technique.

As it stands today, the priest asks a question on behalf of the victim, opens an ancient religious book (not necessarily the Bible) at random, and interprets the text to answer the question. It is commonly used by priests to confirm a diagnosis of witchcraft. People in contemporary Romania are perfectly aware that this technique is officially condemnable: television programs or radio broadcasts treating Orthodox dogma are now accessible even in the most remote villages. The aim of such mediatized efforts undertaken by the Romanian Orthodox Church post-1989 is to reinstruct the parishioners according to the views of a unique and coherent Orthodox dogmatic national center; the impression this whole propaganda could mistakenly create is that it is successful in practice. As the field reality shows, however, this is hardly the case:

> *'You see, it is a somewhat curious fact. The Church states that it is a sin to open the Book; it is a sin for them (for the priests) to tell you about the future. And yet I went to see for my problem three ... no, four priests who opened the Book. I don't know whose sin this is, but you know people in need... At any rate, I felt reassured and with a less guilty conscience. After all, they were priests.' (Miluca, woman, age 55, Bistriţa).*

153 Antoaneta Olteanu, *Şcoala de solomonie. Divinaţie şi vrăjitorie în context comparat* (Bucureşti: Paideia, 1999), p. 186. [My translation].

154 Valer Simion Cosma, p. 112. [My translation].

Unlike the role of the professional fortune teller, the priest's involvement does not end with the diagnosis. Instead, his most important contribution, as the only legitimate *therapist* in an episode of witchcraft, is about to begin. A complex religious ritual dedicated to solving a magical aggression is a long-standing process. It requires the joint efforts of the priest acting as unwitcher and his client and, depending on the particular circumstances, might also require constant ritual involvement from close family and friends.

At the same time, the specific forms of therapeutic religious ritual vary for each situation. Symptoms of illness, delayed marriage, and unexplained, constant misfortune each require different treatments. They also vary according to the personal capabilities of the priests. Religious doctrine holds that all ordained Orthodox priests and monks have the same professional capacity and the same religious means to confront all forms of evil, but the actual situation differs:

> *'Q.: If there is a suspicion of being bewitched, to whom does one appeal?*
> *A.: Well, to priests or monks ... But not any priest or monk. Generally, it is better to appeal to monks. There are some of those who are able to unbind an evil spell—not all of them. In any case, it is better to ask around. People know.' (Floricuța, woman, age 63, Dumitra village).*

> *'There are indeed some priests more recommended than others in dealing with these issues of sorcery ... Maybe that is not a normal situation, as long as they were equally invested by the Church with the same grace, no? Well, maybe this is it: one cannot underestimate the power of the priest's prayer in the face of God. But maybe that particular priest has a bigger, a stronger grace, and his prayers are stronger than the others', you know?' Silvia (woman, age 34, Năsăud).*

The religious term 'grace' ('*har*') has important dogmatic relevance, designating a quality equally shared by all Orthodox clergy and monastics through their professional and religious investment ('*hirotonisire*'). This 'grace' is gained only through ordination and is not linked to the individual person but transcends them and binds them together as representatives of the Orthodox Church. Nevertheless '*harul*' is often perceived as an individual quality or personal power by the people seeking the clergy's help. The term is also employed in reference to the magical power held by fortune tellers, clairvoyants, and other magic specialists. Priests and monks are often approached for dealing with episodes of witchcraft because they are thought to have a supplementary 'gift' or 'grace.' In some cases, priests develop informal specialties, such as curing illnesses caused by a kinship curse, performing exorcisms, and reversing the impossibility of getting married. When in need, people can access true regional oral maps, orientating each individual toward the most suitable religious therapist.

Similar to the role of the annunciator, but even more pronounced, an unwitcher is always a shaping force of the witchcraft discourse.[155] The annunciator him/herself, as a survivor or a direct witness of a witchcraft situation, draws most of their theoretical and explanatory knowledge from the unwitcher they themselves consulted. The fact that it is mostly religious therapists who act as unwitchers means having elements of religious explanatory discourse brought into the very core of the witchcraft discourse and that ethical religious standpoints affect the distribution of actions and roles. Moreover, because these religious unwitchers usually refrain from identifying a particular person,[156] thereby respecting the limits set by the Church's official discourse, the whole aggressor pole is progressively blurring. Whether that might eventually lead to a complete dissolution of the aggressor pole, and thus to the collapse of the witchcraft discourse in Romania, still remains to be seen. Until that time, the magical aggressor mythology is so powerful that it successfully continues to incite people's curiosity and further supplies a myriad of narratives. As the following subchapter will show, the imagined magical aggressor is one of the most complex characters of the contemporary witchcraft discourse; despite its alleged in-

155 Willem de Blécourt, 'The Witch, her Victim, the Unwitcher and the Researcher: the continued existence of traditional witchcraft', p. 184.

156 That's one limit set for the Catholic priests as well in the past, when dealing with witchcraft discourse. Willem de Blécourt, 'Witch Doctors, Soothsayers and Priests: On Cunning Folk in European Historiography and Tradition', p. 299.

existence and mere referential function within the victim's discourse and despite all the religious interdictions to avoid this subject, the aggressor surely still incites the imagination—just as evil always did.

2.3 Who are the Magical Aggressors?

In order to sketch some of the common perceptions regarding magical aggressors, these absent yet virtually indispensable actors of the witchcraft discourse, it might be useful to comparatively examine the material of my research in Romania in contrast to the ethnological studies dedicated to the witchcraft discourse in the second half of the 20th century in France. Contributions by Jeanne Favret-Saada, Dominique Camus, André Julliard, or Owen Davies can highlight significant similarities and important differences.

Dominique Camus' field research in Haute-Bretagne in the 1980s shows that the majority of all the 'professional' unwitchers or sorcerers that he interacted with were men. His informants explained this gender predominance through a shared local perception that links an individual's magical strength to the strength of his or her vital force; and, apparently, men 'have stronger blood running through their veins.'[157] In a patriarchal logic, just as men are generally stronger than women, so too men magical specialists are more powerful than their women counterparts. The disappearance of witchcraft prosecutions and trials between the 17th and 18th centuries had determined, especially in France, a progressive role reversal of the presupposed magical aggressors (the women witches) and their accusers (many of them men), up to the point where 'the witch disappears behind the charlatan'[158] and 'witchcraft becomes masculine.'[159]

---

[157] Dominique Camus, p. 21. [My Translation].

[158] Marie-Sylvie Dupont-Bouchat, 'Diavolul îmblânzit. Vrăjitoria reconsiderată. Magia şi vrăjitoria în secolul al XIX-lea', *Magia şi vrăjitoria în Europa, din Evul Mediu până astăzi*, ed. by Robert Muchembled (Bucureşti: Humanitas, 1997), p. 248.

[159] Marie-Sylvie Dupont-Bouchat., p. 272.

The cases I documented during my research in North Western Transylvania, as well as the historical data presented in specialized ethnological literature, suggest that in Romania the gender distribution between men and the women active in the magical field tends to be strongly in favor of female practitioners. That also seems to be the case for the whole of Europe, from both a historical and a contemporary perspective, with this notable exception of modern and contemporary France. For nowadays Romania, whether we talk about the presupposed magical aggressors or about the actors within the relatively benign area of divination (fortune tellers and clairvoyants), the magical pole appears to be a rather exclusively feminine scene—whose counterpart, integrated into the religious pole, belongs to masculine actors: the unwitching priests and monks of Orthodox denomination.

However, male witches or sorcerers are not something unheard of. For instance, an informant residing today in the village of Reteag remembers vividly the image of an old man who, during her childhood and youth in Agrieş village, was particularly feared for his ability to supposedly steal cows' milk.

> *'My dad was saying that his cows were running from him when they were returning from grazing in the evenings, and he wasn't able to milk them. When he was, then the cows wouldn't give a drop of milk... And they would run to that man's home and just lay their heads on his fence, so he was milking them right there and then. And all of them, my father and his neighbours, they were all just too afraid to go to that man's home and bring their cows back (...). They are all dead now, all those people who knew how to do those things in the past.' (Mărioara, woman, age 62, Reteag/Agrieş village)*

The gender distribution is similar for the supposed victims of witchcraft attacks. As shown in previous chapters, the French research highlights the fact that witchcraft attacks usually target men, the owner of the farm and head of his family. All other people, animals, and resources affected suffer in his stead and in his name, as the male is the ultimate source of the vital force that the magical aggressor seeks to hijack. In the context of the transfer of favorability, the mana (or vital surplus) is the one quality whose possession is disputed in contemporary rural France. Whether it consists of good health, economic prosperity, beauty, abundance, or simply good luck, the possession of such 'goods' has always been considered risky yet highly desirable in a rural-agricultural traditional society. The possessors of mana or vital surplus can easily become targets to witches—always depicted as constitutively 'jealous'[160] beings.

The majority of the cases documented during my Transylvanian field research are not, as mentioned before, based on this principle of magical transfer of favorability any more. The scenario most often encountered today is the one depicting a conflict between an envious, vengeful woman, channeling her aggression through magical means toward another woman. The woman presumably acting as magical aggressor does not seem to gain anything palpable out of her actions (vital, economic, and good luck surplus) but simply the pure satisfaction of causing unhappiness in or even completely destroying the other woman's life.

Several brief examples examined here might clarify this statement better and show the particular mechanism through which the magical aggressor gets named and identified by their presupposed victims.

Miluca, (woman, age 55, Bistrița, nursery teacher) started to suspect in 2006 that her daughter's continuous difficulties in getting married (Ela, 29 years old at that time) might have to be blamed on some spells operated by her mother-in-law (Ela's grandmother). The reason for this designation was the fact that the mother-in-law repeatedly had uttered an extremely serious accusation, namely that her son's premature demise (Miluca's husband and Ela's father) was due to a lethal combination of alcohol and pills, imputable to Miluca either as an accident or a premeditated gesture. In other words, the mother-in-law believed and continued to declare that Miluca had killed her husband. Therefore, in this outrageous accusation, Miluca saw the reason that might have determined the old lady to seek revenge and go as far as to provoke unhappiness in her own grandchildren's lives through witchcraft attacks. It is easy to

[160] Jeanne Favret Saada, p. 343.

observe from this example that the binding of Ela's marriage could not count as a form of proper gain for the supposed magical aggressor (in terms of favorability transfer). Rather, it was simply seen as an action motivated by pure revenge.

Antonia (woman, age 33, Bistrița, shop owner) started to consider in 2007 that the delay in marrying her partner of five years could only be explained through the malevolent witchcraft interventions of her partner's ex-wife, who was residing in Italy at that time. Again, a straightforward motivation of the presupposed magical aggressor was hard to pinpoint, as the suspected woman was living quite far from the couple and was also happily remarried. A transfer of favorability was also unsupported. The magical binding of Antonia's chance to get married had no way to represent a form of gain (such as vital, marital, or bioeconomic surplus) for the ex-wife. The only possible explanation was, once again, vengeful feelings of the ex-wife, the pure desire to cause unhappiness in Antonia's relationship.

Maria (woman, age 56, Bistrița, teacher) diagnosed in the summer of 2007 the general state of unhappiness that had been affecting her life for the previous few years (multiple recurrent illnesses without a coherent medical diagnosis, depression, marital strife, financial difficulties, etc.) as the effect of the maleficent spells operated by his partner's ex-wife, the one he had left for Maria. One interesting aspect of this case is the dimension of personal guilt: The victim internalized an interpretation of the facts pertaining to her life situation that puts a witchcraft attack on an almost equal level to the religious logic of a deserved punishment for sin (in this case, the sin of breaking up a family). This was the only case I encountered where the violence of the witchcraft attack was perceived by the victim as something she almost deserved. Usually, assuming a witchcraft diagnosis and identifying a potential aggressor are intimately linked to a marked feeling of injustice, as an undeserved, exteriorly inflicted violence. Either way, this case also lacks the transfer of favorability principle: the ex-wife had nothing to gain from her presupposed evil magical interventions, other than the satisfaction of revenge rooted in hatred.

Ițu (woman, age 66, Bistrița, retired accountant) started to take notice in 2007 that the repeated visits of her daughter-in-law's mother were always ending in inexplicable, sudden physical pains, or even illness for herself. Both she and her neighbor friend concluded that this could only happen because the unwanted guest was targeting evil spells at her. One possible reason identified by Ițu was the fact that she was initially vehemently opposed to her son's marriage to his current wife; therefore, her daughter-in-law's mother could have employed witchcraft as revenge. Another possible reason was the social status differences between the parties: Her daughter-in-law's family originated from a poor mountain village whereas Ițu's family was a proud Lutheran line of skilled town artisans. Similar to the other cases, the presupposed magical aggressor supposedly obtained only personal satisfaction out of tormenting her victim, rooted in envy.

Mărioara (woman, age 62, Reteag/Agrieș) had suffered the long-term effects of a debilitating magical attack in the 1970s, initiated while visiting her parents in her native village. The magical aggressor was easy to identify: It was an old woman whom Mărioara saw manipulating the dirt in her footprint[161] as she turned to look over her shoulder after exchanging greetings. The actions of that old

161 Manipulating the dirt from a footprint is a well-known technique for a spell. It involves either the removal of some dirt from or the carving out of the footprint altogether. Whatever is taken is then brought home in order to be integrated more into elaborate rituals where it functions on the principle of contiguity (stepped on by the intended target, the footprint dirt retains something of the essence of that human being). Alternatively, it can be worked on right where it has been taken: cutting the imprint with a knife and turning it upside down while reciting the appropriate curse-incantation is still believed to function as powerful harmful magic. Also, during her research in the Maramureș region of northern Transylvania in the 1970s, Aurora Liiceanu documented the apotropaic use of this same technique, this time during an unwitching ritual. The laic therapist digs and carves the footprint with a knife, turns it upside down and places a coin in every hole so that the powers of evil, thus bribed, would stay away from the afflicted individual in the future. Aurora Liiceanu, p. 91.

woman could only be interpreted by Mārioara as compulsive expressions of malice and envy: at that time, she was a healthy, beautiful, happy young wife, easily eliciting jealousy with her involuntary display of vital surplus.

These few examples highlight the fact that, in today's Romania, the loss of vitality caused to the victim through a witchcraft attack does not always follow a compensatory logic, so that the imbalance from the victim's pole would translate as a surplus (vital, marital, and economic) at the aggressor's pole. From the victim's' point of view, the aggressor's actions are sufficiently founded in revenge, hatred, or envy. At the same time, the mechanism of identifying a potential magical aggressor always operates within the wider social perimeter of the presupposed victim. As expressed by Dominique Camus,[162] the reason for naming a certain person as the magical aggressor can be a certain antipathy, even instinctive, felt by the victim toward the person to become the designated witch. After all, the victim is the one choosing her aggressor. The suspected magical aggressor is never a perfect stranger or a very close family member but usually somebody included in the secondary circle of social interactions: a neighbor, a friend, the mother-in-law, a cousin, up to declared and known enemies.

In conclusion, while contemporary French ethnological research describes magical aggression as an attempt of vital force theft directed, ultimately, against the (male) family head of an agricultural exploitation, witchcraft experiences of contemporary Romania nearly exclusively describe a state of war between women, grounded in feelings rather than economical pragmatics, such as revenge, envy, and hatred. As for the actors positioned in the conflict, in rural France, the unwitcher stands in for his client (the victim) so that, in the end, the ones fighting each other through magic means are the sorcerer and the unwitcher (the magic specialists, predominantly men), not the victim and the aggressor. By contrast, in today's Romania, through the same system of delegating competences and purchasing services, it is Orthodox priests or monks who confront,

[162] Dominique Camus, p. 89.

in the victim's name, the magical aggressors, an almost exclusively feminine category.

At this point, some clarifications about specialization and identity might be in order. In theory, there is a distinction between the beneficiary of a magical aggression and the specialist able to accomplish it (the sorcerer or the witch). In some cases, these two analytically distinct roles overlap in practice: The beneficiary is the sorcerer. In other cases, the roles are played by two individuals whose relationship is essentially that of a client requiring a service and a specialist offering that service. The latter is the type of relation that Dominique Camus had in mind when describing a magic war carried out between the professional unwitcher and the professional sorcerer. The role played by the unwitching Orthodox priest or monk in contemporary Romania is similar. The priest is the delegated specialist representing the victim and fighting in her name, with the only reservation that the religious means for unwitching do not permit him to carry out (at least theoretically) actions of counteraggression, and to respond with escalating violence to the magical actions of the aggressor. This necessity of responding to violence with equal or even increased aggression was the hallmark of all Romanian lay unwitchers from the past and still is for the case of contemporary France.

Possessors of 'Grace'

In practice, who exactly carries out the spells is never an issue for the victims of a witchcraft diagnosis. Once they have identified their potential tormentor, i.e., the person who most likely would have reasons to hurt them, little does it matter whether the latter might have hired a specialist sorcerer of some sort or whether they carried out the evil spells themselves. Such a distinction has no meaning and no subsequent stake within the unwitching therapeutic ritual.

Nonetheless, part of the explicative larger discourse surrounding every concrete story is the common conception according to which not everybody who just gives it a go, based on the learning of some charms or spells, would be able to put an aggressive magical force in motion successfully. The classic distinction made by E.E. Evans-Pritchard between a *witch* and a *sorcerer* states that, while a *witch* 'acts without rites and spells and uses hereditary psycho-psychical powers to attain his ends,' a *sorcerer* 'uses the techniques of magic and derives his power from medicines.'[163] The form of this anthropological distinction is a clear dichotomy, whereas the field reality suggests something more along the lines of complementarity.

In Romania, the essential trait that enables individuals to operate in the magical field is believed to be the possession of a type of extrasensory, trans-mundane 'power,' closer to Evans-Pritchard's definition for *witch*. The term most often used for this power in Romanian is '*har*' (>Grace) or '*dar*' (>Gift), equally describing the power attributed to: soothsayers, Orthodox priests or monks, and even magical aggressors. Having said that, possessing specialized knowledge (charms, spells, and rituals) is a part of the condition for ultimately considering someone a specialized magical aggressor. Thus, the portrait of the magical aggressor as common conceptions of yesterday and today's Romania has traits of both, *witch* and *sorcerer*—possessing hereditary psychopsychical powers *and* learning how to use magical techniques and rites.

The mechanical carrying out of a magical ritual is by no means a guarantee of a successful action, because the ritual is seen as merely the instrument, the exterior means to channel the imponderable magical force. For example, in the summer of 2008, an employee of the school in Dumitra confided in her colleagues[164] that she cast some spells to bind her husband in order to prevent him from leaving her, and despite all of her best efforts, he still did leave. After that, she did some spell to try to make her rival ill, still to no avail. The impact of such declarations is to be judged, on the one hand, by the fact that they break the golden rule of secrecy—the prescribed behavior in witchcraft-like subjects does not normally allow for

---

163 E.E. Evans-Pritchard, *Witchcraft, Oracles and Magic among the Azande* (Oxford: Oxford University Press, 1937), p. 387.

164 Fieldwork information, Dumitra, Bistrița-Năsăud County, summer of 2008.

small talk on such a taboo subject. On the other hand, although evolving around a very serious topic, such declarations were never taken seriously by her interlocutors. While they did not doubt her intentions, they definitely doubted her abilities to carry out such spells, because the woman was not credited with possessing the indispensable ability that is the basis of any pretentions to magical action: the power, the gift, or the grace.

Therefore, we are back at the issue of possession of a type of supernatural power, empowering its possessor to operate within the magic field, equally attributed to fortune tellers, unwitching Orthodox priests and monks, or even witches.

In French ethnological literature, this magic power is described as an innate 'gift,' transmitted from one generation to the next within the family, a type of magic force common to both unwitchers and sorcerers, differentiated only through the moral stakes of directing it through magic actions that can be beneficial/curative or malefic/harmful. Another indispensable element is 'the Secret' briefly discussed earlier (in subchapter '**The traditional unwitcher and magical healers**'), a term designating a particular gestural ritual, sometimes doubled by specific incantations, transmitted through the usual traditional channels (from parent to child or received as a gift from a mysterious vagabond passing by). The Secret[165] functions as a personal hallmark for every specialist of the magical field and as a concrete form to attest one's magic abilities from the outside; but without the 'gift,' 'the Secret' has no value.

In contemporary Romania's witchcraft discourse, the term of 'grace,' corresponding to the French 'gift,' is in principle a term refused for the actors placed at the malignant pole of witchcraft, precisely because of its religious connotations. Nevertheless, the indispensability of possessing a special magic force running in one's family is in popular discourse more often linked to the native capacities of the magical aggressors than to any other actor within the witchcraft discourse. As discussed before, for the Orthodox priests or

165 About 'the Secret' and 'the gift', Dominique Camus, p. 29–30; Jeanne Favret-Saada, p. 84–85.

monks, the grace is a type of force invested in them through religious ordination. For magic specialists operating in the field of divination, their ability to foresee and read the signs (in card or Tarot spreads, in coffee, or through clairvoyance) is also linked to a special type of force, designated by the exact same term. But, only one of my informants, a clairvoyant in Bucharest who was originally from the county of Ialomița in the south, explained her ability to foresee things through the previous existence of this ability in her family. She was convinced it had been transmitted from one generation to the next only on the maternal side. All of my other informants who were active as diviners said they just discovered their abilities at a certain time, while the proper learning of the meanings of symbols they handle came as a necessary second phase through experience and repetition.

In contrast, the unnatural gift possessed by magical aggressors is believed to be entirely innate. This perspective highlights the way a witch's existence is conceived to unfold between two markers: At one end, such a person must necessarily come from a family known for the unusual, dangerous abilities of at least one of its members; at the other end, the common idea is that this gift weighs down as a fatality upon the individual's destiny—the witches cannot die without transmitting their power to somebody else.

One common perception about the possession of the witches' gift is that it works rather as an unavoidable force: It is conceived as a fundamental evil overruling the person and even outweighing his/her free will. A story circulating among churchgoers in the town of Baia Mare (Maramureş County) is of interest here. They say that there is a woman from the countryside, always dressed completely in black, who occasionally joins them to take part in the religious service. Always carrying with her a bag filled with heavy prayer books, she is often spotted outside of the town as well, attending most regional religious events: monasteries' special religious services, villages' wakes, religious holiday consecrations, etc. It is said that the old Maramureş Orthodox bishop simply cannot stand her. He spots her in a crowd and, on more than one occasion, interrupted the religious service in order to ask her to move away from him.[166] The reason for her relative notoriety and for the bishop's reaction is that the woman reportedly possesses such a negative energy that even the common people can sense it, let alone the clergy. The talk is that this woman confessed to other devoted churchgoers that she is painfully aware of the evil in her soul, constantly tormenting and oppressing her. But she wishes to do good and not harm, which is why she tries hard to fight against the malefic hereditary predisposition through the means of religious ritual and purification. [167]

The Regionalization of Witchcraft

Within any rural community, identifying potential witches (or, as commonly referred to, 'the ones who know how to handle those things') is relatively easy. The collective ascription works in such a way that it groups them on kinship lines, especially along gendered bloodline affiliation.

What is interesting to see is that a regional ascription of witchcraft is equally operational: The larger the geographical distance between the accuser and the designated witch, the higher the probability to incriminate somebody not based on familial origin, but on the ill reputation of the particular village or region of origin.

> *'Those women from over there, from Agrieş, they really dwell into unclean things. And actually on that whole valley of Târlişua. They are really into that stuff, over there. All the major spell-binders, that's where to be found.' (Mărioara, woman, age 62, Reteag village)*

> *'Look at what happened to me with Maria, my daughter. How long it took until I finally succeeded to break her apart from that good for nothing boy, how many services I've paid and how many priests I had to see in this matter ... Clearly, he's the son of Măria's sister, you know, from Pleş. And everybody knows they dwell into those things over there, they employ sorcerers and do other nasty stuff of the kind. Not necessarily the boy himself, but most likely*

166 The theme of being able to spot, within the churchgoers crowd, those attendees burdened by heavy sins is often present when describing the extraordinary capacities of certain blessed monks or priests.

167 Fieldwork information, Baia-Mare, autumn of 2008.

his mother taught him what and when to do. They know all about this things in Pleş, they do ...' (Rodica, woman, age 53, Râşca village)

'Geta's mother is from Tăure. You know, a renowned region for spell-dwellers and knowledgeable people in these matters. They have a reputation. So, it's transparent to me that she knows how to magically bind. Yes, I bet it's all of her doing.' (Iţu, woman, age 66, Bistriţa)

This regionalization of witchcraft is also documented by Willem de Blécourt for the Netherlands of the first decades of the 1900s: 'Half of the inhabitants of Hornaar were capable of bewitching, it was thought, and it was said that Noordeloos swarmed with witches.'[168] Also, by Julio Caro Baroja for the Basque provinces of 1930s–1950s Spain: 'There are some districts that produce more witches and sorcerers than others.'[169] Therefore, it looks like formulating the suspicion that a certain person might be a witch based mainly on the region of provenance was quite common within the European traditional witchcraft discourse.

What is important to stress here is that the geographic regions or villages imagined as producing more than the reasonable share of those abnormally gifted are never very close (it is rarely the very next village, for instance), nor very far. They are designated within the borders of the reachable or easily imaginable space, a familiar geography not too far to be nameless or lacking in representations within the local community. It is interesting how this type of ascribed witchcraft geography seems to follow the same lines of distance observed during the process of designating an aggressor by the victim: As we saw earlier, it is normally somebody not too close (the spouse or the child) and not a stranger (a passer-by). Therefore, evil seems always to arise from a geographic and existential in-between, marking the transition zone from the most familiar unto the completely unknown.

---

168 Willem de Blécourt, 'Boiling chickens and burning cats: witchcraft in the Western Netherlands', *Witchcraft Continued. Popular Magic in Modern Europe*, p. 94.

169 Julio Caro Baroja, *The World of the Witches* (London: Phoenix Press, 2001), p. 231.

Transmitting the Abnormal Gift

The theme of fatal predestination of those engaged with evil magic is continued with the idea that the possessors of maleficent magic force cannot actually die without first transmitting their power further. The natural direction of transmitting this ambiguous gift lies within the family, especially along the same gender line: from mother to daughter, from grandmother to granddaughter. But, what happens when the magical force possessor does not have any descendants? Apparently, she/he can resort to various forms of replacement:

> *'What I heard is that: if a so-called witch doesn't teach somebody else her skill, she simply cannot die. That's why there were these young girls around the woman from Cepari, she was trying to teach them. Because she's old now and she has no offspring. But now they are gone to Spain, to join their parents. That's what I gathered, that she tried to teach them her ritual or something. They were poorer people, you know, and her neighbours.' Silvia (woman, age 34, Năsăud)*

In the village of Râşca in the Apuseni Mountains, the circumstances of the death of a woman unanimously considered a witch have been lengthily commented on during the summer of 2006. The story went like this: Because she did not have any offspring, the woman agonized alone for two weeks, trying to die. Realizing that she was unable to die, she managed to obtain a black hen from the market of a near-by small town; after she was seen taking the hen into her house, people found out that she had finally passed away. According to the narrative, without direct descendants and without the possibility to find human recipients, the black hen functioned as the perfectly valid replacement and became the depository of the witch's maleficent magic power. This release process finally allowed her to expire.[170] The value of the hen, and particularly a black hen, as a ritual human *alter-ego* or sacrificial replacement is well documented for Eastern Europe.[171] For example, the image of the black hen as protector and human substitute offered to the obscure forces

170 Fieldwork information, Râşca, Cluj County, 2006.

171 Antoaneta Olteanu, *Şcoala de solomonie*, pp. 278–281.

that threaten someone's life is illustrated by the Bulgarian *Namestnik* (Bulg.> *the replacement*) practice of sacrificing a black hen when someone was gravely ill.

The Punishment of Witches

Within the witchcraft discourse and its adjacent narratives, a particular reading of ethical implications is dedicated to the punishment of the witches. The widespread conviction is that proper witches, those marked as such by the possession of a transmitted magical force (either through birth or as receptacles), have to expect to suffer significant consequences from their actions. Not only in the afterlife, but here, on Earth. Interestingly, the same consequences threaten, eventually, the actors foolish enough to dwell into sorcery rituals even when they are not possessors of magical force; and equally, the clients appealing to sorcerers in order to provoke unhappiness in the lives of hated people. They are all to expect the same rightful punishments. In fact, the same consequences attack, through a centrifugal movement akin to the contiguity principle specific to the magic domain in general, the self, the close ones, and the descendants—up to the point of extinction of the whole kinship line.

> *'That man who used to do these things over there, in Agrieş, who was stealing the milk, he's got nobody left in the village. I mean, yeah, he's dead, but also all of his kin is gone, his kids just scattered. He didn't have good children anyway, they were all just good for nothings, scum. Everybody is gone and the house is deserted. You see, that's exactly what people say: those who dwell into those things ... One single daughter remained for a while in that house, and the meat from her bones just came apart little by little, I don't know what kind of an illness is that one. But she also died, several years ago.' (Mărioara, woman, age 62, Reteag village)*

> *'I think that in the end they felt sorry for what they've done and wanted to undo the spells they operated on my sister. But they couldn't any longer, it was too late already. At my sister's funeral, everybody in the village suspected them, everybody was talking ... (...) But her mom [the love rival's mother and the author of the evil spells] developed skin cancer on her leg, and it never healed. Her father went in the forest to bring a carload of wood and the whole load came over him and killed him on the spot. The daughter, the girl*

herself ... well, she probably didn't have any direct fault as such, her mother was the one with the wrongdoings. But she got married and now she's divorced. And many other troubles came over that family after my sister's death. Who knows for how many generations this will hang over their heads ...' (Floricuța, woman, age 63, Dumitra village)

Such representations, linking archaic elements of rural-traditional substratum, the kingship sin logic, religious ethical perspectives, and more modern elements of energy transfers, are all placed in a background area for an actor entering the witchcraft discourse, fighting to reinstate the balance in her/his life. This entire explicative ensemble can be accessed or, equally, simply ignored. Once the aggressor has been identified and named, her/his particular mode of action (directly, through their own magical abilities or indirectly, through resorting to some sort of magic specialist) does not carry any relevance for the afflicted actor. For that matter, the irrelevance is doubled by the ritual interdiction formulated as such by the priest before entering the religious unwitching ritual. Banning the aggressor as a point of reference from the religious ritual is a way of stopping the afflicted actor to ponder upon the former's possible reasons to commit the witchcraft attack. Otherwise, thinking of the evil endured can illicit predominantly negative feelings in the victim's emotional disposition, and those feelings can pollute and unpredictably alter the meanings of a ritual with an otherwise purifying essence.

Chapter 3:
Therapeutic Interventions

As one saying goes, 'an ounce of prevention is worth a pound of cure.' This statement expresses an ever valid attitude toward life—for us, the people of today, as well as for the people of old. A good example is when this idea pertains to contemporary medical thinking: everybody knows it is easier (and wiser) to prevent an illness than to treat it; so, most of us do our best to stay in shape, eat right, go to regular check-ups, sleep eight hours a night, quit smoking and alcohol, etc. Even those who do not do all this are, nonetheless, perfectly familiar with the notion that they should, because this is a discourse that has managed to penetrate all areas of our modern existence (through mass media, official strategies implemented by health-care national services, education, regulated food standards, and so on).

Assessing one's environment, striving to control it, and doing one's best to anticipate factors that might go contrary to the most carefully made plans are parts of being a human anywhere, anytime: 'Life is full of dangers. Our highly developed consciousness makes us, of all living forms in the universe, the most keenly aware of, and the most adept at protecting ourselves from, dangers.'[172]

What we modern people do is to try and control the social, economic, material, and pragmatic reality we experience in everyday life. As a strategic preventative measure, we take out home insurance against fire, life insurance to ensure the financial safety of our loved ones, private pension schemes, and health-care plans. People tend to intervene in a strategic, preventive manner reflecting the current definitions of possible dangers (accidents, old age, illness, and death), the means available for averting or minimizing the impact of misfortune caused by them, and the socially sanctioned

172 Thomas Szasz, 'Psychiatry and the Control of Dangerousness: On the Apotropaic Function of the Term "Mental Illness"', *Journal of Social Work Education*, 39. 3 (2003), pp. 375+, ‹www.questia.com› [accessed May 6, 2009]

main points of interest (the individual, his/her possessions, and the immediate family).

For any past rural-traditional European society, the structure of reality, the means to preventively intervene, and the network of human relations went well beyond the tangible aspects of day-to-day living: 'One should not forget that it is very likely that past worlds were experienced as a web of social relations involving humans, animals and other living beings as much as the dead, ghosts, spirits and different forms of "supernatural" and (im)material beings.'[173] The rural household of old equally incorporated the living members of the family, the dead ancestors, the honored patron saints, the house, the animals, and the land. The source of every misfortune threatening this 'us' was to be found within a vast category of potential evil consisting of what contemporary people would consider a very confusing class of both material and supernatural causes and beings. Wicked fairies, baby snatchers, shapeshifting witches, the undead, etc., were considered dangers just as real as adverse meteorological phenomena, predatory animals (wolves and weasels), or diseases and epidemics. What they all had in common, according to this worldview, was the fact that their manifestations in *this* world were read as unwelcomed intrusions of chaos and disorder from the *other* world. Most rituals practiced in a traditional rural society had precisely the purpose to maintain the right balance between these two worlds in a constant negotiation of boundaries. Practical means to defend against the unknown and any potential dangers were equally employed: for instance, if one stretch of road is known to be haunted, the peasant 'simply avoids using it at night.'[174]

In this chapter, I will begin by discussing ritual prevention on two levels: first, I will offer a short account of the amplitude of the apotropaic-defensive ritual framework in any agricultural traditional society; second, I will examine, based on my Romanian ethnograph-

---

173 Dusan Boric, '«Deep time» metaphor: Mnemonic and apotropaic practices at Lepenski Vir', *Journal of Social Archaeology*, 3 (2003), pp. 46–74, ‹http://jsa.sagepub.com› [accessed July 1, 2008], p. 62.

174 João de Pina-Cabral, *Sons of Adam. Daughters of Eve: The Peasant Worldview of Alto Minho* (Oxford: Clarendon Press), 1986, p. 183.

ic material, the apotropaic strategies in use today mostly focusing on the dangers of falling victim to an evil spell. Prevention, as the core intention and targeted finality embedded in any apotropaic ritual, is inextricably linked to therapy as the proactive step meant to avoid the very need to fall back upon the latter. However, it often happens that prevention fails, sometimes simply because one forgets to employ the recommended apotropaic means; or, on a more general level, because no preventative measures are ever infallible: evil will always find a new way in. That is the logic of the apotropaic: It can be a temporary reprieve from, and constant battle with, the ever-lurking evil. Therefore, therapy functions as the second stand against evil in human lives and the last chance to restore things to normality.

The second section of this chapter will address therapeutic means employed in three concrete instances: means against the evil eye; means against the general '*mal de vivre*' caused by witchcraft attacks; and the religious therapy designed to facilitate marriage. This structure follows the findings of my research in contemporary Romania in a dialog with a relevant comparative material from other European countries.

The last section of this chapter will address the limits of therapeutic means capable of restoring an afflicted person's day-to-day existence. When I say 'limit,' I actually include the possibility of occasional failure, recognized as such by both spellbound victims and their therapists. In the context of the Orthodox religious ritual being the only legitimate therapy for witchcraft in contemporary Romania, the fact that it does not prove infallible needs to be examined in relation to the official religious discourse, the 'illicit' magical practices, and the perceived limits of any kind of therapy, including the medical one.

3.1 The Logic of the Apotropaic

I was mentioning in the first Chapter (in subchapter '**The apotropaic dimension of witchcraft situations: ritual gestures and interior memory**') that *apotropaic* means today, especially in the context of social sciences, 'intended to ward off evil,' routinely translated either as 'turning away from evil' or as 'warding off evil'. I was also mentioning before that the very idea of evil is something not directly present in the etymology of the word.

In a similar vein, 'to turn away from evil'/'to ward off evil' is not necessarily a translation formula that makes it very clear whether the human agent turns himself away from evil (as in a physical back-turning or refuse) or if one acts directly to oppose and block the evil, full-facing the attack. In all likelihood, the *apo-tropos* concept synthesizes, in one single word, both human attitudes possible when confronting evil: avoidance and confrontation, keeping away from or preemptive strike. The fact is that no European language contains a direct translation term that would completely exhaust the meaning of apotropaic. Defense, prevention, and protection represent an assemblage of expressions able to partly equate the meaning of this term in English, but they all suggest a rather defensive approach due to their static and passive connotations. By contrast, the apotropaic observed in ritual contexts, as well as the one denominating a selective function of rememory, always express an active, a volitional, and, arguably, an aggressive side. There are two symbolic images that illustrate this tension well: the magic circle and the Medusa Head.

The magic circle is commonly known as part of sorcery rituals: The magician's safe zone is represented by a circle drawn or imprinted on the floor, in order to protect the performer against the supernatural powers invoked. The best-known image of the magic circle seems to be the Grand Pentacle of Solomon, mostly associated with the sorcery rites of medieval Europe. Regardless of its variants and various modifications, the Great Pentacle is to be found in all Occidental sorcery manuals.[175] As a geometric figure, the circle carves out a secured spatial perimeter, and its limit becomes the interface mediating the interior/exterior rapport. The circle's forms may vary, from cords around towns and churches, to rings and

[175] Dominique Camus, *Puteri şi practici vrăjitoreşti. Anchetă asupra practicilor actuale de vrăjitorie* (Iaşi: Polirom, 2003), p. 145.

bracelets as individual ornaments; yet, the value and function of a magic circle is always the same: to protect within its limits from outside menacing forces, may those be ghosts, epidemics, enemies, or evil spirits. The main apotropaic values expressed through the symbolism of the magic circle are:

- limit,
- circumscription,
- prevention, and
- protection as demarcation.

Its defensive and rather passive characteristics are opposite to the aggression of Medusa's gaze, capable of turning a man into stone. Medusa's Head embodies the apotropaic principle of fighting fire with fire or using the horrible to repel the horrible. As expressed by Marjorie B. Garber and Nancy J. Vickers, Medusa's Head 'has over time been seen as the epitome of the apotropaic object.'[176] Its apotropaic function is the same as the one invested into the graphic representations of the (blue) eye, so common in the Mediterranean regions form Antiquity until today, meant to refract the Evil Eye with an equal, analogous force. The apotropaic coordinates expressed through the symbolism of the Medusa's Head are:

- the look/the sight as action,
- agency, and
- protection as aggression (preemptive strike).

Some examples of apotropaic devices might help illustrate how the purely defensive and the utterly aggressive principles can function independently but mostly mix in order to reach their ritual goal of keeping evil away.

In a broader discussion of the origins and historic developments of bull representations as apotropaic devices (from the Anatolian Neolithic to Greco-Roman antiquity, from the Sumerians to the Etruscans, from Egypt to India), R. Scott Walker and Sigfried J. De Laet mention the contemporary use (in the 1980s) of bull skulls

176 *The Medusa Reader,* ed. by Marjorie B. Garber and Nancy J. Vickers (New York: Routledge, 2003), p. 2.

with horns intact nailed above the doors of farms and barns in the Abruzzi region of Italy. The function of those skulls was to secure the perimeter against the danger of *jettatura* (thrown evil spell). Resorting to the apotropaic symbolism of the bull can be equally achieved through gestural language: when a person is suspected of having the evil eye (*malochhio*), the horn gesture is considered to possess, along with the phallus gesture, a most certain apotropaic value of neutralizing the malefic influences.[177] These two specific gestures, mentioned for their identical apotropaic values also within oral Greek culture,[178] have become rather universal lately while changing their meaning over time. The phallus gesture went from a magical defense gesture to a gestural insult, while the horns are globally recognized as part of heavy-metal popular culture. Until recently, horse skulls were believed to hold a similar apotropaic power in Romanian tradition. Stuck onto fencing stakes around gardens, fountains, and cows' sheds,[179] horse skulls were meant to protect from evil spirits or illnesses[180] or even to magically prevent wolf attacks against livestock.[181] The fact that such devices are spatially located at the interface delimiting the perimeter that needs magic protection (farms, barns, gardens, fountains, etc.) shows how they function on the principle of defense highlighted by the symbolism of the magic circle. For that matter, all talismans and amulets[182] are

---

177 Scott Walker & Sigfried J. De Laet, 'Man and the Bull', *Diogenes*, 29 (1981), pp. 104–132, ‹http://dio.sagepub.com› [accessed November 4, 2007], (p. 132).

178 Marie-Christine Anest-Couffin, 'La relation à l'autre et le geste, dans la culture orale greque', *Premier atelier européen sur la culture orale européene*, (Strasbourg: Conseil de l`Europe, 1990), p. 57. Dominique Camus also mentions the apotropaic meaning attached to the horns gesture, seen as a modality to neutralize the evil intentions of a witch/sorcerer in the French Haute–Bretagne region, p. 92.

179 Ion Ghinoiu, *Vârstele timpului* (Bucureşti: Meridiane, 1988), pp. 96–97.

180 Ion Taloş, *Gândirea magico-religioasă la români. Dicţionar* (Bucureşti: Editura Enciclopedică, 2001), p. 27.

181 Artur Gorovei, *Credinţi şi superstiţii ale poporului român* (Bucureşti: Editura Grai si Suflet), 1995, p. 34.

182 For an in-depth discussion about the differences between talismans and amulets: Don C. Skemer, 'Introduction', *Binding words: textual amulets in*

imagined to work through the principle of magically securing a space, or a person, against exterior evil. At the same time, the fact that bull or horse skulls are invested with symbolic qualities such as virility, masculinity, and aggressiveness suggests that they are imagined to repel evil by scaring it away or neutralizing it through a similar but opposite menacing force. Therefore, they also function along the lines of fighting fire with fire as expressed by the symbolism of the Medusa Head. Whether static or dynamic and defensive or offensive, both dimensions underlined by the symbolisms of the magic circle and the Medusa's Head are equally found in the apotropaic idea and tend to be simultaneously employed by most apotropaic strategies and devices.

Faces of Fear and Cycles of Ritual Defense

The apotropaic princliple is relevant to witchcraft because the fear of witches, evil spells, and evil eye was one of the major ritually negotiated fears in any European traditional agricultural society. Witchcraft-preventing rituals offered concrete modalities to define, actively intervene against, and, therefore, tame this fear. But, the evil to fight against, far from being limited to this single class of supernatural adversity, was culturally represented as coming under many faces.

Any type of magic is anthropocentrical, as long as it defines the human as the center of its action, as both cause and beneficiary of its effects. Apotropaic rituals very much reflect this centrality of the human being. As a relation between the human actor (be it an individual or a community) and the evil that has to be warded off, apotropaic rituals emphasize the faces of this evil as being *anything* that contravenes general human interests and well-being. From mice to fleas, from sparrows to scorpions, from illnesses to epidemics, from evil eye to evil spell, from hail to fire, from strangers, enemies, and ghosts to witches or death—the list of these 'fears of' is potentially endless and yet has a single, unifying meaning: they rep-

---

the Middle Ages, (Pennsylvania: Pennsylvania State University Press, 2006), pp. 1–19.

resent all that is—or might be—contrary to human life, its security, and prosperity. If we agree that each type of ritual represents a specific way for the human actor to relate to the world, apotropaic rituals point toward a negative attitude toward the exterior, as practicing those aims at the evacuation and demonization of the supernatural. The apotropaic attitude thus represents a conflictual approach toward the sacred and the unknown.

The particular forms of human fear, as well as the ritual and social modalities of prevention/protection/defense, varied vastly throughout time and space, depending on the particular social, cultural, economic, or historical circumstances. For instance, the ritual object known in Romania as 'the plague's shirt'[183] (*cămaşa ciumei*) initially responded to the historical circumstances of plague and, later on (19th century), to cholera epidemics.[184] Another example is the scorpion,[185] which is perceived as a menace and embodiment of evil only in those warmer regions where this particular arachnid

183 The plague's shirt is documented for the region of Transylvania up until the beginning of the 20th century. At that time, it was used to fight off any type of epidemic affecting humans or domestic animals. As shown by Pavelescu for the region of the Apuseni Mountains, the process of its making was governed by strict ritualistic prescriptions: seven or nine women (magic numbers) gathered around in a house where they had to complete the shirt in a single night-time—from spinning to weaving to tailoring and sewing. The shirt thus obtained was placed somewhere at the village's boundary before dawn, in order keep away the epidemics haunting neighboring villages. Gheorghe Pavelescu, *Magia la români: Studii şi cercetări despre magie, descântece şi mană* (Bucureşti: Minerva, 1998), p. 52.

184 The last plague epidemic in Transylvania was between 1820 and 1830. The whole 19th century can be described, from the point of view of epidemics, as the time of cholera. Marius Rotar, 'În «afara» discursului asupra morţii: moartea suportată – în «cifră» şi dincolo de ea', vol. II: *Moartea în Transilvania în secolul al XIX-lea, 11 ipostaze ale morţii* (Cluj-Napoca: Accent, 2007), pp. 9–53, p. 13.

185 For further reading upon powerful apotropaic symbols in Muslim folklore and Byzantium, see Finbarr Barry Flood, 'Image against Nature: Spolia as Apotropaia in Byzantium and the dār al-Islām', *The Medieval History Journal*, 9. 1 (2006), pp. 143–166, ‹http://mhj.sagepub.com› [accessed 21th July 2008]; and Jurgen Wassim Frembgen 'The Scorpion in Muslim Folklore', *Asian Folklore Studies*, 63. 1 (2004), pp. 95+, ‹www.questia.com› [accessed January 15, 2009].

lives. By acknowledging the culturally and historically conditioned faces of fear, we understand that the apotropaic is a conventional name for a constant dimension of human behavior in space and time both in an individual's psychological attitudes and in sociocultural mechanisms.

The vast extent to which apotropaic rituals were part of traditional societies can be deduced from the fact that preventive rituals were part of all seasonal crossings (the religious holidays marking the big seasonal thresholds: the solstices and the equinoxes), of all human-life cycle crossings (birth, wedding, and death) and of all significant economic production modes (agricultural and pastoral). Several specific examples from the Romanian traditional rural culture of the past might help illustrate this point. Here, apotropaic rituals occurred all throughout the calendar cycle, from loud noises meant to scare away evil spirits during New Years' Eve[186] to the ritual securing of the household perimeter with wild rose on the eve of Saint George's Day (April 23), meant to prevent mana thieves (witches) from stealing cow's milk.[187] There were apotropaic rituals during life cycle customs, such as the wedding sequence of substituting the bride with a young girl[188] in order to disorientate the evil spirits; or, during a funeral, the placing of garlic inside the coffin in order to prevent the dead from returning as undead. Installing hornbeam poles at every corner of a house and its fence so as to block evil's access[189] was believed to secure the household perimeter, while a cross sign made out of gleanings was meant to magically secure the half-way harvested wheat field during the night.[190] Moments of crossing (in the seasonal cycle or the human-life cycle) of-

186 Ovidiu Bârlea, *Folclor românesc*, vol. I (Bucureşti: Minerva, 1981), p. 293.

187 Gheorghe Pavelescu, p. 215.

188 Dimitrie Cantemir, *Descrierea Moldovei* (Bucureşti: Minerva, 1973), p. 239–240.

189 Aurora Liiceanu, *Povestea unei vrăjitoare* (Bucureşti: Editura ALL, 1996), p. 39.

190 Ion Cuceu, 'Obiceiuri şi credinţe în legătură cu ocupaţiile tradiţionale la Gârbou, judeţul Sălaj', *Anuarul Muzeului Etnografic al Transilvaniei* (Cluj-Napoca: 1973), pp. 435–456, p. 452.

fered perfect opportunities for human agents to intervene through magic means. Each of these crossings came with specific scenarios about certain evils that can potentially be averted at that particular moment. Any crossing has a symbolic association with the threshold principle known in anthropology as liminality,[191] describing a state of unstable and precarious seasonal or existential in-between (no longer here, not there yet). From the point of view of traditional rural communities, the fight with supernatural menacing powers was endless, a perpetual conflict marked by temporary reconciliations achieved through apotropaic practices. Order and chaos, life and death, were the crucial terms of a tensioned dyad in which the human actor strived to take a direct part in through acts of ritual taming of the cosmic, biological, or social rhythms.

Traditional societies had a protective cultural and ritual screen in place, mediating the complex relations between the interior (family; household; and community) and the exterior (the world at large with all its potential dangers). In most European traditional societies, the apotropaic, propitiating, and augural rituals functioned as a constant negotiation of the borders between the human actor and the cosmos. This buffer zone is no longer in place for modern people. Instead of the ritual, protective screen, they are exposed to the nude, direct contact with a reality that is often overwhelming.

When affected personally, unhappiness, misfortune, illness, and death are still felt as inexplicable, violent intrusions from the exterior by the contemporary person. But, the category of evil in itself is no longer the wide and expansive one of traditional societies, where *all* and *only* that which contravened to individual and communitarian interests and well-being were perceived as 'evil.' The potential evils and dangers of today are expected to fall under established, predefined categories that already carry reasonable solutions and corresponding ways of 'fixing' them within them:

[191] More about the importance of liminal rites and the concept of liminality in Arnold van Gennep, *The Rites of Passage* (Chicago: University of Chicago Press, 1960).

'Solutions exist, however, only for mathematical problems and some medical problems. For human problems, there are no solutions. Conflict, disagreement, unhappiness, the proverbial slings and arrows of outrageous fortune are challenges that we must cope with, not solve.'[192]

Drawing Boundaries in Contemporary Witchcraft Discourse

The belief in many of the evil spirits that were traditionally seen as threatening human life security has by and large disappeared. Not many people living in a European agricultural milieu today still take ritual precautions against fairies, supernatural baby snatchers, or the undead. Even in those contexts where witchcraft is a valid explanatory discourse, witches are no longer believed to have the ability to shapeshift, fly, and enter homes through chimneys. Supernatural evil is nowadays considered an abstraction, whereas the localized and individualized evil (the people 'who know how to handle those things') is still as real as it gets for those connected to the witchcraft discourse. To put it differently, for them the evil is no longer 'out there,' it is *in* and *between* people.

In traditional European societies,[193] witches were imagined as human beings endowed (through birth and/or initiation) with supernatural abilities. It was those abilities or 'powers' that were most

---

192 Thomas Szasz, ‹www.questia.com›.

193 Marianne Mesnil defines the premodern European rural traditional society as 'autocephalous' (i.e., independent and self-sufficient) based on three characteristic elements describing its functional mechanisms: the structure of economic activities (an agropastoral subsistence economy based on family units); the political–institutional structure (based on patriarchal familial structures); the ideological–cultural system (the traditional peasant culture, based on oral modes of transmission). Marianne Mesnil, *Trois essais sur la Fête. Du folklore à l'ethno-sémiotique* (Bruxelles: Éditions de l'Université de Bruxelles, 1974), p. 13–14. However, the oral culture specific to the traditional society, representative for the whole European continent, should not be perceived as a historically monadic, isolated entity. Throughout the centuries, it was part of an uninterrupted exchange with the developments of the world at large, with the knowledge circulated through laic or religious writings and, therefore, cannot be described as 'pure' or 'authentic' but fundamentally syncretic.

feared, because of their potential to disrupt human life by causing epidemics, adverse meteorological phenomena, sudden illnesses and accidental deaths, lack of fertility (in humans, livestock, and crops), etc. The stereotype of these witches can be considered the quintessence of antisocial forces threatening the coherence of social life in a rural-traditional, patriarchal society: those most suspected of being witches were, usually, widows or spinsters, rather poor and living at the edge of a village, with a familial and personal history of breaking the social norms of acceptable behaviors, ugly or scary looking, and with a difficult, repulsive, or quarrelsome temperament. Keeping in mind the distinction between practiced witchcraft and ascribed witchcraft,[194] suspecting any person who fit this profile of being prone to witchcraft was always something quite likely to occur in traditional communities. The supernatural powers attributed to such a witch-like older woman were a threat not only for individual households or persons; they were first and foremost a threat for the community as a whole, its' very means of subsistence, and the capacity to perpetuate itself.

The witches portrayed in today's witchcraft discourse of Romania are no longer seen as a general category consisting mostly of maladjusted elderly females. The accusations do not target random members of a stereotyped group but instead follow exclusively the interpersonal lines of social interaction and especially the individual's history of previous problematic relations. More importantly, while these retrospectively identified witches may well be seen to possess the gift of casting a spell, none of them are credited with the supernatural powers previously ascribed to them. They most certainly cannot raise storms and hail, metamorphose into animal form, steal a cow's milk, or fly. Therefore, it is not them who are feared, nor

[194] This distinction operated by Willem de Blécourt highlights the fact that the people whom witchcraft had been ascribed to precisely on the basis of resembling such a cliché-portrait 'do not have to practice witchcraft at all.' Willem de Blécourt, 'The Witch, her Victim, the Unwitcher and the Researcher: the continued existence of traditional witchcraft', *Witchcraft and Magic in Europe. The Twentieth Century,* ed. by Bengt Ankarloo and Stuart Clark (University of Pennsylvania Press, 1999), pp. 141–219, p. 148.

even their powers to put spells in motion: it is the spell itself. *Bozgoana*, as the physical carrier-object of the malefic force, only ever has a 50–50 chance to reach its intended target because, in order to latch onto a victim, it has to be stepped on, touched, or ingested; and the potential target might not do any of that—either through sheer luck or intentional foresight. Between the releaser (the witch) and its potential target, this physical spell gains an independent presence in this world as a tangible carrier of misfortune, initially dedicated to a particular person but, in the end, potentially harmful to anyone: the *bozgoana*, similar to a silent booby trap, releases its malefic potential the moment *any* person comes in direct contact with it. Therefore, in this scenario, it is possible to become the unintended victim of a witchcraft attack simply because, as shown in **Chapter 1: Situations**, a released spell has to eventually cling to somebody, anybody.

> *'My son-in-law had a grandmother. We never approved our daughter marrying him ... They married when they were very young, He was ok, but came from a poor family with a bad reputation, and his father was a drunk. So, they married against our will. First years were hell in our house, always scandal with the son-in-law. After the death of my son, my daughter got pregnant again and went to a fortune teller with a friend. And the fortune teller asked her: "What is it that you did that upset greatly your parents?" My daughter answered that nothing, to her knowledge. But the fortune teller said: "On the contrary, it was a big something, a very big something, but you didn't know about it: somebody had thrown a spell to harm you, right near the house gate, and somebody else, close to you, accidentally stepped into that. That somebody else is now dead... I can see his tomb and it has the number 4 written on it." She was right; it was exactly 4 years since my son has died. And when my daughter came home and told me, I finally understood ...(...) My son-in-law's grandmother knew how to handle these unclean things so, although her grandchildren were coming from broken, bad families, they all miraculously managed to get into very good, illustrious families. But they all misbehaved, once they did: drinking, scandals ...' Floricuța (woman, age 63, Dumitra village)*

Employing various apotropaic strategies specifically addressed to the danger of falling victim to an evil spell is common with actors already connected to this type of explanatory discourse, mostly through having had a similar direct experience in the past. Owing to the spell representing a general threat once released, the first-prescribed attitude is to avoid touching, manipulating, or closely examining any out-of-place suspicious objects.

Other examples of contemporary defense strategies include: wearing one's underwear inside out; domestic amulets (such as pepper, garlic, frankincense, silver, and basil carefully packed in a piece of red tie); religious paraphernalia (small crosses around the neck or hand wrist; small icons in the bag; sprinkling frankincense on the house's threshold, etc.). A house icon, present in most Romanian Orthodox households, is also credited with powerful protective qualities that extend well beyond the threat of witchcraft. Whether we talk about the urban flat or the rural household, the main religious icon of the house opens up the apotropaic theme by providing a generic protection of the domestic perimeter. This particular protection is reinforced by an annual religious hallowing of the interior space, carried on mainly during the Epiphany (6th of January). The apotropaic efficacy of religious blessings on certain dates is seen as generic, offering general protection against any and all forms of evil that can plague a home: illness, familial discord, economical losses, accidents, and so on. Religious rituals, hence, mark a substantial renewal and an annual purification of space. However, in witchcraft situations, the religious hallowing of domestic space is far more targeted. As part of a complex religious unwitching ritual, it aims at fighting off malefic influences already present and at blocking their access in the future, along the same logic of purification of space and the sanctifying of a new beginning. Domestic perimeters can also be protected by sprinkling frankincense granules on a door's threshold. It is even believed that the intended effects of this same apotropaic action can be turned around when a malefic magical intervention is suspected from a known individual:

> *'If you want to throw back the binding spell, you have to go to the home of the person who threw it on you in the first place, and sprinkle frankincense on the threshold and under the door mat. And the spell will go back to that person.' Mrs. Gabor (woman, age 73, Deta, Timiş County).*

Apotropaic amulets forged specifically for averting magical aggression, whether as a counter to a concrete suspicion or just as a generic way of magical securing, belong to the category of 'signs' just as much as *bozgoanele*, the physically thrown object-spells. As shown in **Chaper 1: Situations**, '*bozgoane/blozgoane*' (a collection of substances and things, wrapped in paper; coal; dead frogs; any suspiciously out of place object) are easily recognizable as such, especially in rural communities, because they are limited, through cultural convention, to this single referent. When people see '*bozgoane*' objects, they immediately decipher what those are and instantly assume they are in the presence of a witchcraft situation. These physically thrown spells are not *symbols* (expressions of relatively unknown facts postulated as existing) but *signs*: 'A sign represents the analogue or abbreviated expression of a known thing.'[195] Similarly, the apotropaic devices as cultural signs are read by social actors in a single, unequivocal, interpretative key—carrying instead the opposite reference to the harmful thrown spells: the magical protection. The '*bozgoane*' objects and the witchcraft-targeting apotropaic amulets are, therefore, antinomically opposed (i.e., they function, as signs, in direct mutual contradition) but equally belong to the larger both encompassing context of witchcraft discourse.

One common example for a domestic apotrope is a variety of substances that are each invested with magical protective value (garlic, pepper, frankincense, silver, and basil) wrapped up in a piece of tie whose apotropaic value lies with its red color. This amulet was specially forged by one of my informants' neighbors when both my friend and her neighbor started to suspect that a too persistent visitor comes with unclean intentions into the house.[196] The reason for formulating this suspicion was the fact that, every time after the visitor had left, my informant would suddenly start to experience horrible head and back pains. The visits themselves were hardly welcomed by the host, and contrary to the local informal

195 Victor Turner, *The Forrest of Symbols. Aspects of Ndembu Ritual* (Ithaca: Cornell University Press, 1976), p. 26.

196 Fieldwork information, Bistrița, 2008.

rules of socializing, they would last for hours on end. Therefore, the visitor's behavior was interpreted as suspicious in the context of proper codes of socializing, aggravated by the physical symptoms suddenly starting up every time after the visits were over. Another example is a similar device made of garlic, frankincense, and pepper bound together in a piece of cloth, placed under the door mat, in order to prevent any spell-throwing inside the domestic perimeter, no matter by whom.[197] The necessity of forging and placing such amulet was dictated by the fact that the owner had to leave the village for a while. Even if the house was going to be empty, at least it had to be magically secured. None of the apotropes here mentioned were forged following specific prescriptions regarding the time and space favorable for augmenting their magical properties; their apotropaic value seems to arise exclusively from the defensive values invested in each of the composing elements and from their liminal placement at the point of access to the domestic perimeter.

The individual's protection is assured by various objects of religious provenance, mostly employed as bodily amulets: small icons, crosses, frankincense in envelopes, and small bottles with chrism or holy water. The consecration of such objects during religious service is considered a certain way to augment their protective value. Blessed or not, these talismans are usually worn around the neck or the wrist, in the pockets, or in the purse. One of my informants told me she never leaves the house without a small Virgin Mary icon and an envelope with frankincense in her purse; if she happens to forget either, she always goes back home to get it, otherwise, she feels unprotected and incapable to function. Similarly to that of house icons, the protective value of these religious talismans is a generic one, promising to protect their wearer against any kind of evil—including witchcraft attacks.

However, wearing undergarments inside out[198] represents an individual type of protection targeting specifically the possibility of be-

[197] Fieldwork information, Reteag (Bistrița-Năsăud County), 2008.

[198] Fieldwork information, Deta (Timiş County), 2007; Reteag & Bistrița (Bistrița-Năsăud County), 2008.

ing bewitched. Such a strategy is believed to scare away thrown spells, duping them by causing confusion or simply neutralizing them. It is a purely preventive measure, especially when the actor had been directly involved in a witchcraft situation in the past and is set on not allowing something similar to occur in the future. Wearing the undergarments inside out is also recommended for young, unmarried women, vulnerable to incite jealousy and, thus, of becoming the target of 'binding the marriage' spells. It is also sometimes employed during religious unwitching rituals in order to ensure continuous protection: the afflicted actor starts to wear undergarments inside out at the request of the Orthodox priest or monk so that the supplementary spells launched by the aggressor would be deterred from reaching their intended target.

Just like apotropaic strategies, witchcraft is usually believed to work better in a cumulative manner. The more malefic spells are executed, reproduced, and renewed at certain intervals, the better the chance of reaching the victim. Conversely, the more apotropaic substances and liminal areas there are to intervene with specific magical ways, the better the chance to maintain magical protection.

In contemporary Romania, all these protective measures are known and respected in both rural and urban areas, and they are designed to fight off the always present danger of becoming bewitched.

3.2 Forms of Therapeutic Ritual

The Evil Eye

In all documented cases of my field research, the thrown spell is transmitted *through something* tangible and visible: suspect objects, out of place things, or the proper *bozgoane*. The physicality of the object carrier of a malefic spell suggests that a concrete medium is always necessary to transfer the spell's aggressive intention. If, in a concrete case, it should not be possible to identify a specific physical sign, other means of transfer are taken into consideration, similarly operating by ingestion or touch. The incriminated 'vehicles of transmission' are usually identified retrospectively; they are not something read and interpreted instantaneously like the '*bozgoane*'-signs.

Such carrier objects can be: flowers or chocolate received from a guest (the supposed magical aggressor)[199]; anything to eat or drink[200]; alcohol and cakes consumed at a wedding,[201] etc. The spell catches on like a contagious disease, only by direct contact with its intended victim. Nevertheless, the physicality of the carrier object, eaten, ingested, drunk, stepped on, or touched does not lessen the magical force needed by the aggressor in order to be able to set the spell on motion—that particular supersensible *gift* common to both religious and magical specialists.

The evil eye, a type of magical intervention that is sometimes involuntary, is the only way of operating at a distance, through mere visual transfer. In today's Romania, it is considered to be far easier to remedy than the effects of witchcraft. As opposed to the latter, evil eye afflictions happen without the necessity of being transmitted through a palpable object.

The symptom of being affected by the evil eye is a state of general sickness that cannot be explained by any particular disease:

> *'It's something completely different when you've got the evil eye from, let's say, a gall bladder sickness. All of a sudden, you feel faint, weak, trembling on your feet ... Such a total sickness that you think you'll drop, your head is pounding, your eyes are burning, you feel like throwing up ... Evil energy all the way.' Ițu (woman, age 66, Bistrița).*

Such symptoms are believed to be provoked by the eye contact with a person who has the capacity to negatively affect through the gaze, mostly without even being aware of or wanting to provoke this effect. In a quasi-predestination reading, it is believed that possessors of the evil eye have not been weaned on time (too late or too soon) or have eyebrows that are too close together.[202] The evil eye af-

---

199 Fieldwork infomation, Bistrița, 2008

200 Fieldwork infomation, Râşca, jud. Cluj, 2006.

201 Fieldwork infomation, Dumitra, jud. Bistrița-Năsăud, 2008.

202 Fieldwork infomation, Bistrița, 2008.

fection can also be provoked by anyone's gaze if the potential target arouses a series of feelings in the viewer (envy, amazement, or irrepressible admiration) that causes an uncanny focus of the visual contact.

To diagnose and cure the evil eye, the most common traditional remedy in Romania used to be, until the recent past, the charcoal incantation. In order to establish whether the sick person asking for assistance was suffering from the effects of evil eye or not, a woman knowing magical incantations (Rom.> *descântătoare*) would start by bringing 'unused'[203] water form a fountain or a spring and transfer some into a pitcher. She would then take out nine lumps of charcoal from the burning fireplace and count them in descending order (from nine to one) while throwing them in the water vessel. Next, she would be reciting a traditional incantation of archaic parlance over the pitcher, simultaneously making a gesture of cutting the surface of the water with a knife. If the sick person was indeed suffering from evil eye, the charcoal pieces were supposed to sink to the bottom; if not, they would float on the surface. The more the sunken charcoal lumps were sizzling, the further advanced the evil eye affliction was considered to be. After finishing the incantation, the officiant would ask the sufferer to drink three times from the vessel and then would wet their forehead, eyes, nose, chest, and wrists. The remaining water would be spilled on a fence stake, concomitant with saying: 'how much water remained on the stake, that much evil to remain with X' (the name of the afflicted individual). Finally, the officiant would thrust the knife into the ground and turn the pitcher upside down, saying: 'I don't turn the pitcher upside down, but I turn back the health and all good things to X.'[204]

In a more modern approach, the original text of the traditional incantation is replaced by a religious prayer and the charcoal with matches. For example, in the town of Bistrița, one variation of this

203 Meaning, it had to be water taken early in the morning, before anyone else had a chance to use water from that source.

204 Aurel I. Candrea, *Folclorul medical român comparat. Privire generală: medicina magică* (Iaşi: Polirom, 1999), p. 216–217.

cure starts by putting out nine successively lit matches in a small water cup, while reciting every time the Lord's Prayer (therefore, also nine times in total). The evil eye diagnosis is usually confirmed as positive when all the lit matches sink to the bottom of the cup. Before drinking, the person conducting the ritual says: 'as this cup will never be affected by the evil eye, so X (the name of the suppliant) too should never be affected again.' The water in the cup must be drunk by the sufferer immediately after in nine sips split into three rounds. From the water left in the cup the officiant takes a bit on the index finger and draws a cross on the door frame while saying: 'as this frame will never be affected by the evil eye, so X should never be affected again.' The remaining water is thrown in the direction of the house's roof, a gesture accompanied by: 'as this house will never be affected by the evil eye, so X should never be affected again.' The evil affliction is thus progressively pushed further and further away from the sufferer through three consecutive actions: in a centrifugal motion, the evil eye is expelled from the victim to its immediate vicinity, then toward the interior border of the domestic perimeter (the door frame illustrates the liminality principle) so that, in the end, it is banished to the furthermost exterior border, directing this evil 'out there.' The ritual can be finished by the officiant with sprinkling the now-cured victim with the remaining drops in the cup and/or with drawing the sign of the cross with the same water on the afflicted person's forehead. In the Mediterranean area, a far more popular diagnose-cure seems to be the dripping of an uneven number of oil drops in water, accompanied by a prayer or incantation: if the drops dissipate, the symptoms are confirmed as the result of the evil eye; if they maintain their shape, the cause of illness needs to be looked for elsewhere. The cure could simply result from the evil eye being diagnosed or, similar to the Romanian example, by the sufferer being sprinkled with and drinking some of the water used in the ritual.[205]

[205] Willem de Blécourt, p. 194; Regina Dionisopoulos-Mass, 'The Evil Eye and Bewitchment in a Peasant Village', *The Evil Eye*, ed. by Clarence Maloney (New York: Columbia University Press, 1976), pp. 42–62, p. 47; Enrique

Protection against the evil eye is considered most important for people who are liminally placed, which makes them particularly vulnerable. The first to be taken into consideration are infants and little children, who can arouse various intense feelings (envy, admiration, or delight) even during casual interactions. Their magical protection is based on the apotropaic emphasis of the color red, either as a red thread tied to the baby's wrist or ankle or as red piece of clothing (particularly the ones worn directly on the baby's skin). The inherent apotropaic quality invested into the red color can be doubled by placing a clove of garlic in the buggy, complying with the logic of cumulative defensive ritual actions.

From a gestural and interactional point of view, seeing a small baby can trigger a series of feelings in the onlooker. Aware of the negative impact that these feelings can have upon the magically vulnerable baby, an adult running into a baby and his/her parents by chance would always commence the interaction with an apotropaic precaution: he/she verbalizes the standard formula *'ptiu, ptiu*[206]*, so that I won't give you the evil eye!'*, usually accompanied by miming the customary triple spitting on the child. The same spitting gesture sometimes accompanies greetings between adults in oral Greek culture,[207] either as personal protection against the met person (evil eye or possible spells) or as averting the magical acts possibly put in action by a third party in order to prevent that meeting from taking place.

The bride is another liminal, vulnerable being that needs protection because she can arouse the same set of intense, dangerous feelings within wedding participants or casual onlookers. It is recommended that the bride wears something red on her body, either a red thread, a piece of lingerie, or a piece of jewelry. In Romania, this custom is scrupulously respected, but the actors are not always mo-

Perdiguero, 'Magical Healing in Spain (1875–1936): medical pluralism and the search for hegemony', *Witchcraft Continued. Popular Magic in Modern Europe*, ed. by Willem de Blécourt & Owen Davies (Manchester& New York: Manchester University Press, 2004), pp. 133–150, p. 141.

206 'Ptiu, ptiu' it's an imitative interjection illustrating the sound of spitting.

207 Marie-Christine Anest-Couffin, p. 56.

tivated by apotropaic reasons. Especially in the cities (Cluj, Bistrița, and Baia Mare), the custom of the bride always wearing something red is explained with a more general 'that's the right thing to do' or sometimes it is motivated by the bride's desire of having a girl as the first child (when a boy is wanted, the bride wears something blue). In the villages, however, enquiring about the same custom usually leads to a different type of answer: the bride wears red in order to scare away the evil spirits[208] or to avoid getting the evil eye from envious women.[209]

Envy always seems to have played a crucial role in the understanding of the evil eye, especially in the rural-traditional societies of Europe where the ideology of egalitarianism was contradicted by the day-to-day processes of economic stratification and competition. Someone's good fortune, health, beauty, or abundance was always susceptible to be met with a type of admiration combined with jealousy from one's peers because all this 'good' (economic success; a successful marriage; a newborn baby; a healthy cow, and so on) actually meant 'better' than someone else's. That is why 'the compliment is a threat, one expressing the envy for the admired one's good fortune,'[210] and it has to be met with the appropriate apotropaic strategies meant to nullify the dangerous sentiment channeled by it. Envy can cause the evil eye affliction (intended or not); it can make the admired one the target of sorcery attacks from jealous people, especially neighbors; it could generate gossip and slander, damaging the social reputation of the more fortunate individual or family.[211] As noticed by João de Pina-Cabral in the context of his research in Portugal (between 1978 and 1980), for the Portuguese peasants, the concept of envy represents a profoundly death-dealing, antisocial

---

208 Fieldwork infomation, Năsăud,. Bistrița-Năsăud County, 2007.

209 Fieldwork infomation, Dumitra & Reteag, Bistrița-Năsăud County, 2008.

210 Regina Dionisopoulos-Mass, p. 44.

211 Regina Dionisopoulos-Mass discusses the three possible outcomes of envy (the evil eye, the gossip, and magic) as 'controlled dynamics of power' stressing out 'the socioeconomic unity of the society' and reinforcing the norms, p. 60.

force, crucial in explaining rare open conflicts and any significant misfortune[212] imputable to other people.

The evil eye is known and feared in many parts of the world but not all. Clarence Maloney put together a world map with the known distribution of the belief in the evil eye,[213] which shows the evil eye not being known mostly in North and South America (but present in Central America), southwestern Africa, Australia, and central and northeastern Asia. Beyond all the local differences in understanding, defining, and treating it, it can be seen as 'the simple belief that one's eye power can cause sudden harm to another's property or person.'[214] One interesting aspect is that, in anthropology, there remains an analytical distinction between the evil eye and witchcraft, whereas, as suggested by Willem de Blécourt, 'there is little in the description of the evil eye that justifies its separation from witchcraft in general.'[215] Furthermore, research suggests that the actors themselves seldom operate this distinction.[216] After all, the perceived effects of the evil eye and those of witchcraft in a rural traditional society were similar, ranging from physical illness-like symptoms to accidents, cows not giving milk any more, women losing their pregnancies, or unexplained deaths. One difference that is relevant for the researcher of a certain society, but probably less so for the insiders of that society, is that of the transfer medium necessary to channel the aggressive intention: through the eyes in the case of the evil eye or through the spell in the case of sorcery attacks. The degree of intentionality is another element that sets aside the evil eye from the sorcery attacks: the evil eye could be given by an innocent passer-by, unaware of their unwanted ability to harm through sight.

212 João de Pina-Cabral, *Sons of Adam, Daughters of Eve. The Peasant Worldview of the Alto Mihno* (Oxford: Clarendon Press, 1986), pp. 176–177.

213 Clarence Maloney, 'Introduction', *The Evil Eye*, ed. by Clarence Maloney (New York: Columbia University Press, 1976), pp. V–XVI, pp. XII–XIII.

214 Clarence Maloney, p. VI.

215 Willem de Blécourt, p. 196.

216 Richard Jenkins, 'Witches and Fairies: Supernatural Aggression and Deviance among the Irish Peasantry', *The Good People: New Fairylore Essays*, ed. by Peter Narváez (Lexington:University Press of Kentucky, 1997), pp. 302–335, p. 307.

At the other end of the scale, closer to witchcraft, the evil eye could be projected by a jealous witch with the equal malefic intentionality required by the sending of a complicated evil spell.

In today's Romania, the forms, the imagined range of action, and the preventive and therapeutic means to counter the evil eye are quite diminished when compared to those of traditional societies or even to the variety of protective means still in use in the Mediterranean region. Not so long ago, it was believed that the evil eye can affect livestock and humans well beyond the unpleasant but rather minor physical symptoms described today and much more similar to the potentially catastrophic effects of sorcery. As for the therapeutic approach of the evil eye, 'the boundaries between diagnosis and cure are blurred'[217]: in most cases, the diagnosis is also the cure; once named it is fairly easy to treat. Treating the effects of sorcery, however, was never something equally unproblematic. As my next subchapters will show, unwitching, whether laic or religious, is a complicated, long-standing process with no guarantees of success.

Religious Unwitching

In the Transylvanian region of today, complex religious rituals meant to undo a magical aggression combine the efforts of a priest with those of the victim and, if necessary, even the ritual involvement of the victim's close family and friends.

This is typified by the experience of Maria (woman, age 56, Bistrița). In the summer of 2007, she appealed to a priest from S., a nearby village, who was renowned for his triumphs against witchcraft. She had first suspected that she had been bewitched two years earlier on the basis of recurrent nervous breakdowns, continuous and unexplained illnesses, and constant conflict with her partner, John. A neighbor who had a previous personal experience with witchcraft was the first to identify this general '*mal de vivre*' as an effect of evil magical interventions. Both the neighbor and Maria identified the aggressor as John's ex-wife, the one John had left for

[217] Willem de Blécourt, p. 194.

Maria: therefore, the supposed magical aggressor's actions were sufficiently explained as rooted in hatred and revenge.

One August morning, Maria finally worked up the courage to address the issue. So, instead of checking herself in (again) at the hospital as she had at first intended, she got into her neighbor's car and they both traveled to the priest's village. It was very early in the morning, as they were supposed to arrive before the priest would start the liturgy. By midway, Maria started to feel really sick.[218] She was dizzy, shaky, nauseous, shivery, and foggy. When they arrived, she barely managed to get out of the car. A lot of people were already in the churchyard, waiting for a consultation with the priest and for the liturgy to begin. Many of them, just like Maria and her neighbor, were not locals but people traveling from various distances in need of the priest's particular expertise. When the priest arrived, people queued, waiting for their turn to confession: especially for those like Maria, with sensitive issues to address, confession is the first compulsory step to assure ritual purification. During the confession, the priest advised Maria to continue her effort by participating in the following liturgy and the customary communion rite. Confession, liturgy, and communion would ensure that she gradually became ritually cleansed; only then would she be able to address the evil tormenting her together with the priest. Maria's first impulse was to give up and leave, convinced that she could not possibly stand up for a further three hours (the standard duration of Orthodox liturgy). Nonetheless, with help and encouragement from her neighbor, she somehow managed to pull through. She continued to feel physically ill and quite confused about everything going on

---

218 The theme of evil infestation manifesting itself as physical, illness-like symptoms when getting closer to something holy (a church; an icon; a priest; a rosary) is quite common in Romania. As shown in the second chapter, someone feeling sick when holding a blessed rosary can be a clue for the diviner that s/he is most likely bewitched. Similar to this, it is believed that people suffering the effects of a magical aggression cannot stand the smell of frankincense: therefore, if one feels particularly sick from that smell during liturgy in the church, it can be an indication that s/he is afflicted.

around her during the liturgy until the moment of the communion: once she swallowed the host and wine, she suddenly realized that her state was gradually improving.

> *'I remember that, after stepping away from the priest, my friend helped me get out to the church's porch. And I remember that, while I was leaning against one of the lateral columns, it was like a fog was lifting from my eyes … Literally, it was like I was finally seeing—colours, shapes, sun light. And I felt relieved, like a dark burden has been lifted away from my soul …' (Maria, woman, age 56, Bistrița)*

A private consultation with the priest followed. He did not have any difficulty in confirming the witchcraft diagnosis, based on Maria's story and, more importantly, based on seeing her feeling so sick in contact with holy spaces and objects that morning. The sufferer's narrative is used to establish what kind of evil exactly was in place (witchcraft; kinship curse; a hidden sin; even demonic possession requiring exorcism). Maria's story supported the witchcraft diagnosis, but, before formulating the next steps necessary for the ritual healing, the priest insisted that she recognized the fact that she was not an altogether innocent victim: her actions of breaking a family through seducing John are, from the Church's point of view, a grave sin. She was advised to repent for that sin and warned that impurity was the back door to her soul allowing the witchcraft attacks to succeed; they would have been far less successful for somebody with a clearer conscience.

The first compulsory step of any religious therapeutic ritual, namely the general ritual purification through confession and communion, had already been accomplished that morning. The next step consisted in the priest reciting a special type of unwitching-prayer over the kneeled repentant, effectively marking the beginning of the unwitching ritual. From there on, Maria was to comply with a complex 40-day ritual. She had to read the *The Acatist of Saint Pantelimon* every morning and *The Acatist in Times of Adversity and Temptation* when needed. She had to read a selection of psalms from the *Psalms of David* by candle light and in front of a religious icon every night at midnight. She had to observe a strict fasting[219] every Monday, Wednesday, and Friday. She attended the evening religious service[220] (*Maslu*) at least three times during the observed period, bringing along three liturgical pieces of bread (*prescuri*), a bottle of red wine, and clothes to be blessed during the ritual. In addition, the priest prayed and held masses in the name of his solicitor, and after the first half of the ritual period, he came into town and hallowed Maria's apartment as a religious means to ward off evil spirits and influences. She was also advised at that point, by both the priest and her neighbor, to wear her underwear inside out as protection against further witchcraft attacks.

The hardest part of the process was, for Maria, reading the Psalter at midnight, kneeling before an icon with a lit candle. Especially during the first two weeks, the midnight reading proved to be quite a challenge every single time: after reciting few verses, she would start to feel sick, unable to focus or see the letters, sleepy, and having to fight really hard in order to continue. Both she and the priest took this as a sure confirmation of the diagnosis, interpreting it as *'the Devil's struggle to hang on to a soul where he thought he's got a foothold.'* For her neighbor, who continued to offer support, Maria's struggle at midnight was also a clear sign that John's ex-wife, the presupposed attacker, was still sending out evil spells. Reading the Psalter at midnight is perceived by both clergy and the faithful as a double-edged sword; a powerful but dangerous way of purifying oneself from evil. It has to be done under strict supervision, and only when a member of the clergy recommends it—a layman might not

219 Wednesdays and Fridays are recommended weekly fasting days in Orthodox Christianity in order to commemorate the day when Christ had been betrayed by Judas and the day of his crucifixion. Fasting in this religious context means abstaining from certain foods (especially diary and meat), but the appropriate behavior also includes refraining from intimate relations and limiting entertainment, for instance. 'Certainly, it is a time when there is increased focus on refraining from evil actions and thoughts' - ‹http://en.orthodoxwiki.org/Fasting›.

220 *Maslul* is an Orthodox religious service that is considered helpful for resolving health problems and earning the forgiveness of sins.

be able to handle its ambiguous power. Also, talking about the ritual or simply mentioning it is strictly forbidden.

For Maria, reading the Psalter became easier only after the first half of the ritual period. The only ones aware of the fact that she was going through an unwitching ritual were her neighbor friend and John, her partner. Nobody else knew: not her mother, not her children, and none of her closest friends. She had to carry on with her teaching job and to do her best to accommodate the ritual requirements with the profane rhythms of everyday life. She struggled hard to dissimulate from the exterior that anything out of the ordinary was happening in her life at that point. Also, Maria had to find the financial resources required by the various stages of the ritual process. The initial consultation, the liturgies, and prayers held by the priest in her name, his traveling to her town to blessing the apartment, these were all services needing compensation: the unwitching priest, just like any other specialist, had to be paid every step of the way.

Did she feel better after going through the ritual period? She did feel a lot better and had an immediate, spectacular recovery from illness with no further need for hospitalization—at least at that time. When I interviewed her one year and a half later, some of the somatic symptoms had started to reappear. But, as the priest had told her at the time of the unwitching, evil can always find a new way in—as that is the nature of evil. In her particular case, the priest confirmed from the very first moment that they were dealing with a particularly strong type of sorcery and that Maria might need to go through unwitchments again and again if this evil finds its way back to her. The only way to protect against it is to repent for one's sins and scrupulously follow the everyday religious duty as prescribed to the faithful.

Informal Specialization

The previous example of an Orthodox religious unwitching ritual was addressed strictly to curing a type of '*mal de vivre*' affliction, one of the more complicated effects of witchcraft due to the fact that it instantiates itself as a long-term crisis, usually for years at a time, and affects the actor comprehensively, in all the aspects of existence: health; ability to function; relationships and family; financial situation; continuous misfortunes; unhappiness, etc.

The prescribed steps of an unwitching process can be different when dealing with, for instance, delayed marriage. The priest I. from the village C. in Bistrița-Năsăud County, much-praised locally for his ability to solve young women's difficulties in getting married, has a shorter standard formula for these specific cases. In general, the priest recommends the *Paraclisul Maicii Domnului* (*Paraklesis to the Mother of God*)[221] to be recited on three consecutive Wednesdays, accompanied each time by severe fasting, followed by the *Acatistul Domnului Nostru Isus Hristos* (*Akathist to our Lord Jesus Christ*) every Wednesday and Friday, also with fasting. Then, the cycle is repeated for a minimum of three times and a maximum of nine times in a row, depending on the priest's recommendation, until the eventual successful outcome. The dedication by the client is supplemented by the priest's own involvement: he prays and conducts various liturgical acts in her name and for her benefit. This shorter formula normally addresses less-complicated situations, such as delaying of marriage as momentary setbacks in the life of the young women requiring ritual assistance.

As Maria's example shows for the *'mal de vivre'* situation, religious therapists tend to rate the witchcraft they are up against, considering some situations more serious than others. If the priest I has reasons to believe that, in a specific case, the sorcery affecting his client is stronger and more threatening to her general well-being than the momentary difficulty of getting married, he may recommend a 40-day ritual based on the reading of the *Acatistul Sfântului Ciprian* (*Akathist to Saint Cyprian*), with severe fasting every Monday, Wednesday, and Friday.[222] The iconic figure of Saint Cyprian

221 *Parakleses* and *Akathists* are special types of Eastern Orthodox prayers used to seek the intercessions of Jesus Christ, Virgin Mary, or any saint.

222 Severe fasting means, in this context, not only the avoidance of animal-based food and restrains on one's behavior and thoughts but the practice of

(celebrated in the Orthodox calendar on the 2nd of October) is particularly relevant for Orthodox Christianity as a symbol for the fight against witchcraft. His hagiography insists on his spectacular conversion to Christianity from being a powerful, ruthless sorcerer. Therefore, prayers bearing his name and all symbols associated with him often play a part in religious therapies against witchcraft as a symbolic investment in the afflicted actor's capacity to defeat the powers of evil.

Another saint associated with unwitchments is Saint Basil the Great, celebrated by the Orthodox Church on the 1st of January, when it is also customary for most churches in Romania to hold *The Divine Liturgy of Saint Basil the Great* instead of the more frequently used *Divine Liturgy of Saint John Chrysostom.* But, Saint Basil's connection to witchcraft comes from *Moliftele Sfântului Vasile cel Mare* (the three Prayers of Exorcism), popularly also known as *The Curses of Saint Basil the Great.* These prayer–curses can be held by the Orthodox priest or monk at the end of Saint Basil's liturgy, after the *Maslu* service, or even in individual homes after blessing and purifying the space if there is a case of illness or another type of adversity in one's family. Very dramatic in tone and display, these exorcisms–prayer–curses are customarily held at midnight with the whole audience kneeling. They have indeed an ambiguous fame among the faithful, seen as a source of power so dangerous that reciting them can have a disastrous boomerang effect upon the priests who use them when they are not sufficiently strong or ill prepared:

> *'S: There are those [priests] who employ those payers of Saint Basil. But that's very dangerous ... He shouldn't be married, or have kids. Monks are safer to use it, of course. They can read these curses at 12 o'clock at night on the night of the 1st January towards the 2nd of January, or any Friday at midnight. And that means they exorcize. They exorcize all evil spells, all witchcraft, and chase away the Devil. But if the priest is married and he's not strong enough, all his family will die.*

---

not eating or drinking anything preferably all day or, in a milder version, until noon. That is sometimes called in Romanian *'post negru,'* word-by-word translated as *'black fasting.'*

M: Then how do you explain that the priest A. reads them pretty often? He's married ...

S: He must be courageous, but ... Our old priest from Mocod, he was courageous too, and then all of his sons died, and some of his grandkids, one by one. That's why the new young priest, although he actually used to be a monk, stays away from it. He simply refuses to do it, he has a wife to think about.

L: And after all, the priest A. is very ill, isn't he? More and more so by the day. People say it's precisely because he insists to employ these prayers, although he shouldn't ... They are too powerful for him. And you know what they say: the evil is banished from somebody during the ritual, but then it enters back ... in whom it enters.' Maria (woman, age 56, Bistrița); Silvia (woman, age 34, Năsăud); Lenuța (woman, age 28, Dumitra village)

Presented as 'the cure' in any discussion about witchcraft, these curses of Saint Basil are a weapon exclusive to the religious therapists' arsenal. They do not get to be used privately by victims of witchcraft, like the other prayers or rituals mentioned earlier. The bewitched get to participate in collective ritual readings of these curses (in a monastery or a church) only when/if the unwitching priest asks them to.

According to religious doctrine, all ordained Orthodox priests and monks have the same professional means at their disposal to confront all forms of evil, and one of the most important tools in this respect is the book known as *Molifielnic* (*Euchologion*), *The Slavonic Great Book of Needs*. Effectively a collection of all the essential texts needed by the officiant in his daily activity (sacraments; Divine Liturgy; blessings; rites for minor orders, etc.), the second section of this book is dedicated to short prayers for various needs. For instance, there are prayers for various afflictions and illnesses, against evil spirits or evil spells, against the evil eye, for those who suffer the effects of a curse, and so on. *Moliftele Sfântului Vasile cel Mare* (Saint Basil's three Prayers of Exorcism), along with those of Saint Chrysostom's, are also included in the last section. But, as the previous examples show, there is no single standard approach prescribed for witchcraft situations. Which prayers the client is to use, at what times, and combined with which ritual steps and fasting, what religious services she or he has to attend—these are all selected and dosed in careful combinations by the intervening religious therapist depending on the particular case they are being presented with. Also, as shown in **Chapter 2**, all Orthodox priests and monks are supposed to have the same professional capacity to fight off the evil in this world, precisely through their ordination investing them equally with 'grace' ('*har*'). Whereas, outside the doctrine, most laical actors perceive this quality of *grace* as a form of personal power explaining some monks' or priests' higher success rate when dealing with forms of evil.

Therefore, the prescribed steps of a religious unwitching process can vary, depending on the nature of each case and on the personal capabilities of the respective priest in curing a certain form of affliction. This results in two types of informal specialization within the religious therapy of unwitching:

- informal specialization according to the specific affliction needing intervention and its gravity: '*mal de vivre*'; delayed marriage; problematic love relationship; kinship sin; and weaker or stronger sorcery involved (as rated by the priest);
- informal specialization according to the personal capabilities of the priests.

When in need, people can access veritable oral maps of their region, orientating each individual toward the most-suited religious therapist for her/his particular case. For example, everybody in Bistrița knows that if you need help regarding a delayed marriage or a problematic love relationship, the one to go to is the priest I. from village C. But if the problem is of a different sort, such as a general '*mal de vivre*' incapacitating the sufferer, which is probably the result of stronger witchcraft, the one to consult is the priest from village S. Many other priests and monasteries can be singled out as subsequent alternatives for the afflicted individual, mostly from neighboring counties.

Episodes of witchcraft are characterized by spatial mobility, represented as vast networks of movement that cut across rural and urban social environments. The febrile rhythm of each search is based on the necessity of identifying the best specialist[223] able to offer answers and strategies for solving the crisis. People feel motivated to travel far and frequently anywhere in Romania where they hear they might find a capable therapist:

> *'Whatever adversity one faces, there are gifted people out there, monks or priests, who can help. There is one in Stejaru, Maramureş County, who also opens the Psalter. There is one in the village Chintelnic, and there used to be another very good one in Cociu. Fact is, once you find yourself in one of these desperate situations, you go ... to the end of the world, if you have to. You hear from here and there, about one priest able to help you or another maybe better, and you go ...' Floricuța (woman, age 63, Dumitra village)*

The dynamic pattern of mobility, guided by particular needs and renewed hopes of finding the right solutions, is equally reflected by the fact that local[224] specialists tend to be avoided. This tendency is also noted by Jeanne Favret-Saada[225] in the context of her research in rural France: her informants always preferred to choose their therapist from a neighboring district, since too few of the most difficult witchcraft affairs were ever presented to the local unwitcher. Dominique Camus,[226] also noting the fact that the sorcerers and unwitchers of his French research lived, on average, at about 20 km away from their clientele, saw this as the effect of the value attached to the witchcraft discourse: more precisely, the illegitimate character of the latter by reference to the dominant ideologies. Thus, victims or clients of witchcraft stay away from known social circles in order to avoid being judged by their peers for their personal beliefs. All my informants in Romania explained the preference for religious therapists from localities other than their own as a measure to prevent

223 In this context, I am referring only to magic and religious specialists, although the same dynamic spatial mobility describes the search for identifying the most suitable ('the best') medical doctor, especially in cases of chronic illnesses with little chances of healing.

224 By 'local,' I mean from the very same village or town as the victim.

225 Jeanne Favret-Saada, *Les mots, la mort, les sorts* (Paris: Gallimard, 1977), p. 44.

226 Dominique Camus, p. 72.

the unwanted public visibility of their personal problems. Another connected reason, also mentioned by Camus, is that the client looking for unwitchment would rather stay away from the sorcerer's immediate social reach. As the presumed witch is always part of the victim's personal network of family, friends, or relations, he/she would easily learn of the victim's intentions and efforts; this, my informants insisted, would give the evil-doers an unfair advantage and a reason to renew or intensify their attacks.

3.3 Protection and Combat Limits

In official Orthodox discourse, the best prevention against falling victim to witchcraft (and the only efficient apotropaic mechanism) is to follow every good Christian's daily religious duty devotedly.

Informally, priests, monks, and lay actors assume that not all evil spells can be definitively unbound by religious therapy:

> *'That evil spell once thrown ... I do not know, the priest said that it might come back periodically. Once thrown, if it is powerful enough, you have to fight it ... maybe continuously.' Maria (woman, age 56, Bistrița)*

> *'There are cases in which not even a powerful monk can undo an evil spell. There are some of those made as such, unbreakable.' Floricuța (woman, age 63, Dumitra village)*

Such acknowledgments of the limits of the religious ritual can be a bit surprising, seeing that this is the only legitimate therapy in contemporary witchcraft cases. However, it can be linked to the common rural-traditional belief that an evil spell or charm, once triggered, has to cling to somebody. Or, in Dominique Camus' terms: 'no spell is ever lost.'[227] The spell is seen as loaded with a dangerous power of its own, independent from its target and equally independent from the one launching it. It can stray from the initial target but eventually will find somebody else to attach itself to. It can also come back to the emitter, which is why any sorcerer takes precautions against it. And, finally, a spell is rated according to the amount of destructive power it carries, not only in terms of its po-

---

[227] Dominique Camus, p. 80. [My translation].

tential effects (illness, accident, and dying) but also by duration in time (years). In extreme cases, the best that a religious therapeutic ritual can offer is to generate a sort of continuous protective halo shielding the victim until the evil spell expires by itself. Nonetheless, there are some evil spells, particularly those using corpses in the ritual, which are thought to never expire. The analogy at work here is fairly simple and always uttered by the witch in the form of an incantation sealing the spell: 'Just as the part of the corpse's body will never be alive again, so too' the addressee's targeted attributes (beauty; health; marriage or choice in marrying; good fortune; luck; or life) 'will not.'

> *'The day of the burial, before taking the deceased out of the house, the women have to break a glass or something there, in the house, in order to scare away the evil spirits. At the same time, you have to unbind the thread from around the deceased's feet, and hide that thread under the shroud. If you're not careful, somebody might steal that thread. And use it in witchcraft later on. For instance, if she wants to bind a good looking young woman's chances of getting married, so that her own daughter might marry: she goes on a barren field and binds together two thorny weeds, saying: "Just as these thorns will never untie, so too X will never get married" and "This spell will dissolve only when this dead will walk again." You can imagine, as the dead is dead, the bewitched's chances to ever get married can remain cursed ... forever.' Silvia (woman, age 34, Năsăud)*

The traditional solution to these situations was to throw back the evil spell to the original aggressor. This was a type of returned magical aggression usually employed by the laical rural therapist (*dezlegătoarea*), who normally supplemented the process of 'unbinding' (undoing) the evil spell by this act. Especially when dealing with a powerful spell that is never lost and is unlikely to dissolve on its own, finding a new target for it (other than the suffering client) seemed to be the only solution. And what better other target than the very author of the evil attack? Therefore, in one process of unwitchment, healing was paralleled by revenge, showing how, in the domain of traditional magic, efficiency was customarily linked to aggression.

The difference between the religious therapies employed today and the earlier laic unwitchment of the rural-traditional kind lies precisely in the way each related discourse rates aggression. A religious intervention of any kind cannot make the voluntary aggressive act of throwing back the evil spell a part of its ritual. Committing a magical aggression is a deliberate, condemnable act of violence and, thus, cannot play any part in a religious ritual.

During the religious therapeutic unwitching ritual, there are special precautions to be taken against the potential discharge of destructive-aggressive powers. For example, immediately after identifying the potential aggressor, the priest tells the victim to pay masses for that sinner, to pray for their soul, to write them down in their diptychs[228] along the names of the alive and departed loved ones, so that *'maybe God will enlighten them and straighten them out.'*[229] Such recommendations are equally voiced by the fortune teller who, along the same religious ethics, also advises her client to avoid prolonged meditations on the aggressor's reasons to harm; one should not be thinking badly of anybody in order to avoid causing harm to that person: *'Let them be punished by God, not us.'*[230] Furthermore, in the cases where the process of the religious unwitching is based upon the afflicted actors' reading of the Psalter at midnight, one interdiction is always explicitly and firmly expressed by the priest: the 108 Psalm is not to be read while thinking of a person, and especially the presupposed attacker. For that reason, skipping the 108 Psalm altogether is, sometimes, the recommended course of action. All of these precautions are based on the idea of a harmful magic force possible to unleash not only through words or ritual means but also through the simplest thought. In a religious perspective, causing harm to somebody else, even when done un-

---

228 In this context, diptychs refer to a very common practice of every Eastern Orthodox faithful to write down a list of people he/she would like to be read out loud by the priest at the end of the liturgical service. This equates, more or less, to having both the devoted and the priest praying for the people named in this way. The names put down on a diptych are mostly the closest loved ones, alive or dead. But, in a similar manner to the one described earlier, people can put down the names of their enemies so that God might turn them around.

229 Fieldwork infomation, Bistrița, summer of 2008.

230 Fieldwork infomation, Cluj-Napoca, September 2008.

consciously (the mean thoughts) or apparently legitimate (as instinctive reaction or defensive attitude), is a danger of impurity threatening the ritual outcome and the actor's moral quality. The right to punish somebody for evil doings lies well outside the human's right to action and resides exclusively with the divinity.

Chapter 4: Magic and Religion

Magic, religion, and science are three major categories we can use to define our reality, and each corresponds to a different mode of action. Today, these domains of human existence are most often understood to stand in tension with one another. Magic is set in opposition to religion as a form of dangerous superstition or even blasphemy against the deity. Magic is plain absurd to scientists as it fails any standard of empiricism. Religion also is seen as irrational from the scientific point of view due to the investment of belief instead of tested proof. In short, we all think of these three categories of being fixed, impossible to reconcile, and opposed to one other. More than that, we attach implicit values to each according to the dominant frame of reference of our time and culture—according to this, magic is currently the big loser, religion lies somewhere in the middle, while science is the big winner.

Claude Lévi-Strauss showed how no category can be fully conceptualized unless inscribed in a series of binary oppositions: 'Any classification proceeds through pairs of contrasts.'[231] The human understanding of the world is based upon the way a word or a notion is implicitly opposed to another, a fundamental relationship between contrasting ideas whose operational character resides in the way this dichotomic structure elicits the automatic mental evocation of the opposed term to the one directly presented. In a dialog for instance, one speaker says 'white,' and its interlocutor will also think of 'black.' The apparent innocence of these operational dichotomies is cast into doubt at the point where this classificatory mode of thought proves to be insidiously doubled by a ranking process. In a binary pair, one term is always valorized as positive, superior to its opposing one, so that the history of that opposition is actually the

231 Claude Lévi–Strauss, *La Pensée Sauvage* (Paris: Librairie Plon, 1964), p. 287. [My translation].

expression of a ceaseless fight for hierarchic position.[232] In the long line of oppositions that historically marked the Western thought, such as: woman/man, body/soul, black/white, praxis/theory, magic/religion, night/day, belief/reason, etc., only one term is, every time, the one carrying the + sign. The binary way of thinking is not simply a way to classify and organize the world; it comes under the form of a dilemma,[233] which subconsciously invites a choice, owing to the previous tacit understanding of the binary terms as being mutually exclusive.

Therefore, in any explanatory frame, some terms fare better than others, or the reality they claim to express is culturally ranked higher than another. This is also a matter of historical developments. Simply put, some modes of thought, frames of reference, and dominant lines of enquiries can be prevalent at certain times in history, while losing their salience at others. The fact that, in contemporary Western civilization, positive science is held to be the quintessential form of rationality and that this type of rationality is seen to be the ultimate mode of knowledge is the result of localized historical process of separation between Christianity and science during the 16th and 17th centuries in Europe,[234] culminating in the 18th century with the Enlightenment. Up to that point, religion had been the main generator of normative social discourse. However, with rationalization becoming the dominant mode of thought, all of the others had to be defined, classified, converted, or explained in the exclusive terms of scientific rationality. Furthermore, the way we perceive magic today—as occult, mysterious, illicit, and irrational—has more to do with 'a Western (especially Victorian) fascination with magic and witchcraft (wicca),' as an 'invention of a Post-Enlightenment

---

232 Jaques Derrida, *Diseminarea* (Bucureşti: Univers Enciclopedic, 1997), p. 10.

233 François Laplatine, *Descrierea etnografică* (Iaşi Polirom, 2000), p. 67.

234 Stanley Jeyaraja Tambiah, *Magic, Science and Religion and the Scope of Rationality* (Cambridge: Cambridge University Press, 1990), p. 140.

secularism'[235] rather than representing immutable traits of an easily definable magic domain.

The history of Western anthropology underlying the magic/religion/science debate of modern times is intimately linked to the historical successive periods of defining reality in the Western world. A very brief account illustrating successive stages of defining magic, religion, and science in anthropology shows how much these debates inform the way we think about these three fields of knowledge today.

4.1 Magic, Religion, and Science as Key Concepts in Anthropology

From the authors of classical anthropology (19th century) to more modern research, magic is either analyzed as somewhat akin to science, focusing on its empiricist and technical aspects, or as similar to religion due to its beliefs ('superstitions') and its belonging to the sphere of the sacred. One of the earliest ways for anthropologists to establish rapports between religion, magic, and science was to do so in terms of antagonism, similarity, or derivation. An initial corollary to anthropology's enquiries into the specific traits of these modes of thought was the assumption that they correspond to certain types of societies. The magical and religious modes of thought were taken to best characterize 'primitive' people and those of traditional rural societies, whereas the scientific, rational, and causal thinking would describe the people of modern industrial societies, the Occidental man. Or, in Marcel Mass's terms, members of outer-European societies can be described as *homo religiosus*, replaced in 'our society' by *homo economicus*.[236] Therefore, the preoccupation with establishing hierarchies and derivative schemes between the religious, the magical, and the scientific thinking effectively meant

235 Bruce Kapferer, 'Introduction: Outside all reason – Magic, Sorcery and Epistemology in Anthropology', *Beyond Rationalism. Rethinking Magic, Witchcraft and Sorcery*, ed. by Bruce Kapferer (New York & Oxford: Berghahn Books, 2003), pp. 1–30, p. 4.

236 Marcel Mauss, *Manuel d'ethnographie* (Paris: Éditions sociales, 1967), p. 173.

to qualitatively rank the Western world against any other type of society and culture.

The emblematic evolutionist scheme drawn up by Fraser[237] (at the end of the 19th century and beginning of the 20th century) still informs contemporary perceptions about the place, or the value, held by each of these phenomena in social life to a significant extent. Fraser starts with magic as the first step of human mental evolution, emblematic for 'primitive' societies, arrives at religion as the first significant attempt to outgrow simplistic magical associations, and finally reaches science as the highest stage of human thought. This scheme of evolutionist anthropology endured as the mark par excellence of most anthropological discussions about religion, magic, and science, even for authors who explicitly distanced themselves from evolutionism. The main controversies in this context were the rapports that can be established between the three terms—in other words, which is closer to which, and what exactly sets them apart.

Another popular dichotomy in the late 19th and early 20th centuries was aiming to establish the relations between myth and rite (as stand-ins for the 'thought' vs. 'action'). Initially, these theoretical approaches were similar to the religion/magic/science model in the sense that the core stake was, more often than not, establishing hierarchies and primordialities between the two terms. Whether the premise was that the ritual translates a preexistent myth into action, or vice versa, that the myth was just the secondary by-pass explaining ritual action, the relations between the two were seen as a perfect homology, such as cause and effect or original and copy. J.G. Frazer, similar to other authors, found himself oscillating between these opposite approaches, generically known as mythological orientation versus ritualism.[238] Émile Durkheim wrote a theoretical differentiation that persisted for a long time within the social sciences: He equates rituals to modes of action, as opposed to representa-

237 Sir James George Frazer, 'Chapter 4: Magic and Religion', *The Golden Bough. A Study in Magic and Religion* (New York: Macmillan, 1922), ‹http://www.bartleby.com/196/9.html› [accessed October 5, 2015]

238 Robert Ackerman, 'Frazer on Myth and Ritual', *Journal of the History of Ideas*, 36. 1 (1975), pp. 115–134, ‹http://www.jstor.org› [accessed March 2007]

tions, which correspond to thought.[239] This mechanical, mirroring equalization, reflecting well the rationalistic period to which it belonged, left a long-standing imprint in subsequent anthropological enquiries, known as 'intellectualism.'[240] The term refers to what will later on be pointed out as a typical aspect of Western theoretical approaches: the positive valorization of the theoretical, rational, and abstract, to the detriment of action, the actual/concrete, and the lived.

Few theoreticians of the classical period managed to sound as definitive as Lévy-Bruhl when he stated that 'the primitive man' has no rational or secular thought and that he is hopelessly caught up in an exclusively mystical frame of mind.[241] Even if he went on to make this point of view subsequently more nuanced, it did not go much beyond granting this 'primitive man' *some* empirical capacities but maintaining that he is definitely more religious, more mystical, and more superstitious than the Occidental man. In other words, the implicit hierarchy at work here was not only that of magic/religion/science but also pertaining to the tension between 'sacred' and 'profane,' defined through their corollaries 'belief' versus 'reason.' Needless to say, only 'profane' and 'reason' are the terms carrying positive values.

Closer to the first half of 20th century, various authors start to break free from these trends dictating the approaches to this subject area. One of those was Arnold Van Gennep. He states that the evo-

239 'Religious phenomena consist of two categories: the beliefs and the rituals. The first are states of opinion, consisting of representations. The others are determined modalities of action. Between the two categories, there is a distance similar to the distance between thought and movement.' Émile Durkheim, *Formele elementare ale vieții religioase* (Iași: Polirom, 1995), p. 45. [My translation].

240 Fionna Bowie, 'Chapter 6: Ritual Theory, Rites of Passage, Ritual and Violence', *The Anthropology of Religion: An Introduction (*Oxford: Blackwell Publishing, 2006), pp. 138–173, p. 143.

241 Lucien Lévy-Bruhl, 'Introduction', *La mentalité primitive* (Paris: Les Presses Universitaires de France, 1922), pp. 9–17, ‹http://classiques.uqac.ca/classiques/levy_bruhl/mentalite_primitive/mentalite.html› [accessed February 2006]

lutionist view opposing a 'participationist' to a 'logical' way of thinking, i.e., a 'savage' to a 'civilized' way, is plainly nonsensical because, in reality, everywhere and always human beings have relied on both modes of thinking, depending on circumstances.[242] Malinowski also states that the 'primitive' man has, just like the 'civilized' one, a profane world for practical activities and a rational perspective, set apart from the realm of magical–religious beliefs and ritual practices.[243] Newer studies, either from the anthropology of science or the anthropology of witchcraft, point to the fact that the so-called civilized people of the industrial era continue to resort to magic and religion when they are being overtaken by difficult life situations that they cannot handle through the means of rational discourse; more than that, there seems to be a consistent dose of faith around the newest technical discoveries. For instance, Gusterson cites the case of the lie detector that proved empirically inconclusive, but the popular faith in this device is unmoved, concluding that today 'technology itself has an aura of infallibility that makes it an instrument of magic.'[244]

Slowly moving away from defining the relations between religion, magic, and science and equally abandoning the 'myth versus ritual' topic, another frame of reference became relevant by the 1960s, namely that of 'religious versus secular.' The discourse about modernity as breakage, mutation, and de-sacralization (seen as the effect of urbanization, the prestige of science and the collapse of former social structures) also had to rely on its opposed, correlative term: that of tradition. In contrast to modernity, tradition is characterized through linear continuity, invariance, and sacrality. Magic and religion are tightly associated with tradition as the two main cultural forms defining an exotic, outer-European or a European ru-

242 Arnold Van Gennep, *Manuel de folklore Français contemporain*, tome premier (Paris: A. & J. Picard, 1972), p. 97.

243 Bronislaw Malinowski, *Magie, știință și religie* (Iași: Moldova, 1993), p. 44.

244 Hugh Gusterson, 'How far have we traveled? Magic, Science and Religion revisited', *American Anthropological Association, Anthropology News,* November 2004, ‹http://www.aaanet.org/press/an/0408Gusterson.htm› [accessed July 15, 2005].

ral-traditional society—which effectively disqualifies them as possible sites of modernity.

During the evolutionist period of anthropology, secularism was one of the key terms taken to define the Occidental society, opposed, as shown earlier, to the superstitious attitude defining magic and religion (emblematic for primitive/traditional societies). However, Mary Douglas states that every society consists of a mixture between skepticism, materialism, and fervent faith, meaning that secularism proves to be, historically, an old type of product of social life.[245] The root of defining secularism as something fundamentally different from religion and Church is to be found with St. Augustine's distinction between the city of man and the city of God from the early dawn of Christianity[246] and nothing makes it universal.

Later on, the postmodern deconstructive phase of anthropology brought with it a great deal of critical reflexivity and assessment of previous orientations and approaches, and a greater attention to the ideological charge of key concepts. By analyzing the meaning of 'modernity' in specific contexts, Lionel Obadia showed how it is synonymous with: Occident, democracy, industrialization, secularism, science, and clearly opposed to the 'traditional' or 'primitive' nonmodernities, characterized by religiosity, superstition, participationist thinking, and material backwardness. Through this implicit axiality, the old evolutionist terms are reinvested in a new formula. This time, modernity is geographic in nature, while nonmodernity is evolutionist in nature.[247] One proposition I find particularly appealing is to cease approaching 'tradition' and 'modernity' as monadic realities or tangible phenomena in their own right but to take them as concepts expressing cultural phenomena among others. 'It ap-

---

245 Mary Douglas, *Natural Symbols: Explorations in Cosmology* (New York: Routledge, 1996), p. 17.

246 Martine Segalen, *Etnologie. Concepte şi arii culturale* (Timişoara: Amarcord, 2002), p. 52.

247 Lionel Obadia, 'Religion(s) et modernité(s): Anciens débats, enjeux présents, nouvelles perspectives', *Socio-Anthropologie*, N° 17–18 (Religions et modernités, 2006), ‹http://socioanthropologie.revues.org/document448.html› [accessed March 2007]

pears appropriate, on a hermeneutical level, to submit modernity to its own regime of historicity. Not modernity as **reality**, but modernity as **discourse on reality**. (...) In short, bringing back the (human) science to that which it never ceased to be: a cultural discourse, historically and socially contextualized within the world.'[248] In other words, we could attempt to examine the relationships between modern and traditional as well as between secular and magical/religious not as modalities to illustrate the reality of historical changes but rather as the key concepts of the main frame of discourse built around those changes: yet another way of the industrial society to conceptualize itself.

In a similar manner, we could try to imagine magic, religion, and science, not as depicting stages in the evolution of humanity or historically irrevocably divorced modes of thought or as objective terms directly expressing real, palpable realities, but as one of the main narratives through which modern Occidental thought progressively aimed to define itself by projecting/creating differences against all sorts of alterities (geographical, historical, cultural, and social).

What I hope to have been able to highlight through this brief and by no means exhaustive account is the fact that the ways in which we think today about magic (as exotic, illicit, and occult), about religion (as Church, private matter, investment of belief, and personal choice), and science (as the highest type of knowledge, able to explain our world to us) is socially contextualized and temporally conditioned: historically, through the different stages of perceiving and forging these concepts in Western world; and socioculturally, by the concrete realities of today, globalization processes, the dominant frames of thought of the moment, etc. The extra-European anthropological studies were the first to indicate that, more often than not, magic and religious attitudes are so consubstantial in practice that it is very hard to separate them and decide which fragment of custom or belief falls under what label. This is an aspect that post-1950s was met head-on in Europe as well, once anthropology had to

[248] Lionel Obadia, ‹http://socioanthropologie.revues.org/document448.html› [My translation]

move away from the former colonies and research its own societies. In addition, the category of a religion, which was defined initially according to the model of monotheist religions, characterized as Church[249], and dissociated through the same model from an inferior and antinomical magic, is a perspective that cannot hold pretentions to universality, not even of general applicability for the European territories. Abandoning the restrictive religion/magic/science model can offer the chance of looking at aspects of popular culture in their phenomenality, without needing to classify them under artificial headings. Otherwise, we can simply address the magical–religious dynamic as subtle forces at work in all societies, at all times, and not as objective, immutable institutions swept away by the progress of civilization. It is true that, in the specific context of European societies, magic and religion did function as fields historically engaged in competition. And yet, as suggested by Robert Muchembled,[250] this rivalry had less to do with their essence and much more with the status acquired within the societies as such, especially the position gained by their representatives.

4.2 Social Change and Insecurity: Three Examples

Witchcraft and sorcery, as a distinct subdomain of the larger field of magical phenomena, have a long tradition in anthropology of being interpreted in terms relating to conflict. If we agree that the traditional witchcraft of rural Europe can be best described as 'misfortune ascribed to other human beings'[251] or as 'personified evil,'[252]

---

249 Émile Durkheim, p. 51.

250 Robert Muchembled, *Magia şi vrăjitoria în Europa, din Evul Mediu până astăzi* (Bucureşti: Humanitas, 1997), p. 328.

251 Willem de Blécourt, 'The Witch, her Victim, the Unwitcher and the Researcher: the continued existence of traditional witchcraft', *Witchcraft and Magic in Europe. The Twentieth Century,* ed. by Bengt Ankarloo and Stuart Clark (University of Pennsylvania Press, 1999), pp. 141–219, p. 151.

252 Niels Freytag, 'Witchcraft, witch doctors and the fight against superstition in nineteen-century Germany', *Popular Magic in Modern Europe*, ed. by Willem de Blécourt & Owen Davies (Manchester& New York: Manchester University Press, 2004), pp. 29–45, p. 40.

then interpersonal and social tensions do seem to occupy the core of the witchcraft discourse's manifestations.

Researchers of a functionalist orientation within anthropology took the conflict hypothesis and looked at the ways in which witchcraft accusations play out in particular social settings and what exact function they have within the societies or communities in which they occurred. For Gluckman, for example, witchcraft beliefs have to be seen as a 'part of a positive philosophy, culturally established, and transcending and constraining individuals, used to explain the occurrence of misfortune in terms of personal animosities (...). Indeed, hatred, anger, and fear are often positive emotions in social systems, depending on contexts; while frustration is positively valuable both in socialisation and in maintaining some order in social life.'[253] Similar to this, for Regina Dionisopoulos-Mass 'witchcraft is defined as potentially harmful power, yet power that has a socially acceptable role and works to promote some type of harmony in society. The social utility stems either from the exercise of these powers or the fear that they will be exercised.'[254] The aspect these authors highlight is the witchcraft discourse's potential to function as method of social control in societies where the ideology of egalitarianism is contradicted by day-to-day dynamics of competition and economic inequalities. Other research approaches centered, on the contrary, on the disruptive potential of witchcraft, especially of harm-centered sorcery. The merit of all these functionalist perspectives was the fact that they managed to extract discussions about witchcraft and sorcery from the magic/religion/science frame of debate, looking instead exclusively at their social relevance and function.

The theory of witchcraft as management of social conflicts would always work best, at least for the territory of Europe, when applied

253 Max Gluckman, 'Psychological, Sociological and Anthropological Explanations of Witchcraft and Gossip: A Clarification', *Man, New Series*, 3.1 (March 1968), pp. 20–34, ‹http://www.jstor.org/stable/2799409› [accesed October 2007], p. 26.

254 Regina Dionisopoulos-Mass, 'The Evil Eye and Bewitchment in a Peasant Village', *The Evil Eye*, ed. by Clarence Maloney (New York: Columbia University Press, 1976), pp. 42–62, p. 44.

to peasant communities, where there is little privacy due to an observant community and which is restricted geographically, socially, and economically.[255] This description fits contemporary communities, even rural ones, less and less. Also, the witchcraft discourse of northern Transylvania addressed in this book is, as we saw, equally manifest in cities, towns, and villages. It seems to be no longer conditioned by adversarial vicinity (competing households), economic competition, or a small and tight community. The bewitched women of my fieldwork might feel antipathy toward their designated aggressor, but this animosity hardly takes the form of an open, mutual state of conflict, and the unwitchments do not seem to aim at solving these interpersonal antagonism. Distance between the accuser and the accused, in terms of geographical distance, might also be a factor in determining this physiognomy of muted antipathies rather than explicit conflicts.

The old approach of 'delegating unhappiness' along the lines of the scapegoating theory[256] might seem to fit better to the manifestations of contemporary witchcraft in north Transylvania. However, as pointed out by Gluckman,[257] this particular theory is applied for too wide a range of disparate social phenomena in the social sciences, called on, for instance, to equally explain the Nazi attacks on the Jewish people and the victim's reasons to name an aggressor within the witchcraft discourse; therefore, it cannot function as singular explanatory mechanism for either. It has to be at least corroborated with the respective actors' particular actions and their sociocultural context. From my point of view, the explanatory insufficiency of this particular theory also lies with another, maybe more subversive, implication, namely, a tacit but obvious underlying hierarchy. Equating the witchcraft discourse exclusively with a surrogate modality, an outward projection of negative feelings (in the sense of

255 Willem de Blécourt, 'The Witch, her Victim, the Unwitcher and the Researcher: the continued existence of traditional witchcraft', p. 211.

256 An in-depth account of the social function of scapegoating, particularly in the context of sacrifice, can be followed in René Girard, *La violence et le sacré* (Paris: Éditions Bernard Grasset, 1972).

257 Max Gluckman, p. 24.

displacing aggression from the victim's closest toward more distant people), actually means to say that witchcraft situations are fictions eagerly grabbed by those incapable to confront their personal issues with objectivity. The limit of the scapegoating theory is the point where it confiscates the bewitched's own terminology of their drama by attempting to convert it into rationalistic, academic terms. As rightfully pointed out by Willem de Blécourt and Owen Davies, assuming a diagnosis of witchcraft in 20th-century Europe is, from the point of view of the bewitched, a **choice** to interpret events in a particular way and to resolve misfortune.[258] But, for this choice to present itself as the valid one against others, there are some conditions to be met: the personal sensibilities of the individual; the witchcraft diagnosis has to already be part of the local cultural repertoire of explaining misfortune and be sustained by relevant actors; and the recent life experiences of the afflicted present themselves as a mosaic of adversities, unhappiness, and duress, inexplicable through the more conventional discourses (the rationalistic–medical or the religious one). And there is one more aspect highlighted by several commentaries: The witchcraft discourse can be linked to times of radical social change.

In the following pages, I would like to examine three examples of social contexts that underwent massive structural transformations in recent years in Europe. Each is known for forms of readapting the witchcraft discourse or for reinventing a public magic phenomenon able to respond to conditions of challenging exterior circumstances.

France

As mentioned in the introductory notes to **Chapter 1**, the processes of industrialization, urbanization, and linguistic homogenization deeply affected the peasant population of rural France during the 19th and 20th centuries. These processes, as observed by Owen

---

258 Willem de Blécourt and Owen Davies, 'Introduction: Witchcraft continued', *Witchcraft Continued. Popular Magic in Modern Europe*, pp. 1–13, p. 7.

Davies,[259] were still well underway in France during the first half of the 20th century, whereas in England, the industrialization had been completely finished at least 50 years earlier. In particular, the period after the Second World War was marked by a sustained effort of the state to modernize agriculture in France's rural areas, mostly by encouraging the transformation of family-scale, subsistence agriculture to models of entrepreneurial, industrial, large-scale agricultural exploitations. This had a most direct effect on the social and economic life of the peasantry, as it facilitated a gradual but fast dissolution of the rural local community and a fragmentation of the social tissue,[260] which was described by Dupont as a chain transformation of the peasantry into the proletariat, the employee, and, ultimately, the unemployed.[261] The sanctioned discourses of the postwar period, observable through public debates, newspaper articles, philosophical inquiries, and social scientific frameworks, created a public image of this peasantry as either stubborn antiprogressive, reactionary forces or as the soul and essence of the nation. The paradox at work here relies on the double meaning attached to the term 'tradition': It can be taken to mean the sum of elements impeding the progress of modern society (negative connotation) or the cultural essence of a European culture (positive connotation). The same double meaning can be observed within Mediterranean studies, which was one of the first institutionalized forms of post-1950s European anthropology. Some researchers of this orientation highlight the inertia of Mediterranean traditions, effectively obstructing the process of integrating this area into European progress, while

259 Owen Davies, 'Witchcraft accusations in France, 1850–1990', *Witchcraft Continued. Popular Magic in Modern Europe*, ed. by Willem de Blécourt & Owen Davies (Manchester& New York: Manchester University Press, 2004), pp. 107–132, p. 122.

260 André Mary, 'Sorcellerie bocaine, sorcellerie africaine: le social, le symbolique et l'imaginaire', *Les Cahiers du LASA, Sorcellerie: bocage et modernité*, 17 (1987), pp. 125–152, ‹https://halshs.archives-ouvertes.fr/halshs-00137125› [accessed September 12, 2015], p. 144.

261 Yves Dupont, 'Pourquoi faut-il pleurer les paysans?', *Ecologie & politique*, 2 (2005), ‹http://www.ecologie-et-politique.info/IMG/pdf/31_Pourquoi_faut-il_pleurer_les_paysans.pdf› [accessed June 2015], p. 13.

others consider the archaism of the customs surviving here as guarantors of the persistence of a millennial European rural culture.[262] This paradox can also be seen in many European nation-building processes, where the official discourse insists on national identity being dependent upon the value of peasant traditions (archaic, pure, and always unique) at the same time with putting into effect precise economic, social, and political strategies directed at rapidly modernizing, therefore effectively pulverizing this rural-traditional social milieu.

As Owen Davis' study shows,[263] in France, the peasants themselves reacted by opposing to these superimposed processes of modernization and adopted a self-chosen identity as '*paysan*' (Engl.> 'peasant'), a badge of honor expressing their distrust with the new, modern values and ways of life. By all accounts, the '*paysan*' as an economic reality ceased to exist by the 1960s. And yet, the identity of '*paysan*' was proudly and purposefully maintained by actors, even when their own social or economic situation could not technically sustain it—even when living in a town or city, employed as a laborer, trader, or artisan, which had little, if anything, to do with agricultural production. The identity of the '*paysan*' was defined in moral terms as attachment to the 'true' values of the traditional rural society, against the consumerism and the nonvalues of modern globalist society. One crucial dichotomy reflecting the self-defined French peasants' universe of cherished values is the dichotomy between the old rural-traditional agriculture (subsistence-orientated, organic, and ecological in modern terms), and the industrial, large-scale agricultural enterprises, profit and productivity oriented, with serious environmental impact.

The witchcraft beliefs and accusations documented in western France, or more precisely their endurance in contemporary times as valid explanations for misfortune, are usually linked precisely to this local and voluntary maintenance of traditional peasantry val-

---

262 John W. Cole, 'Anthropology comes Part-Way Home: Community Studies in Europe', *Annual Review of Anthropology*, 6 (1977), pp. 349–378.

263 Owen Davies, p. 122–123.

ues. By being 'linked,' however, I do not mean that witchcraft beliefs can be explained mechanically as linear, transgenerational remnants. The emphasis is, on the contrary, on change. The people of western France who continue to employ the witchcraft diagnosis for personally challenging times do so not because they hang on stubbornly to a lost way of life, not because they see this type of explanatory frame as a cherished traditional value, but because this outside-of-the-norm type of explaining unhappiness seems to be, at times of duress, the only one able to express their own challenged (and marginal) social, economic, and political situation. Camus' short depiction[264] of postwar Western France is one of continuous transformations, where small family-run businesses go bankrupt and small family farms gradually disappear to make space for the new large-scale, entrepreneurial agriculture. Therefore, when put in a larger historical and social context, being bewitched can be seen as 'a both conscious and subconscious response to broad social developments, a withdrawal into the traditional past,' or even as 'a psychosomatic response to the helplessness felt in the face of sociocultural change.'[265]

Some commentators of Jeanne Favre-Saada's research in Bocage[266] have turned this line of interpretation into a more simplistic leftist-inspired approach, where the witchcraft discourse is seen as the rural world's clandestine way of maintaining their local identity, as an ideological expression and underground resistance against the capitalist logic of accumulation and the dissolving effects of globalist values.[267] The problem with this misguided glorification of the Bocage witchcraft discourse is not simply that it is pretty far-fetched. According to André Mary,[268] a witchcraft crisis stresses first and foremost the afflicted family's **rupture** with dominant discourses (the rationalist and the religious ones) but equally with their own

264 Dominique Camus, *Puteri şi practici vrăjitoreşti. Anchetă asupra practicilor actuale de vrăjitorie* (Iaşi: Polirom, 2003), p. 23.

265 Owen Davies, p. 125.

266 Jeanne Favret-Saada, *Les mots, la mort, les sorts* (Paris: Gallimard, 1977).

267 André Mary, p. 142.

268 André Mary, p. 142.

peers and support network and, therefore, an effective isolation from their own social group. Rather than a form of peculiar behind-the-scene collective resistance, entering a witchcraft discourse might be interpreted as an individualized commentary on major social change, illustrating through its very processes (the social isolation; accusing one's peers) the ripping away of the structures underlying the rural tradition and the dissolution of socialization systems built on solidarity.

There is another aspect pertaining to the contemporary witchcraft discourse of rural western France, besides the rapid social and economic changes altering the structure of traditionally defined reality: The historical role played by the Church in addressing a witchcraft crisis in France and its modern progressive withdrawal from sustaining, treating, or addressing this type of discourse is also of great importance.

Although there are strong Protestant communities in France, it has always been perceived as a Catholic country.[269] During and after the period of the French Revolution (1789–1799), the Catholic grip has been constantly challenged by secular liberal forces. At the level of popular faith, this was illustrated as a tension, or even radical conflict, between Catholic devotion and anticlericalism. By 1880, all education had been placed under state authority, effectively removing it from clerical control, culminating with the 1905 law officially sanctioning the separation of church and state.[270] But, the end of official witchcraft persecutions between the end of the 17th and 18th centuries[271] not only did not mark the end of witchcraft accusations; it was actually followed, in the 18th, 19th, and 20th centuries, by occasional phases of witchcraft-motivated violent inci-

269 Ellen Badone, 'Breton Folklore of Anticlericalism', *Religious Orthodoxy and Popular Faith in European Society*, ed. by Ellen Badone (Princeton, New Jersey: Princeton University Press, 1990), pp. 140–160, p. 140.

270 Ellen Badone, 141.

271 Marie-Sylvie Dupont-Bouchat, 'Diavolul îmblânzit. Vrăjitoria reconsiderată. Magia şi vrăjitoria în secolul al XIX-lea', *Magia şi vrăjitoria în Europa, din Evul Mediu până astăzi*, ed. by Robert Muchembled (Bucureşti: Humanitas, 1997), p. 245.

dents, when people suspected of witchcraft fell victim to physical attacks from members of the local communities. The motivation of these collective attacks upon people suspected of witchcraft had to do, more often than not, with a widespread belief in Europe that the witch had the power to reverse her/his own spell,[272] thus effectively making the retrieval of the spell the first and shortest path to healing. However, the problem faced by the attackers was, in their interpretation, to convince the supposed witch to do just that. The violence based on this belief showed that, in many instances, trying to convince the witch to undo his/her spell often escalated to physical aggression. The same authorities that in previous centuries prosecuted the crime of witchcraft were now, in the 19th and early 20th centuries, completely on the side of the designated 'witches,' adamantly condemning their attackers as ignorant, superstitious, and backward. As pointed out by Dupont-Bouchat, the justice system's approach was completely reversed at this point: The law was now the protector of those it once prosecuted, and sanctioned the aggressors formerly treated as perfectly credible witnesses.[273] The times had changed, the morality had changed, and the whole jurisprudence system had changed. Not only was witchcraft no longer a crime under the definitions of law, it was also no longer a socially acceptable explanation for misfortune. This also reflects a conflict in world view between the elites and the popular classes, between which a gap had been steadily growing from Enlightenment onward, with the educated classes assuming the role of civilizing the peasant masses all over Europe. As shown by Freytag for the case of 19th-century Germany,[274] the state authorities coordinated their anti-magic, antiwitchcraft, and antisuperstitions campaigns with corresponding efforts from the press, a prime role assigned to education, and an equally active involvement from the Catholic clergy.

[272] Willem de Blécourt, 'The Witch, her Victim, the Unwitcher and the Researcher: the continued existence of traditional witchcraft', p. 152.

[273] Marie-Sylvie Dupont-Bouchat, p. 253.

[274] Niels Freytag, p. 31.

Responding to this general context of laicization and rationalization of thought, the Catholic Church entered a gradual process of extracting itself from such contexts that were from a strict doctrinal point of view marked by dangerous slips toward a rather magical or mystical attitude. More precisely, particularly during the 19th and 20th centuries, in a general European context of universal emancipation from retrograde superstition, the Catholic Church strived to demarcate its system of beliefs and ritual practices from some the practices of the popular faiths, especially those using religion for practical means rather than genuine spiritual edification. Here, it was the use of religious paraphernalia, rituals, and prayers in unwitchments, exorcism, or healings that were on top of the list of practices to be strongly discouraged. From the 1960s onward (after the Second Vatican Council), this general tendency became explicit Church politics. A new generation of priests was then educated in the spirit of the newly envisioned role of the Church, that of making Catholic religion 'more relevant to a modern, urban world view turned critical to the faith by the advances of science, technology and industrialism (...).'[275]

The result, in France, was that Catholic clergy no longer took part in the witchcraft discourse, just as they tried to discourage the popular cults of saints not approved by the church, or the use of religious consecrated items in contexts now deemed condemnable and superstitious. When the witchcraft discourse persisted, nonetheless, particularly in the rural areas confronted with abrupt social and economic changes, the place of the retreating religious unwitchers was progressively occupied by laic unwitchers. The few Catholic priests still agreeing to be involved in healing, exorcism, or witchcraft discourse[276] did so individually, without the knowledge of their superiors, risking serious sanctions.

---

275 Ruth Behar, 'The Struggle for the Church: Popular Anticlericalism and Religiosity in Post-Franco Spain', *Religious Orthodoxy and Popular Faith in European Society*, ed. by Ellen Badone (Princeton, New Jersey: Princeton University Press, 1990), pp. 76–112, p. 80.

276 Dominique Camus mentions in passing a priest as one of the 18 unwitchers and sorcerers he met during his fieldwork, p. 23. Jeanne Favret-Saada

The particular profile of western France's rural witchcraft described by Favret-Saada and by Camus in the 1970s and 1980s is clearly a product of historical changes impacting on the local structures. Arising from the traditional witchcraft discourse in a rural world that is dissolving and recomposing under the processes of modernization, with actors apprehensive to jump on the 'train of progress'[277] and morally opposed to these transformations, being bewitched in rural western France may be interpreted as the afflicted actors' ways to symptomize the drama of losing control over the fabric of their reality.

Russia

Magic in contemporary Russia, as described by Galina Lindquist after her 1999 field research in Moscow, has little to do with the traditional witchcraft discourse as discussed in this book for the French and Romanian settings. And yet, in Russia, it is a widespread phenomenon of social significance, linked once again to the contexts of profound changes and insecurity following the demise of the USSR (Union of Soviet Socialist Republics) in 1991.

The central figures of this phenomenon are the magi, specialists of magical practice, and charismatic individuals able to assist their clients in a wide variety of circumstances, whose common denominator is a life crisis. The clients see the magis to deal with loss of control and power over their own lives, series of misfortunes annulling personal efforts, serial personal tragedies, pain, and despair. The type of diagnosis[278] that magi place upon such a situation can include, depending on the circumstances:

---

mentions the priest from Torcé who, on one occasion, cured eczema through prayer and yeast; when asked to bless a witchcraft afflicted farm, its animals and people, he did so but stated his complete disbelief in the notion of witchcraft. Jeanne Favret-Saada, *Deadly Words. Witchcraft in the Bocage* (Cambridge: Cambridge University Press, 2010), pp. 268 and 270.

277 Yves Dupont, p. 12.

278 Galina Lindquist, *Conjuring Hope. Healing and Magic in contemporary Russia* (New York, Oxford: Berghahn Books, 2009), pp. 53–80.

- the evil eye;
- *'porcha'*, translated as 'spoiling,' considered a negative force sent, with persistent focus and clear intent to deeply harm its addressee, by someone envious or resentful;
- 'the crown of celibacy,' with its more serious variant 'the seal of loneliness,' manifested as the impossibility to establish and maintain love and friendship relations mostly due to immoral deeds of an ancestor;
- kinship curses; and
- demonic settlements, when the actor manifests bursts of uncontrollable, uncharacteristic rages believed to be caused by the presence of a demonic agency inserted in one's home, etc.

Interpersonal negativity (horizontal web of social relations), the sins of the ancestors (the diachronic kinship line), and demons (supernatural evil) seem to be the three main causes identified by this discourse as possible causes for affliction. In contemporary Russia, the traditional witchcraft discourse as 'device for ascribing misfortune to others'[279] can be traced mainly under the *'porcha'* diagnosis, reflecting problematic social relationships, as well as the capacity for evil inherent in all human beings. But, the assumption that the culprit operated through spells does not seem to represent a concern, as it is the case for the French and Romanian witchcraft discourses. For both the Russian magi and the client, proper spells (operated in person by the magical aggressor or through hiring a black magi) are no different in effect from a truly intense, hateful thought that is being directed with powerful intentionality toward the potential victim. Therefore, such a distinction is, in this discourse, inconsequential.

Regardless of the particular terms of diagnosis, magi describe their clients' source of affliction as visible disturbances in the 'energy field' or 'thin body'[280] caused by all sorts of impurities able to pollute this bioenergetic field, manifested exteriorly as either affection of the physical and emotional body (illness) or as troubles in social

---

279 Willem de Blécourt and Owen Davies, 'Introduction: Witchcraft continued', p. 2.

280 Galina Lindquist, 'Not my will but thine be done: Church versus magic in contemporary Russia', *Culture and Religion: An Interdisciplinary Journal*, 1:2 (2000), pp. 247–276, p. 257.

life. The role of the magi is to repair this compromised bioenergetic field during a long-term intervention of channeling their supersensitive and extra-sensorial abilities through appropriate rituals and techniques. This discourse of affliction is similar to Western New Age definitions of individual bioenergetic field blockages, conceptualized by the Russian magi as a kind of rot in the nonphysical body of the client. And indeed, the sources of the contemporary Russian magic discourse are incredibly varied, combining to create, in the end, a quite unique phenomenon. Folk medicine, local rural traditions of healing, and folk magic mixed in late Soviet times with bioenergy healing and studies of the paranormal, along with established non-Russian complementary therapies (homeopathy, acupuncture, reiki, ayurvedic, and Tibetan medicine).[281] During the Soviet regime, these types of healing approaches were mostly urban practices cultivated or accessed privately, semi-illicitly, and never publicly advertised by their practitioners.

The big change came in post-communist times. For magic and healing practices, the newly found freedom translated into an unprecedented opportunity to establish themselves publicly, advertise through mass media channels, and turn into profitable, respectable businesses. And even though magical practices have always been conventionally marked, both by practitioners and clients, as secret and secretive, the new urban post-perestroika magic and healing businesses were a 'conspicuously public phenomenon'[282] of unprecedented success. Translated into the new jargon of the free market, these entrepreneurial initiatives were not, however, a simple case of savvy 'business shamans'[283] enthusiastically responding to the newly established conditions of capitalist democracy, preying on the new consumers' naivety (common to all post-communist people). On

---

281 Galina Lindquist, *Conjuring Hope. Healing and Magic in contemporary Russia*, pp. 30–40.

282 Galina Lindquist, *Conjuring Hope. Healing and Magic in contemporary Russia*, p. 23.

283 André Julliard, 'Urgia Sorților. Vrăjitoria zilelor noastre în Franța', *Magia și vrăjitoria în Europa, din Evul Mediu până astăzi*, ed. by Robert Muchembled (București: Humanitas, 1997), pp. 274–326, p. 278.

the contrary, this phenomenon of visible, even institutionalized magic practice is a direct response to a context of social, political, and economic radical changes within the post-USSR world that left individual actors with too few means to survive, respond, or fight back.

If life under communist regime was often described by the Russian people as living in a prison, the period that followed the dissolution of the USSR in 1991, conventionally known as 'transition' all over the post-communist world, was routinely described as a 'jungle'[284]: the jungle of democracy. For most analysts of the Eastern bloc, the 'transition' was supposed to represent a more-or-less smooth passage from the dark ages of a repressive regime toward the new age of civilization and the implementation of the ultimate Western values: democracy, free market, and capitalism. However, for most, it was anything but. One widespread popular comparison regarding living standards during communist and post-communist times, in both Russia and Romania, was that 'before' people had money but not much to buy with it, as the shops were virtually empty; whereas in democracy, there was an inflation of products on offer but no money to buy them with. Between 1991 and 1993, the real average wage fell by half in Russia and Ukraine, and most life savings had been wiped out by hyperinflation.[285] By 2007, the World Bank estimated that 30% of residents in Russia and Ukraine had incomes below the subsistence level.[286]

Official statistics on income levels, however, can do little to illuminate the real struggles of day-to-day living in a rapidly changing world; when estimating the monthly expenses of a household, no official statistic will, for example, take into account the extra routine expenditure of paying for services which, in theory, are free for all citizens (such as healthcare, schooling, and bureaucratic necessi-

---

284 Galina Lindquist, *Conjuring Hope. Healing and Magic in contemporary Russia*, p. XIII.

285 John Round & Colin Williams, 'Coping with the social costs of "transition": Everyday life in post-Soviet Russia and Ukraine', *European Urban and Regional Studies*, 17 (2010), pp. 183–196, p. 184.

286 John Round & Colin Williams, p. 193.

ties). Or, shortly put, the forms of bribery based on the former structures of informal economy and informal networks of mutual help developed during communist times. As shown in **Chapter 2: Actors (The 'incidental diagnostician'** subchapter), the secondary economy and informal networks have proven crucial in assuring access to otherwise scarce goods and services for citizens under communist rule. On an everyday basis, this often meant that one informal favor for a friend or acquaintance (such as repairing their car using the state's resources, during working hours) was going to be responded to when needed, according to what that person could offer in exchange (access to clothing, food, better hospital care, etc.). As observed by Chris Hann,[287] citizens all over Eastern Europe Communist block developed such networks not only to help each other to surpass economic crises but also to provide themselves with positive values and authentic social solidarities otherwise absent under socialism. The big change after the fall of communism was that these networks of mutual favors reconverted, to a certain extent, to monetary terms[288]: not only as bribes demanded for access to services but also as opportunities for extra income for impoverished households. Therefore, the informal economy perpetuated itself in this cash-for-service form as a crucial practice for supplementing the regularly low wages, as well as extra expenditure for services otherwise defined, at macro- and theoretical levels, as free of charge. Also, 'the changing significance of money altered the fabric of sociality itself'[289] by replacing friendship ties and the value attached to friendships.

Discussing the widely spread economic marginalization of households in post-Soviet Russia and the microlevel social tactics employed for ensuring day-to-day necessities (if not plain survival) might not sufficiently reflect the individual costs of a period when all

---

287 Chris Hann, 'Antropologie socială şi socialism', *Întâlniri multiple. Antropologi occidentali în Europa de Est,* ed. by Enikö Magyari-Vincze, Collin Quiglei, Gabriel Troc (Cluj-Napoca: Efes, 2000), pp. 89–130, p. 116.

288 John Round & Colin Williams, p. 188.

289 Galina Lindquist, *Conjuring Hope. Healing and Magic in contemporary Russia*, p. 209.

previous contexts that offered a minimum of coherence to the world quickly disintegrated under the impact of a chaotic, tormented, and often dangerous new world. The way this transition unfolded in some of the post-communist countries quickly contradicted the previous expectations of both observers and local actors who had hoped for a smooth, progressive societal reconstruction and a natural falling on the path of Western democracies by following their example and lead. In reality, just as every communist regime in Eastern Europe had its personal profile, its particular historical developments, and even unique repressive methods of social control, so every period of local transition presented its individual challenges, proving in the end that, if democracy was ever going to be successful, it was going to be so in local terms—redefined, refined, and adapted to local circumstances.

In order to illustrate the social turmoil and the cultural entropy of Eastern Europe's postsocialist transitions, Katherine Verdery draws a suggestive parallel between some of those local processes and feudalism.[290] The collapse of the USSR, immediately followed by general insecurity and violence, led to the de-structuration of the state's central power into multiple local narrow forms of suzerainty, quickly built around local men of power, mainly the previous leaders of former Soviet enterprises. Just like feudal lords, these local figures of authority rationalized food for exclusively the benefit of locals and took measures to protect people from violence, and in some cases, they even emitted their own money. Owing to inflation, barter became more reliable: people from Moscow would work the fields of former collective farms, receiving in exchange several bags of potatoes. It was hard to guess where a valid unique authority lied, under these conditions. Life in Russia had become precarious, with very little to offer to regular actors in terms of external channels of agency. And that's where the new popular phenomenon of magic fitted.

---

290 Katherine Verdey, 'O tranziție de la socialism la feudalism? Reflecții despre statul postsocialist', *Întâlniri multiple. Antropologi occidentali în Europa de Est*, ed. by Enikö Magyari–Vincze, Collin Quiglei, Gabriel Troc (Cluj–Napoca: Efes, 2000), pp. 217–260.

Agency is understood, in Western philosophy, mainly as 'the individual's capacity to act consciously and voluntarily upon the world,' therefore, a formula to celebrate, in Asad's terms, 'self-empowerment, history-making and individualism.'[291] In this view, 'the desire and ability to act are taken as unproblematic'[292] because the exterior structures and contexts allow, or even enable, individual action. That is, in fact, mostly the case of the Occidental world, and, therefore, the definitions of agency in this vein simply reflect, and are limited to, the social realities of the West. What happens, though, in a society where the ability to act is highly problematic, where self-empowerment is not automatically granted and does not reflect exterior circumstances, or where individualism is not necessarily a value or does not reflect local constructions of identity? Russia, just like many other countries in Eastern Europe or other parts of the world, is a society where the exterior structures are constraining, not at all facilitating.[293] People did not put their trust in the system of Soviet times, repressive and eliciting fear, just as they cannot trust the powers-that-be of present times, where 'a monstrous bureaucracy is enmeshed with individual inclinations and agendas and steered by emotional impulses and pragmatic considerations.'[294]

When living in a world that only offers, in terms of exterior conditions, extreme uncertainty, chaos, and entrapment, people usually try to bypass the structural limitations and create alternative structures where they can channel their agency—such as the informal networks or the use of raw power. And, as Galina Lindquist argues, the appeal to post-Soviet magi is another way for individual actors to regrasp their agency, to regain control over their lived-in worlds, and to reshape the very basis of their self-representation as empow-

291 Talal Asad, 'Agency and pain: An exploration', *Culture and Religion*, 1:1 (2000), pp. 29–60, p. 29.

292 Talal Asad, p. 30.

293 Galina Lindquist, 'Not my will but thine be done: Church versus magic in contemporary Russia', p. 250.

294 Galina Lindquist, *Conjuring Hope. Healing and Magic in contemporary Russia*, p. X.

ered individuals. The consumption of magic, as costly[295] services offered through both modern healthcare-like clinics and individually rented spaces, became so popular in post-communist Russia because it offers some of the things that the social reality of a radically changing world cannot offer: hope, a way to act efficiently, and the promise of personal happiness.

Romania

Romania, similar to many states in central and southeastern Europe, is a fairly recent state, with Transylvania[296] joining previously unified Moldavia and Wallachia[297] at the end of First World War, in 1918. Between the two World Wars, the advance of capitalism, urbanism, and modernization was rather slow in Romania, a predominantly rural-agrarian state with 76.6%[298] of its population living in villages. At the end of the Second World War, under full Soviet Army occupation, Romania became a communist country under the rule of a single party, PCR (the Romanian Communist Party). With virtually no working class to speak of, the first project of the newly established socialist hegemony was to create one—out of the rural population. Through forced massive-scale industrialization and urbanization, by 1966, the urban population of Romania had already grown

295 In 1999, a good salary was 1,500 rubles, the minimum wage was 800 rubles, and a diagnosis consultation at one of Moscow's most popular magic parlor (to be followed by subsequent sessions) was 500 rubles. Galina Lindquist, *Conjuring Hope. Healing and Magic in contemporary Russia*, p. 42.

296 Transylvania joined the state of Romania in 1918 together with Bukovina and Bessarabia. Today, the Southern region of Bukovina is part of Romania, while the Northern region is part of Ukraine. Bessarabia is today the independent ex-Soviet Republic of Moldova.

297 Wallachia and Moldavia joined in a union in 1859, officially called 'Romania' since 1866, but only gained independence from the Ottoman Empire in 1877.

298 Dr A. Golopenția and Dr D. C. Georgescu, *Populația Republicii Populare Române la 25 ianuarie 1948. Rezultatele provizorii ale recensamântului*, ‹http://sas.unibuc.ro/uploads_ro/1147/51/AG48a.RECENSAMANT48.pdf› [accessed June 2015], p. 11.

to 38.2%[299] (compared to only 23.4% in 1948). Part of the social project of creating the 'New Man' of the Socialist order, the peasant was to become the worker, and the old patriarchal familial values and ties were to be replaced with the loyalty toward the Father State and its ruler. By 1970s, the rural–urban internal migration pattern had proven so popular that the state decided to officially close the big cities to migrants.[300] At the time of 1975 population census, the rural–urban distribution had reached 56.8–43.2%,[301] close enough to an even distribution as to sustain the image of total urbanization success in Romania.

The pre-communist minimal unity of production was represented by the rural household familial cell owning land and livestock, aiming more at subsistence and self-sufficiency rather than surplus. Similar to the surrounding communist states, the new regime brought in Romania, as soon as 1948, full-scale nationalization (placing all industry, commerce, agriculture, finances, etc., under the state's exclusive control) and collectivization (dissolving ownership of the land and creating state-owned local collective farms). By the beginning of 1960s, 30% of all land was controlled by IAS (Agricultural Enterprises of State), 60% by CAP (Collective Agricultural Farms of Production), while only 10% was still privately owned.[302]

December 1989 marked, in Romania, the end of the totalitarian regime of Nicolae Ceausescu through youth-led street protests and bloody confrontations. This 1989 Romanian Revolution, a dramatic and violent moment in itself, was followed by the first free multiparties elections, the retrocession of private property, and the collective aspiration to create a free, democratic state similar to those of West-

299 Gail Kligman, 'Construirea socialismului în România lui Ceauşescu. Politica văzută ca performanţă', *Întâlniri multiple. Antropologi occidentali în Europa de Est*, edited by Enikö Magyari-Vincze, Collin Quiglei, Gabriel Troc (Cluj-Napoca: Efes, 2000), pp. 131–182, p. 136.

300 David A. Kidekel, 'Socialismul românesc ca sistem social şi cultural', *Întâlniri multiple,* pp. 183–216, p. 197.

301 Marius Silveşan, 'Consideraţii de ordin demografic privind oraşul românesc între 1960–1975', *Studia Universitatis Cibiniensis. Series Historica*, 6 (2009), pp. 199–215, p. 208.

302 David A. Kidekel, 'Socialismul românesc ca sistem social şi cultural', p. 189.

ern Europe. The transition period post-1990 was lived by most Romanians as a cultural shock, when the magic of Western abundance and values were perceived exclusively through mass media, and the miracle of getting rich overnight was becoming almost the new popular mythology. The mass consumerism was to replace the egalitarian-socialist mode of consumption/production, while the shrewd entrepreneur was to replace the proletarian 'New Man'. From a social and a political point of views, the 1990s came to Romania as the beginning of a new age. But, the pursuit of democratic ideal and capitalist dream soon found itself challenged by confusion and bitter reality checks. By 1991, inflation rose to a whopping 170% (compared to only 5% in 1990) and remained exceedingly high until 1995.[303] Similar to Russia, 'democracy' quickly stopped to signify 'the dream' for the population of Romania and turned to being described as 'jungle,' thus illustrating the collapse of structures, the insecurity of everyday living, the lack of legitimate central power, and the collision of values.

The genuine progress in economy and administration, the implementation of democratic values and institutions, and the mechanisms set in place to fight off the structural corruption were all considered to be on a promising ascendant path by international observers, so that, in 2007, Romania joined the European Union. Institutional macrolevel progress, however, is not the same thing as deep-level, structural changes. Although the general economic climate improved significantly, Romania still figures in all post-2007 international statistics as one of the poorest countries in the EU[304] and fares equally problematic in the Corruption Perceptions indexes

303 Institutul Național de Statistică, ‹http://www.insse.ro/cms/ro/content/ipc-serii-de-date›.

304 Peeter Leetmaa, Dennis Leythienne, Fabienne Montaigne, Pascal Wolf, 'The 9 poorest countries catching up on income per capita', *EUROSTAT. Statistics in focus*, 16 (2011), ‹http://ec.europa.eu/eurostat/documents/3433488/5578692/KS-SF-11-016-EN.PDF/0b17e544-c7d4-4be0-9012-0399bde343c9›

of Transparency International[305] (in 2014, Romania, along with Bulgaria, Greece, and Italy scored the last place in EU in terms of how corrupt their public sector is perceived to be, by both local actors and foreign observers). In day-to-day living terms, this continues to translate as economic difficulties, jobs scarcity, bureaucratic nightmares, general distrust in the system, the government, and the political class, and not enough hope for a better future.

Fifty-four percent of today's Romania's population live in the cities, while only 46%[306] reside in rural areas. The pattern of migration of the past years is not so much the rural–urban, but one that was not an option during the communist regime: emigrating toward better-off EU countries, even USA or Canada (under stricter regulations), mainly as economic migration toward better paid jobs. Interestingly, to this day, Romanians use to express the geography of emigration-targeted countries as *dincolo*, an adverb reflecting the idea of 'the other side' or 'across the border,' showing how, 25 years after the collapse of the Communist bloc, the old frontiers persist as cultural landmarks in people's general orientation in this world.

The urban actors of today's northern Transylvania feel they have better job opportunities than they did in recent past years, access to a larger range of services and goods, freedom of movement, and more ways to channel their agency. But, in a country where the minimum net wage has just been raised, in 2015, to £130 per month, with an average income seldom exceeding £300 and yet similar prices to other EU countries, the familial financial situation is still the first one to function as frustrating exterior limitation to action. The rural actors are skeptical and waiting for genuinely applicable reforms that never seem to come. For the time being, they seem trapped between the bygone model of the self-sufficient peasant, the peasant-worker model contributing to the rise of socialist

---

305 Transparency International, *Corruption Perceptions Index 2014: Results*, ‹http://www.transparency.org/cpi2014/results›

306 *Rezultate definitive ale Recensământului Populației şi al Locuințelor (caracteristici demografice ale populației) – 2011*, (Institutul Național de Statistică, 2011), ‹http://www.recensamantromania.ro/wp-content/uploads/2013/07/REZULTATE-DEFINITIVE-RPL_2011.pdf› [accessed December 2014], p. 1.

world, and the ideal of the know-how agricultural entrepreneur/farmer able to capitalize on his possessions—with a little bit of each but no definitive contemporary profile. In other words, even after the 2007 EU integration, the rural world of Romania is still trapped in an in-between where only the past models are something certain. A promising, different future is still to come—just as it was 20 and 15 years ago, during the official transition.

Social Change and Witchcraft Discourse: Concluding Remarks

As these examples show, the persistence of witchcraft accusations in western France can be placed in the context of deep changes still affecting the local rural population in the second half of the 20th century. The witchcraft discourse of northern Transylvania cannot be foreign to the general processes of social transformation at work in contemporary post-communist Romania. The conspicuously public phenomenon of magical services on offer in Russia today is a direct effect of the restructuration of society in post-Soviet times. Similarly, Willem de Blécourt[307] cites the case of postwar Germany, when the rise in witchcraft cases has been linked to the influx of single women in village communities and, more generally, to the overthrow of Nazi power. The pervasiveness of *inveja* (envy) in the daily life of 1980s Portugal, a 'profoundly death-dealing, antisocial force'[308] often translated into accusations of the evil eye, witchcraft, and sorcery, seems to have a lot to do with 'increasing commoditisation and industrialization that have introduced new divisions and intensified competition among maritime women.'[309]

The social relevance of witchcraft discourses and magical practices in various contemporary contexts that witness structural social changes should not be taken, however, as a causal explanation. To

---

307 Willem de Blécourt, 'The Witch, her Victim, the Unwitcher and the Researcher: the continued existence of traditional witchcraft', p. 214.

308 João de Pina-Cabral, *Sons of Adam. Daughters of Eve: The Peasant Worldview of Alto Minho* (Oxford: Clarendon Press, 1986), p. 177.

309 Sally Cole, *Women of the Praia. Work and Lives in a Portuguese Coastal Community* (Princeton, New Jersey: Princeton University Press, 1991), pp. 122–123.

put it in a simplistic manner, not all societies undergoing massive transformations suddenly experience an increase in phenomena of this type. To discuss magical practices and beliefs as part of wider social contexts offers a change in focus, a zoom-out from an actor-centric to a social or societal level, which helps in illuminating further aspects that are otherwise easy to miss. But, there is simply no golden bullet to explain witchcraft discourses, not even in the sense of multiple concurrent factors and their combination. Furthermore, as the previous examples of social change show, even when the process of social restructuring acts as a unifying factor, the particular local conditions of those changes forge differently the profile of magic and witchcraft discourses. In other words, conditions of disruptive social change can favor but not automatically determine a renewed interest in alternative means to gain agency under the form of magical practices and witchcraft. At the same time, preexistent conditions join with the particular dynamics of the local changes to shape a magic discourse uniquely responding to its settings.

Nonetheless, it is true that changes such as those affecting post-communist countries or peasant communities pressured to alter their structures and adapt to the conditions of an urbanized and globalized world, carry with them a tremendous potential of disrupting not only the day-to-day life of human actors but also their representations about the world. To borrow a very suggestive image from Galina Lindquist,[310] it is all about crossing the minefield: When changes come not as gradually flowing lines of forward movement but as violent breakages of societies and systems, when everyday life security is challenged, the social reinvention, or reinterpretation of magical–religious practices might help people to navigate adversities. After all, magical–religious perspectives have always played the role of 'constant representatives of the fight against unhappiness'[311]—in European societies and everywhere else. It is all a mat-

310 Galina Lindquist, *Conjuring Hope. Healing and Magic in contemporary Russia*, p. 236.

311 André Julliard, p. 282.

ter of activating or reshaping them, dependent on exterior conditions.

4.3 Orthodox Religion and Magical Practice

In the previous subchapter, we have seen how conditions of profound social change can sometimes translate into a higher valorization of witchcraft discourses and magical practices at a social level, resorted to by individual actors as a last-stand mechanism for difficult life situations. The case of France shows how institutionalized religion, especially the Catholic Church, also played a major role in shaping the discourse of affliction. As the representatives of the Church gradually withdrew from witchcraft situations, male laic unwitchers stepped in to fill the gaps until they became the near-exclusive holders and shapers of the discourse. Religious paraphernalia, such as blessed salt and water, religious icons, and prayer books have always played, and continue to play, a central role in unwitching therapies.

Similarly, the relationship between religion as dogma and institution, represented in Romania and Russia mainly by the Eastern Orthodox Church, and the magical practices and beliefs held at a popular level, played a key role in determining the form of these contemporary phenomena in each country. Both institutionalized religion and magical phenomena respond today to conditions of major post-communist social change. They both aim to address unhappiness and they both, discursively and in practice, relate to each other. I would like to explore further how this interaction shaped the contemporary profile of witchcraft discourses in northern Transylvania as well as the phenomenon of public magic in Russia. The line of discourse employed by the Church is similar in both countries (i.e., the irrevocable condemnation of all magic), but the practical ways in which this conflict is addressed is what has had the most direct effect on what the local profiles look like today.

As shown in **Chapter 2** (**subchapter 5: The Orthodox priest or monk**), the Orthodox Christianity in Eastern Europe and traditional rural magical practices evolved over centuries in a 'genetic relation'[312] intermingled and competing with one another. Conflicts and accommodations between theological dogmatism and the practices of everyday life throughout eastern European Orthodoxy lead to a striking similarity of Church rituals with peasant practices and customs. The latter would only ever be defined as 'magical' by trained theologians. This tense spiritual synthesis was described by Mircea Eliade as 'Cosmic Christianity,' a religious folklore that is not quite that of the Church, emblematic for Oriental Europe, and characterized by the presence of numerous pagan, barely Christianized, archaic religious elements.[313]

Even as early as the Byzantine period[314] (which all Orthodox Christian theological tradition follows), the 'very broad and obvious grey area'[315] of practices sitting in between the definitely Orthodox and the certainly non-Orthodox were forming the bulk of daily attitudes for common people. Exorcisms, prayers, blessings, icons, relics, etc., were used not as means of spiritual edification but as operations to obtain certain requested outcomes in the same fashion we define magical acts today. People were then, just as they continued to be throughout the centuries, much less interested in sharp theological distinctions (or simply unaware of them, in the context of local customs) and much more interested in practical solutions capable to respond to concrete life predicaments: illness, famine, adverse weather, love, marriage, fecundity, etc. That the Orthodox Church, much like the Catholic, occasionally adapted and made concessions to popular pressure still does not mean it abandoned

312 Charles Stewart, 'Magic and Orthodoxy', *Greek Magic. Ancient, Medieval and Modern*, ed. by J.C.B. Petropoulos (New York: Routledge, 2008), pp. 87–94, p. 93.

313 Mircea Eliade, *De la Zalmoxis la Ginghis-han* (București: Editura Ştiinţifică şi Enciclopedică, 1980), p. 246.

314 The Byzantine Empire, or Eastern Roman Empire, is historically seen as an autonomous entity revolving around the city of Constantinople/Byzantium from 330 (the year when Constantine the Great transferred here the capital from Rome) to 1453 (when it was conquered by Ottoman Turks).

315 Richard P.H. Greenfield, 'A Contribution to the Study of Palaeologan Magic', *Byzantine Magic*, ed. by Henry Maguire (Washington, DC: Dumbarton Oaks, 1995), pp. 117–154, p. 148.

its own stand points and ceased to fight against doctrinally suspicious phenomena altogether. However, unlike Catholic and Protestant Churches, the historically uninterrupted, virulent condemnation of all magic within Orthodoxy never took the form of demonology (which is what led in Catholic and Protestant Europe to the well-known witch hunts). In late Byzantine ecclesiastic law of the 14th century, the harshest punishment for sorcerers and magicians was banishment, actually mentioned as being put in effect on only a few occasions.[316] In Slavic Orthodoxy, the penalties under canon law typically involved several years of religious penitence, with excommunication as the most extreme measure.[317] In all Orthodox Romanian medieval and premodern books of canon law, the stipulated punishment for practicing witchcraft and sorcery is consistently the same: banning from communion for 20 years, according to St. Basil's canon no. 65 from the 4th century.[318] These were all harsh punishments, effectively pulverizing the social and moral persona of any individual defined at that time first and foremost as Christian—and yet, this seems quite mild when compared to the fate suffered by most of the accused individuals during the witch hunts. Although recognizing the importance of the Devil as concrete evil presence meddling in our very real world, it looks as though Easter Orthodoxy never overemphasized this threat: the Enemy **can** be kept at bay through the force of prayers, exorcisms, fasting, and all the rituals of the Church,[319] thus proving time and time again the self-evident truth of God's eternal power to defeat His arch enemy. The human agents of evil (sorcerers, witches, diviners, astrologers, healers, etc.) were souls in error, to be reconverted and cured of their folly, rather than signers of a fatal pact with the demons re-

---

316 Marie Theres Fögen, 'Balsamon on Magic: from Roman Secular Law to Byzantine Canon Law', *Byzantine Magic*, ed. by Henry Maguire, pp. 99–117, p. 114.

317 Robert Mathiesen, 'Magic in Slavia Orthodoxa: The Written Tradition', *Byzantine Magic*, ed. by Henry Maguire, pp. 155–177, p. 174.

318 Ioan Pop-Curşeu, *Magie şi vrăjitorie în cultura română* (Iaşi: Polirom, 2013), p. 70.

319 Ioan Pop-Curşeu, p. 51.

nouncing God and placing them beyond any salvation—like in the medieval demonologist interpretations that informed the witch hunts.

At a popular level, this relative tolerance toward magic was mirrored by the inability or even plain refusal of local communities to renounce customs condemned by the Church as 'devilish' (i.e., non-Orthodox). Forms of divination, love magic, protecting the mana/fertility magic, healing incantations, apotropaic practices, throwing spells, curing spells, and the effects of evil eye were all part of daily life, intensified at liminal moments of life cycle (birth, wedding, and funeral) or seasonal crossings (holidays marking the fertility cycles), validated through the unquestionable morality of the forefathers who passed down this way of life through generations. It was customary for most rural priests to become parishioners in their villages of origin, so that their own dogmatic discernment was often saturated with elements belonging, as per scrupulous academic disjunctions, to the magical pole.

Magic, Religion, and Processes of Secularization

All across Romania, by the end of 18th century, this encompassing popular religiosity started to be criticized not only by rigorous theologians from within the Orthodox Church but also by representatives of a new secular movement making its way from the West: the Enlightenment. The first mission of Romanian Enlightenment intellectuals was to wage war with the superstitious mentalities of peasantry, militating against their pagan retrograde customs and in favor of a more enlightened Christianity, better aligned to the Western secular revolutions of thought. Throughout the 19th century, the progressive project of this Enlightenment elite became a general project of all clerical and laic Romanian elites, motivated at this point by the perspective of nation-building and to help the nation of Romania rise to a level comparable to other European nations.[320]

---

[320] Valer Simion Cosma, 'Preotul ca "intelectual" in lumea țărănească a romanilor din Transilvania secolului al XIX-lea', *Seminatores in Artium Liberalium Agro. Studia in Honorem et Memoriam Barbu Ștefănescu*, ed. by Aurel Chi-

Campaigns of mass education led in formal education settings (schools) or through various publications and ecclesiastical channels also heavily relied on intellectuals with direct access to the rural life: teachers, doctors, and priests. But, from the point of view of 19th-century intelligentsia, the priests were proving to be quite imperfect tools in disseminating the progressive type of knowledge among the masses. Insufficiently theologically trained, more peasant-like than enlightened, predominantly from families with priesthood tradition well anchored in the cultural visions of the village, they themselves had to be 'perfected'[321] first through proper dogmatic instruction.

The growing gap between the elites' vision of building the nation by enlightening the ignorant masses and the reluctance of the latter to follow suit is suggestively illustrated by an incident from 1802, reported critically by a representative of the Enlightenment, Dimitrie Țichindel. A protopope of Banat[322] heard that a new witch had just established herself in a local village. He immediately proceeded to confiscate all that woman's possessions, which were then redistributed to the poor and saw to that, that the authorities removed her from the village. The reported reaction of the villagers: 'they were all shouting in anger, saying that our protopope has no law and he's worse than a Turk, to not let the witches into the village like that.'[323] 'Having no law' meant, in this context, that the Orthodox protopope was accused of not respecting the **proper** Orthodox religion. Far from seeing him as the official representative of religious authority, the villagers saw him as behaving worse than a pagan ('a Turk'),[324]

---

riac & Sorin Șipoș (Oradea: Editura Academiei Române, 2014), pp. 101–110, p. 105.

321 Valer Simion Cosma, p. 106.

322 Banat represents the Western-most province of Romania, at that time (1802) part of the Habsburg Kingdom of Hungary.

323 Dimitrie Țichindel, reprised by Ioan Pop-Curşeu, p. 175–176. [My translation].

324 'The Turk' was, at the time, the prototype of all non-Christian believers, based on the historical contact with the Ottoman Empire.

purposely defying the only valid religious authority for them, the law of old.

Modernization efforts were, over time, moderately successful. By the second half of the 19th century, there was a public education system that deserved this name in place, so that the literacy of the population slowly rose from 22% in 1899 to roughly 40% in 1912.[325] But, in a predominantly rural country, the rationalistic urban censorship operated by the elites throughout the 18th and 19th centuries[326] could only go as far as the fertility-based cultural rhythms and the practical needs of an agricultural–pastoral existence would allow them to. The more a new idea contradicted those, the less it was likely to succeed. This was not the case because the peasants were opposing in principle to the new but because they simply considered some of their customs more concretely relevant to (or, at any rate, more proven in) their living conditions and means of production. Some examples might help illustrate the point.

At the beginning of the 19th century, a letter denouncing the superstitious ringing of church bells in the municipality of Wichterich in Germany was followed by an immediate investigation and the subsequent ban of the custom. Even so, the ringing of the church bells in order to announce hailstorms, as well as witches, continued in the Rhine province throughout the 19th century.[327] Romanian ethnological material often mentions the customary ringing of church bells during Easter[328] as one of the sacral, beneficial times of passage symbolically comprising the whole positive potential of the near future. Therefore, ringing bells in such a sacral interval would magically assure the warding off of thunder, lightning fires, hail-

---

325 Vintilă Mihăilescu, 'Istoria României: noul val?', *Contributors.ro. Texte cu valoare adăugată*, April (2015), ‹http://www.contributors.ro/cultura/istoria-romaniei-noul-val/› [accessed June 2015]

326 Ioan Pop-Curşeu, p. 215.

327 Niels Freytag, 'Witchcraft, witch doctors and the fight against superstition in nineteen-century Germany', *Popular Magic in Modern Europe*, pp. 29–45, p. 38.

328 Antoaneta Olteanu, *Şcoala de solomonie. Divinaţie şi vrăjitorie în context comparat* (Bucureşti: Paideia, 1999), p. 439.

storms, etc., thus allowing the crops and the hemp fields to prosper throughout the following year.[329] In the summer of 2008, the locals of Giurgeşti (Bistriţa-Năsăud) were impatiently waiting for a new church bell. The old one had just cracked during Easter, after one too many a zealous chiming from one of the men carrying out the old custom. In Piatra-Fântânele (Bistriţa-Năsăud County), the nuns from the local cloister managed to build a chapel exclusively dedicated to the thunder bell therein, serviced in 2008 by one appointed sister with the precise task to run and ring the bell before the storms begin. Since the village is placed at a high altitude, the summer storms here are highly dangerous and quite destructive.[330] It is fair to say that if the campaign of the secular and clerical authorities in 19th Germany to eradicate this 'superstitious' popular custom proved to be, in the end, successful, in Transylvania it simply endured, with or without official approval, and even integrated into local religious practices. The danger represented by violent storms continues to be a serious concern for people in rural areas, who are largely dependent on subsistence agriculture, even today, just as it always was. This rather pragmatic factor seems to override any official ban or condemnation.

Religion and Magical Practices under Communism

Up until the end of the Second World War and the subsequent abrupt instalment of the communist regime, numerous ethnological studies suggest a continued coexistence between the fields of magic and the religion in Romania, either as very similar types of practices in everyday culture or as suggestive overlapping of social functions between the magical specialists and the local Orthodox priests.[331]

---

329 Elena Niculiţă-Voronca, *Datinile şi credinţele poporului român, adunate şi aşezate în ordine mitologică,* vol. I (Iaşi: Polirom, 1998), p. 289; Ion Taloş, *Gândirea magico-religioasă la români. Dicţionar* (Bucureşti: Editura Enciclopedică, 2001), p. 113.

330 Fieldwork information, Giurgeşti and Piatra-Fântânele, Bistriţa-Năsăud County, summer of 2008.

331 Ştefania Cristescu-Golopenţia, *Gospodăria şi credinţele magice ale femeilor din Drăguş (Făgăraş),* (Bucureşti: Paideia, 2002); Gheorghe Pavelescu,

However, during communism, religious life as such was discouraged, if not completely forbidden in Romania. It is true that only Communist Albania (and Cambodia) went as far as to formally ban any form of institutionalized religion, effectively outlawing all forms of worship.[332] Still, in Romania and in Russia, the radical atheist ideology of the communist–socialist state clashed with all forms of religiosity. The periods of state-sanctioned, open persecutions against religious leaders, believers, and institutional structures of Churches alternated in both countries with periods of the tacit allowing of some aspects of religious life, albeit under strict state surveillance. In Romania, the Greek-Catholic United with Rome Church, one of the main religious confessions in Transylvania, was the only one to be officially outlawed by decree from 1948.[333] All of its properties were confiscated and either taken over by the state or given to the Orthodox Church, effectively disbanding it. Many hierarches were persecuted, killed, or went to prison, especially when refusing to convert to Orthodoxy. At the same time, the Orthodox Church itself was being purged from all anticommunist forces, with both members of the clergy and faithful church members executed or imprisoned. A similar fate of persecution and systematic purge awaited religious leaders and devotees from all major remaining Churches (Romano-Catholic, Protestant, and Neo-Protestant) until the communist regime felt satisfied that they were left with a controllable, docile, nonpublic religious scene. Just like in Russia, the repressive socialist regimes realized they could not ban religiosity altogether and transform an enduring popular mentality overnight. But, they strived to achieve exactly that over time through the teaching of atheism in schools, by publicly ridiculing and quietly controlling religious people and institutions under the threat of repressions, and by well-orchestrated indoctrination campaigns at all levels of society, using all available channels. The public censorship

Magia la români: Studii şi cercetări despre magie, descântece şi mană (Bucureşti: Minerva, 1998).

332 Chris Hann, 'Antropologie socială şi socialism', p. 100.

333 The Greek-Catholic United with Rome Romanian Church was reinstated, through the abolition of 1948 decree, only in December 1989.

launched against religious discourse in order to completely evacuate it from the category of public discourses was combined with the lack of free access to information and systematic state-sanctioned campaigns of disinformation.

Socialism and nationalism are both often conceptualized as forms of laic religions because they strived to replace traditional religions with their respective ideologies through the readaptation or invention of ritual and symbolic forms (staged public demonstrations; worshipping of the leader; salient symbols, like the national flag of the hammer and sickle; public commemorations of relevant historical events, etc.) able to legitimize and to make these atheist ideologies appealing to the masses. However, the historical success of these strategies remains doubtful.[334]

At the everyday level, people under communist rule in Eastern Europe, for better or for worse, simply got on with their lives and did their best to adapt to the exterior conditions. Most of them never joined the Communist Party, despite the advantages that could bring, just as they did not join any dissident groups.[335] Participating in cultic religious activities was problematic for all citizens. In particular, for those in the military or members of Communist Party, such activities were strictly forbidden. There were only few categories of citizens who were not risking serious consequences when insisting to practice religion in a visible way, i.e., by frequenting the church. The effect seems to have been, in the long run, a simple 'getting used to it':

> *'We lived like this, with a fear and an imposed restriction, and it's like it became a reflex ...' Ioana (woman, age 49, Râşca village)*

Anthropological and ethnological studies carried out in Romania mostly by foreign researchers[336] throughout the 1970s, 1980s, and

---

334 Chris Hann, 'Antropologie socială şi socialism', p. 99.

335 Chris Hann, 'Antropologie socială şi socialism', p. 100.

336 Gail Kligman, *The Wedding of the Dead. Ritual, Poetics and Popular Culture in Transylvania* (Berkeley, Los Angeles & London: University of California Press, 1988); Jean Cuisinier, *Memoria Carpaţilor. România milenară: o privire interioară* (Cluj: Echinox, 2002); Marianne Mesnil, *Etnologul, între*

the beginning of the 1990s following a momentary relaxation of Communist Romania's politics of foreign affairs show how traditional values and customs were still pretty functional despite the ideological pressures of the political regime. For most rural communities, magic–religious life was one of those major values that, in some parts of Romania, somehow managed to endure. The social project of the Party to recreate a working class out of the peasantry, to urbanize and industrialize Romania, to create city people out of village people, and to have almost everybody singing to the same sheet of the proletarian atheist credo was indeed (at least apparently) quite successful. But, apart from special exterior conditions, such as villages that were left untouched by collectivism because of their isolated location in rough mountain areas, the persistence of certain traditional rural mentalities and traditions can be linked to the general dissimulative tactics of everyday life.

The emblematic popular phrase *'They pretend to be paying us, we pretend to be working,'*[337] which expresses the motivations underlying the secondary economy, is a good illustrator of an increasing separation between the ideological propaganda on the one side and people's personal beliefs facing the harsh realities of daily life on the other. With fear of repression and of being denounced always on people's minds, double-talk and double-thinking became the most common form of interpersonal everyday exchanges, as well as the exclusive form of addressing representatives of official power. The more the State tried to intervene in private affairs (redefining family structures; regulating reproduction[338]), the more people were

---

şarpe şi balaur/ Marianne Mesnil şi Assia Popova – *Eseuri de mitologie balcanică* (Bucureşti: Paideia, 1997).

337 Gail Kigman, 'Construcţia socialismului în România lui Ceauşescu', *Întâlniri multiple. Antropologi occidentali în Europa de Est,* ed. by Enikö Magyari–Vincze, Collin Quiglei, Gabriel Troc (Cluj–Napoca: Efes, 2000), pp. 131–182, p. 139.

338 The famous decree of 1966 effectively outlawed abortion in Romania, aiming to ensure demographic growth for the utopian socialist project of future dedicated work force. Through this decree, 'the physical bodies of the citizens were instrumentalized for the purpose of the political economy of the state'. Gail Kligman, *The Politics of Duplicity: Controlling Reproduction in*

trying to keep their private affairs under lock and key. This was also true for personal convictions and practices. If one was a religious believer, a provider of magical services, or a client of the latter, one would be careful not to advertise this and even be prepared to deny it—but, as long as no real threat of exposure would come from institutionalized level, one would simply carry on with it. Also, the hated system was, in real life, experienced through people: Similar to the mentioned case of the 19th-century priests, who were criticized by the intelligentsia for their insufficient abilities to educate the rural milieu precisely because they were part of it, Communist Party members and local authorities were people taking part in informal support networks, native members of the community, or simply outsiders needing to adapt to it on an unofficial level. The case study of Anuța, one of the last famous specialist witches of Maramureş County (northern Transylvania), shows how she managed to maintain a busy, demanding service of magical expertise (of traditional rural type) in her village throughout the 1970s, fearful of official sanction but quite hopeful that two aspects might help in averting that possibility: first, the fact that she opportunistically had joined the Communist Party and had become a communist activist ever since she was young; and second, the fact that she was well-known by local policemen, whose wives were coming to seek her help—even prominent figures from the regional Party had been her clients.[339] On the basis of the protection offered by these informal networks, she was fairly sure she was safe from official repercussions.

Similar to this case, my own field material suggests, as shown in **Chapter 2: Actors**, that, although people in need were occasionally resorting to the clergy, in 1970s and 1980s Communist Romania, they were predominantly appealing to magic specialists, such as laic unwitchers or specialists of magic incantations (*descântătoare*). Today, for both witchcraft situations and magical healing, my inform-

Ceausescu's Romania (Berkley, Los Angeles, London: University of California Press, 1998), pp. 24–25.

339 Aurora Liiceanu, *Povestea unei vrăjitoare* (Bucureşti: Editura ALL, 1996), pp. 27–29.

ants can only appeal to religious unwitchers simply because these are the only ones available now (explained as generational shift by my informants). It looks like during Communism, the magical field continued to unfold more or less on the same road as it did before Communism, in clear opposition to the public discontinuance of the religious field. Magic was regarded by the official ideology as distasteful superstition, and its study in social sciences was strongly discouraged—unless saved by the use of an ahistorical perspective —void of any reference to a concrete social and historical context. But, the communist regime never made the magical domain an ideological preoccupation or a target for repression and control, as it did with the institutionalized religions.

Post-communist Developments

When communism fell throughout Eastern Europe, it felt like 'overnight, Christianity "was in"':[340] after 44 years of religious suppression in Bulgaria, 42 in Romania and 73 in Russia, the citizens of former communist atheist states woke up to democracy and a world of religious freedom. All across the post-communist Orthodox states where Eastern Orthodoxy was the dominant religion, the Orthodox Church immediately started a process of repositioning in the public sphere, and it is very interesting to note how similarly these strategies unfolded in different national settings.

One such crucial strategy was (and continues to be) to play the 'church of the nation' card: In Bulgaria, Russia, and Romania, public secular authorities and Church authorities rarely skip the opportunity to recognize the Orthodox Church's contribution to national identity and its historical role in the building of their respective nation. In Russia, a 1997 law formally recognized the Russian Orthodox Church's contribution to 'the history of Russia and to the establishment and development of Russia's spirituality and culture,'[341] af-

340 Milena Kirova, 'Religion and Post-Communism: a Chronicle of Absurdity', *Critical Research on Religion*, April 1 (2013), pp. 102–107, ‹http://crr.sagepub.com/content/1/1/102› [accessed September 2014], p. 103.

341 More about the actual implications of this law, especially the ones concerning other confessions and faiths, can be found in *Eastern Europe, Russia*

ter stating that the Russian Federation is a secular state. In all three countries, suddenly, the Church was everywhere: Every public event (opening sessions in Parliament; opening of the new school year; opening of businesses, or inaugurations of a football pitch) was marked by the participation of Orthodox Clergy and the holding of adequate rituals (from simple collective prayers to elaborate religious blessings). Ex-communists, quickly reconverted as socialists, were among the first politicians to be seen crossing themselves and diligently kissing the hands of high prelates. To this day, being seen at religious events or inviting priests to hold such events is a political strategy copiously employed by political candidates as a means to prove their moral quality and their devotion to national identity. Another category that made ample use of religious symbols and behavior was, as rightly pointed out by Milena Kirova,[342] the nouveau-riche, many of whom acquired their wealth through involvement in criminal activities. In order to publicly express their moral quality as good Christians and to expiate their sins, such characters publicly donated to churches and built chapels in Bulgaria, as well as in Romania and Russia.

In all three post-communist countries, there was one common accusation coming from members of the civil society concerning the Church. Many complained that Orthodox hierarchs had actively collaborated during communist times with the KGB or the Romanian and Bulgarian State Securities. As one theologian put it, these collaborations 'may have been a compromise made with the political authorities judged necessary for the sake of the survival of the Church,'[343] and that is usually where the discussion stops. Another accusation is that Orthodox Churches, having been set up by public consensus as symbolic churches of the nations, actually overshadow other confessions and faiths in terms of both concrete access to

and Central Asia 2003, 3rd edition, ed. by Imogen Bell (London: Europa Publications, Taylor & Francis Group, 2002), pp. 47–48.

342 Milena Kirova, pp. 103–104.

343 Vladimir Feodorov, 'Religious Freedom in Russia today', *The Ecumenical Reviews*, 50.4 (1998), ‹*www.questia.com*› [accessed October 2009]

resources from the state and due recognition for their own historical contributions.

However, the success the post-communist reinstatement of Orthodox Churches in public spheres had cannot be exclusively explained by the favorable political climate at the macrolevel. Another crucial factor is the genuine 'post-communist revival of interest in any nonmaterialistic world-view'[344] at the popular level. The Orthodox revival was paralleled by unprecedented popular access and interest in a plethora of pseudoreligious and quasi-sciences, a very confusing field of information all equally pertaining to the 'sacred' and the 'supernatural.' These had a large impact—in a world where, for most people, only atheism was a clear notion. It was in this field that the Orthodox Churches in Bulgaria, Russia, and Romania had to establish their moral supremacy, competing against other historically established Christian denominations (Catholicism; Protestantism; The Greek-Catholic United with Rome); against the so-called 'sects' (neo-protestant proselytism-based denominations); the so-called 'cults' (yoga and 'Oriental' organizations); Western-based New-Age and occult theories; magical practices and beliefs, etc. This religious entropy was initially fought against by Orthodox Churches in their respective countries, but later on, it became a field to organize, lead, and control.

Looking at the available statistics, it seems like the general process to reimpose the Orthodox Church as a pole of undeniable authority on the public scene of those post-communist countries where it can profess to be the 'church of the nation' was largely successful. For instance, in Russia, various surveys (previous to 2006) showed that between 55% and 59% of all Russian citizens, or up to 82% of ethnic Russians, identify themselves as Orthodox.[345] In Ro-

344 Elizabeth A. Warner, 'Russian Peasant Beliefs and Practices concerning Death and the Supernatural Collected in Novosokol'niki Region, Pskov Province, Russia, 1995. Part I: The Restless Dead, Wizards and Spirit Beings', *Folklore*, 111. 1 (2000), ‹*www.questia.com*› [accessed March 2012].

345 Serghei Filatov & Roman Lunkin, Statistics on Religion in Russia: The Reality behind the Figures, *Religion, State & Society*, 34. 1 (March 2006), pp. 33–49, p. 35.

mania, 86.45% Romanian citizens declared themselves Orthodox at the 2011 population census.[346] In Bulgaria, the percentage of citizens to self-identify in 2011 as Orthodox was 76%.[347] But, as rightly pointed out by Serghei Filatov and Roman Lunkin,[348] self-identification in religious terms does not mean that a person actually subscribes to the doctrine of that religion or follows the relevant religious practices. More often than not, such a self-identification might have less to do with personal religious beliefs and more with other factors, such as ethnic, national, and family line arguments (usually condensed under the formula 'the religion of our forefathers'). Therefore, people who in everyday life think of themselves as atheists, agnostics, or are interested in various Oriental religious approaches far removed from Christianity might still self-identify as Orthodox because of their family background and ethnic line.

And yet, if religious identification needs to be further discussed in terms of proper religious observance, then Romania seems to be the one standing out at this point: In a 2010 statistic inquiry at national level, 95% of the respondents declared they believed in God, 88% in the power of prayer, and 53% stated that they attend mass in church at least once a month. The last figure, relating to actual religious observance, might not look particularly impressive; but when compared to other countries, Romania proves to be 'the Orthodox country with the highest active religious practice.'[349]

In post-communist Romania, the Orthodox Church gained an unprecedented direct access to the faithful through mass media channels. Television programs and radio broadcasts treating Orthodox dogma are now accessible even in otherwise-isolated villages. Their immediately observable effect is the abandonment, or at least

346 *Ce ne spune recensamântul din 2011 despre religie?* Institutul Național de Statistică, ‹http://www.insse.ro/cms/files/publicatii/pliante%20statistice/08-Recensamintele%20despre%20religie_n.pdf›

347 *Population Census in the Republic of Bulgaria. Final Results 2011*, ‹http://www.nsi.bg/census2011/PDOCS2/Census2011final_en.pdf›

348 Serghei Filatov & Roman Lunkin, p. 40.

349 *STISOC 2010: Raport de Cercetare - Publicul şi Ştiința* (Bucureşti: 2010), ‹http://www.stisoc.ro› [accessed July, 2011], p. 52.

decrease in relevance, of some local ritual practices that can be classed by the religious authority as superstitious or dogmatically equivocal. Also, reinstructing the parishioners according to a unique and coherent dogmatic national center can easily lead to the undermining of the local priests' authority. In this context, employing a strict 'magic versus religion' dichotomy continues to come, just like in previous centuries, from an elite of trained theologians looking to reconfigure the dogmatic religious pole. Only that this time they benefit from an unprecedented range of channels to reach the faithful.

Despite these efforts of dogmatic propaganda coming from the institutional centers of the Orthodox Church, various social analysts also point to the fact that, in many instances, the impressive numbers of churchgoers actually consist of people who, insufficiently educated in the proper spiritual functions of religion, treat it similar to magic. They seek healing of the body and not that of the soul through mass rituals, drinking holy water for treatment of various affections, and venerating icons and holy relics for purely mundane or bodily needs.[350] What is usually blamed for this confusion at the very core of popular religious practices in post-communist Orthodox Churches is the insufficient efforts on the part of trained theologians to educate the masses combined with the general ignorance in dogmatic matters of populations descending directly from communism and its strictly atheist ideology. When compared to the discussions in previous subchapters, this discourse sounds not unlike that of the elites' Enlightenment call to fight magical–religious superstition at a popular level from the 18th and 19th centuries. Then as well as now, it would seem people tend to treat religion more like a source of concrete (albeit supernatural) help with everyday predicaments rather than a source of spiritual edification—with or without factoring in the influence atheism had as a cause of people's ignorance, or naivety, in religious matters.

In this post-communist context, the existence of magic in forms that are considered maleficent (harmful spells and evil charms) but

350 Serghei Filatov & Roman Lunkin, pp. 42–43.

equally in forms that can be considered benign (divination, astrology, and protective spells) are part of a discourse that is always present in the Church's dogmas as one of the faces of evil most present in this world with which the representatives of Orthodox clergy consider themselves to be engaged in direct combat. One argument often presented by observers to explain this virulence is that institutionalized religion is now placed in a consumerist world, where magic specialists are, simply, business competitors. They address the same clients, and, therefore, they are competing over the same sources of income. This argument might hold some truth. However, magic specialists tend to legitimate themselves precisely by resorting to religious elements. The fortune tellers of Romania always prove to their clients, as shown in **Chapter 2: Actors**, extensive religious knowledge. They are able to orientate each client toward the best-suited religious therapist for their particular case, they indicate the repertoire of religious prayers appropriate for their client's situation, and they can provide small portable icons or encourage their clients to purchase similar ones from the church. Similarly, the magi in Russia encourage their clients to start frequenting the church as part of their treatment, go to confession, be baptized if they have not been yet, and procure holy water, crucifixes, icons, etc.[351] These examples show that, far from stealing the Church's clients, these magic specialists actually have a most interesting role of leading people in need *toward* the Church, thus increasing the latter's public visibility.

As argued by Galina Linquist,[352] the reason for the post-communist Orthodox Church's ideological offensive against magic practices and specialists must be looked for elsewhere. Linquist argues that one has to look at the radical incompatibility between religious and magical ontologies of self and the corresponding constructions of agency, an issue that is now more pressing than ever, as the

351 Galina Lindquist, *Conjuring Hope. Healing and Magic in contemporary Russia*, p. 29.

352 Galina Lindquist, 'Not my will but thine be done: Church versus magic in contemporary Russia', p. 247.

Church is in the process of reassuming its long-lost role as moral arbiter and source of coherent ontological foundation in society. Agency, seen as the human ability to intervene in this world in order to produce a desired effect, is something portrayed by the religious dogma as placed well outside the individual self. Not the human can be a source of intentionality and power, but only God. To think and attempt otherwise means to follow Lucifer's footsteps, the one fallen angel who questioned the will of God. The humans have to understand that the trials in their lives express God's will, make peace with the inevitable pain of this world, and have faith that their humbleness and acceptance will be recompensed in the next, better world. The Church is the legitimate active mediator between the only source of power (the divinity) and the human beings.

This image of the religious self as being conditioned exclusively by an external authority, defined by obedience, and humbly subordinated to higher powers, is very similar to the image of the Soviet self.[353] Here, too, the individual was defined as selfless part of the utopian brotherhood of working men and women, dedicated to the common goal of rising up the Socialist state, under the approving gaze of the Father of the Nation. As shown previously, communism unsuccessfully aimed at creating a laic religion through borrowing some of the exterior ritual and symbolic signs associated with practicing traditional religions. Lindquist's argument highlights this other similar project to institutionalized religions: the communist ideol ogy's ambition to have the supra-individual state system as the exclusive locus of agency and power.

Therefore, in this long history of macrodiscourses officially placing the locus of agency outside of the individual, the public and advertised Russian magi practices reintroduce the opposite message always carried by magic into new, post-communist consumerist market-oriented settings: the self-empowering, self-forging project of regrasping individual agency, similar to the Western New Age defini-

353 Galina Lindquist, 'Not my will but thine be done: Church versus magic in contemporary Russia', p. 266.

tions of 'self as a locus of agency and a seat of the Divine.'[354] The Orthodox Church's and the magi's interpretations of the human beings' place in this world, of their power to act and of their right to go ahead and try to change their life conditions could not be more divergent. In a world changing as dramatically as that of post-communist Russia, one has to either accept unhappiness and misfortune as the will of God or turn around to regain agency through supramundane means of power.

The witchcraft discourse of Romania does not cut such an irreversible gap between institutionalized religion and magical practices. It is true that diviners (the only ones actively practicing magic in today's northern Transylvania) and any other imaginable kind of magic or healing specialist of yesterday and today (astrologers, sorcerers, witches, users of magic healing incantations, clairvoyants, etc.) are often the discursive target of collective rituals, church sermons, and clerical educative projects. The Romanian Orthodox Church's nonnegotiable stand point is, at this level, the same as that of the Russian Orthodox Church. Both are the exclusive possessors of moral and existential truth. But, while the Russian Orthodox Church seems to maintain the irreconcilable disjunction toward the magical field beyond the discursive level by wanting nothing to do with the magi, the Romanian Church is now actually placed at the core of the witchcraft discourse, effectively having confiscated the unwitchment pole, thus being able to shape this discourse from the interior. When I made a note, sometimes in 2005, to describe today's Romanian Orthodox Church's strategy of reimposing itself on the Romanian public scene by combining the 'church of the nation' strategy with a monopoly of the sacred, I was meaning to express the terms of intentional politics on the part of the Church, not the actual effects. And yet, after several years of fieldwork, I think that this statement sums up pretty well the bottom line of my observations.

---

354 Galina Lindquist, 'Not my will but thine be done: Church versus magic in contemporary Russia', p. 269.

However, it would be a simplistic mistake to interpret this development as an orchestrated strategic move made by the institutionalized religions with the explicit purpose of infiltrating and pulverizing from the interior the magic discourse. The situation in France, where Catholic religious unwitchers exited the witchcraft discourse and were gradually replaced by laic unwitchers, is probably the closest example, only the other way around: As laic unwitchers left the discourse in Romania, the Orthodox clergy, already quite well connected to the discourse, progressively occupied the empty spaces until they became exclusive holders of unwitcher positions. The Catholic French priests had a reason to evacuate the discourse: the progressive, Protestant-inspired secularization of views on magical practices and beliefs,[355] culminating in the politics established by the Vatican Council of 1966 aiming to delimitate the Catholic Church from superstitions. By contrast, the reasons for the quiet disappearance of Romanian laic unwitchers sometime between 1980 and today are far from clear. Social science research on magic and religion had been clearly discouraged during communist times; so, there is not much hope of finding answers there. My informants insist that the people who knew how 'to handle those things,' for good or for evil, simply died out without transmitting their knowledge, just as their world was shifting from communism to post-communism.

For the Romanian Orthodox clergy, confiscating one pole of the witchcraft discourse means indeed to gain a position of power within the magical domain because, as shown in **Chapter 2**, unwitchers are the main shapers of the discourse and the ones to define the terms of affliction. From this perspective, the progressive blurring of the aggressor pole under the requirements of the religious discourse (discouraging the victim's anger or need for revenge) might eventually lead to a collapse of the discourse altogether. However, we are seeing a two-way avenue here: The witchcraft discourse and its specific perspectives, requirements, and distribution of roles also get to play a part in influencing the religious discourse from the interior.

355 Stanley Jeyaraja Tambiah, p. 13.

For instance, from a religious perspective, the root of illness is always a sin.[356] To cure the body, the penitent must cure the soul through the appropriate religious means. Also, adversities in human life come as God-sent trials to test the faithful. Conversely, participating in the witchcraft discourse means accepting its initial premise, that adversities are send through evil spells by enemies, which affirms human agency, the power of evil in the real world, and the human ability to manipulate and control supernatural evil—all of which are placed in a whole other register than the customary religious interpretation of God, agency, sin, illness, and evil. In other words, to take part in the witchcraft discourse means, from a dogmatic religious perspective, to make a compromise and adapt to this discourse's terms of affliction even if they contradict some theological distinctions. It also means to lend religious rituals and prayers for magical means.

This is simply one aspect of a larger social strategy that was always present within the Romanian Orthodox Church—the same that was in the past, and is now once again, criticized for allowing popular devotion to take forms contrary to pure faith. At the level of the public sphere, the Church's efforts are directed to present itself as a public, active, involved church of the nation, able to play the role of moral arbiter. Equally visible are the efforts of instructed theologians from the institutional core to educate believers according to the correct principles of true faith. But, a whole different level, effectively in contradiction with the former, is what Gabi Troc calls 'cultic manifestations placed at the outer edge of dogmatic permissiveness.'[357] Exorcisms, unwitchments, and various religious healings are theoretically and dogmatically discouraged but tacitly tolerated by the church hierarchy (as long as they do not cause a public scandal) for the simple reason that they maintain and augment the social prestige of the Orthodox Church. Looking at these phenome-

356 Valer Simion Cosma, 'Preotul, tămăduirea şi cartea în lumea ţărănească a secolului al XIX-lea', *Conferinţele de vară de la Telciu*, ed. by de Valer Simion Cosma and Edit Szegedi (Cluj Napoca: Eikon, 2014), pp. 97–112, p. 99.

357 Gabriel Troc, 'Exorcism şi vindecare în Biserica Ortodoxă', *Caietele Tranziţiei*, 2.3 (Cluj–Napoca, 1998).

na on a microlevel, the Orthodox clergy are now, just like they always were, part of local communities. They have to respond to concrete needs and requests of the members of their congregation pertaining to life, love, death, illness, wishes, unhappiness, etc. In market terms, social prestige means financial success. Moreover, in post-communist Romania, the churches are very well attended. Turning a bit of a blind eye to questionable practices and to the type of popular religiosity more interested in the tasks of everyday living and the practical realities than the 'intellectual hair-splitting'[358] is also a contemporary strategy of the Romanian Orthodox Church to get a firm foothold in the social reality of the post-communist world. It is not hard to imagine a scenario in which clear interdictions of practices and a more aggressive dogmatic education of devotees from the theological center would actually result in the emptying of the churches.

358 Stanley Jeyaraja Tambiah, p. 31.

Concluding Remarks

The traditional witchcraft discourse, defined as 'a device for ascribing misfortune to others'[359] is not something of the past in Europe. On the contrary, it is perfectly functional in some social contexts, like in the two examples of Romania and western France, which I was able to provide in this book. Also, in other social milieus, mostly from the Mediterranean region (such as Greece, Italy, or Portugal), the evil eye continues to serve as the answer for otherwise inexplicable misfortunes in people's lives. In Russia, the new magi phenomenon of magic advertised as a commodity reflects a recent, post-communist development combining various sources of local and rural witchcrafts with Western New Age discourse. And, although modern paganism that has its roots in 1950s England had little to do with the traditional witchcraft of the rural milieu as such, it is interesting to note the success this city-based form of religion has had worldwide,[360] which goes to show the large extent to which contemporary people continue to be interested in various forms of (re-)enchantment of the world.

Richard Jenkins uses the term 're-enchantment' as 'taken to refer to two linked tendencies: one which insists that there are more things in the universe than are dreamt of by the rationalist epistemologies and ontologies of science, the other which rejects the notion that calculative, procedural, formal rationality is always the "best way."'[361] The contemporary witchcraft discourse, the existence

---

359 Willem de Blécourt and Owen Davies, 'Introduction: Witchcraft continued', *Witchcraft Continued. Popular Magic in Modern Europe*, pp. 1–13, p. 2.

360 'It is England which is the heartland, exporting ideas and practices to the rest of the British Isles and of Europe, and (above all) to North America. Twentieth-century pagan witchcraft, known in its most established form as Wicca, is in fact the only religion which the English can claim to have given to the world.' Ronald Hutton, 'Modern Pagan Witchcraft', *Witchcraft and Magic in Europe. The Twentieth Century,* ed. by Bengt Ankarloo and Stuart Clark (University of Pennsylvania Press, 1999), pp. 1–80, p. 1.

361 Richard Jenkins, 'Disenchantment, Enchantment and Re-Enchantment: Max Weber at the Millennium', *Max Weber Studies,* 1 (2000), pp. 11–32,

of diverse magical and occult practices in every European metropolis, the renewed popular interest in spiritual and religious practices all over the continent—all of this seems to point toward the constant human need for mystery and a deeper meaning of existence beyond the confines of materiality. At the same time, it is interesting to note that discussing witchcraft discourse always involves talking about human feelings. Accusations of witchcraft aggressions express, on the sufferer's side, fear, anxiety, pain, despair, loss of control, and antipathy against the designated aggressor; on the presupposed witch's side, they express envy, hatred, revenge, greed, and anger. In sorcery (seen as proper spells leveled against a targeted victim or in order to coerce supernatural powers), everything is about desire and the wanting to impose human will above and beyond the limits of tangible reality. Maybe that is why the talks of witchcraft and sorcery are felt today (and have always been) as something quite uncomfortable: They feed from this realm of powerful emotions that stands in contrast to the province of reason and the standard morality of everyday life, which they threaten with the a constant subversive potential to question and contradict. In Kapferer's terms: 'Sorcery unsettles complacency and is a disturber of systems of control and order,'[362] which might account for its historical niche placement, as well as for being resorted to especially in crisis situations when people need to re-create their avenues for agency.

Witchcraft discourses as described in this book and understood throughout as 'the whole complex of thinking and acting in terms of witchcraft'[363] contain sorcery at the aggressor pole as an indispensable starting point of the victim's interior narrative: more specifically, as the imagined immoral actions of the designated witch. This sequence is meant to sustain for the sufferer the coherence of the whole witchcraft scenario. The very fact that, during my research in

‹http://maxweberstudies.org/kcfinder/upload/files/MWSJournal/1.1pdfs/1.1%2011-32.pdf› [accessed October 12, 2014], p. 12.

362 Bruce Kapferer, *The Feast of the Sorcerer: Practices of Consciousness and Power* (Chicago and London: The University of Chicago Press, 1997), p. 9.

363 Willem de Blécourt and Owen Davies, 'Introduction: Witchcraft continued', p. 3.

northern Transylvania, I have only encountered victims' words of accusation toward presupposed magical aggressors but never sorcerers or any declared interest in sorcery as such shows how disreputable this domain is perceived to be in popular conscience. No one would ever want to openly play the part of 'those who know how to handle those things.' The bewitched, on the other hand, always represent not simply the pole of the sufferers of magical aggressions but also the unquestionably moral pole: The victims always describe themselves as deeply virtuous people, churchgoers, not guilty of any wrongdoings, and good, decent people conforming to the social standards of acceptable behavior. By entering the witchcraft discourse, they have to empirically confront the undeniable existence of 'the proverbial human wickedness'[364] as a generic social predisposition to cause harm without sufficient cause. Sorcery is, in this context, the key concept imagined to embed the essence of human malevolence as hubris against the social order, a stepping outside of all predefined boundaries—always imputable to the presupposed witch, never to the victim.

The witchcraft discourse in Europe has always been, with the remarkable exception of the example of contemporary rural western France, a mostly feminine scene. Especially in a rural-traditional context, the main actors of a witchcraft drama—the accused witches, the victims (the accusers), and, to some extent, even the laic unwitchers—were usually women and rather infrequently men. This had a lot to do with the underlying patriarchal social order of any European rural-traditional society. Accusations of witchcraft and sorcery formulated against certain women in rural communities were used to 'direct them to their "proper" place in society.'[365] In

364 André Julliard, 'Urgia Sorților. Vrăjitoria zilelor noastre în Franța', *Magia și vrăjitoria în Europa, din Evul Mediu până astăzi*, ed. by Robert Muchembled (București: Humanitas, 1997), pp. 274–326, p. 307. [My translation].

365 Willem de Blécourt, 'The Witch, her Victim, the Unwitcher and the Researcher: the continued existence of traditional witchcraft', *Witchcraft and Magic in Europe. The Twentieth Century*, ed. by Bengt Ankarloo and Stuart Clark (University of Pennsylvania Press, 1999), pp. 141–219, p. 151.

most[366] European traditional social contexts, to be suspected of sorcery interests and activities was a certain way to stigmatize someone (and their kin) and to socially isolate the person in question.

Women were seen as responsible for the private sphere and the domestic activities of production and reproduction. In many regions, such as, e.g., the historical provinces of nowadays Romania or Ireland, marriage was patrilocal (the women were leaving their family after marriage, moving in with the husband's family). As Richard Jenkins showed,[367] this created a perpetual ambiguity about the social perception of the women's role, arising from the tension between the women's position as outsiders on the one hand and their crucial role as guardians of prosperity on the other, caught in between the explicit authority of the husband and the implicit importance of the wife in the household economy. When expressed as accusations of witchcraft against certain women, this ambiguous social anxiety was translated through the framework of the witchcraft discourse as a way of exercising control and as reinforcement of the sanctioned, patriarchal social rules. These accusations were made possible in the first place by the very fact that women were responsible, as an extension of the domestic sphere designated to them, for the spiritual and physical well-being of their household components (the family members, livestock, and fertility of the crops). The magic–religious knowledge and actions meant to promote domestic health and prosperity was, hence, exclusively a feminine domain. Every married woman had to know certain elements of everyday magical practice like minor healing incantations and spells, medicinal herbs,

---

366 However, not everywhere. In late 19th- and early 20th-century Finland, for instance, by being accused of witchcraft or sorcery people would not lose their social position or face: 'to be known as a witch was not neccessarily a stigma to be avoided at all costs'. Laura Stark, 'Narrative and the social dynamics of magical harm in late nineteenth- and early twentieth-century Finland', *Witchcraft Continued. Popular Magic in Modern Europe*, pp. 69–88, p. 85.

367 Richard Jenkins, 'Witches and Fairies: Supernatural Aggression and Deviance among the Irish Peasantry', *The Good People: New Fairylore Essays*, ed. by Peter Narváez (Lexington: University Press of Kentucky, 1997), pp. 302–335, p. 327.

apotropaic means, religious holidays to respect, key moments of the calendar cycle, cunning people to consult when her knowledge proved insufficient, etc. However, it is important to stress that this type of common magic–religious repertoire employed mainly by women in their daily living did not represent some sort of secret knowledge, nor some type of protofeminist organization,[368] as it is sometimes imagined by the discourses of modern paganisms. It was pure and simple knowledge for living—but of a kind adding to the ambiguity of the place of women within a rural traditional society, and likely to inflame, at times, targeted accusations of witchcraft. As a parenthesis, the difference between this necessary everyday magic–religious knowledge held by most women and that of a more specialized village witch or cunning woman was defined by the degree of interest invested in this field by the latter. Judged according to the level of personal attraction toward the magical domain (people would say, on the basis of the 'gift' or abnormal force driving her), a magic specialist of any kind was a person actively pursuing and gathering elements of this common magic repertoire, pushing it further and further toward more refined and purpose-dedicated techniques.

One very interesting aspect to highlight here is the fact that the witchcraft discourses of today display elements of the patriarchal order of old. For instance, in the example of rural western France, a witchcraft attack is imagined as directed exclusively toward the man: the wife, the children, the tools of production, or livestock are always affected in his stead because they together constitute the man's property, the topologic and vital domain bearing his unique name. In this type of witchcraft example, the male head of the family is indubitably the ultimate familial authority and, therefore, the targeted source of power of any witchcraft attack. Even the general perception explaining the contemporary predominance of male unwitchers and their perceived bigger power over their female counter-

---

368 Willem de Blécourt, 'The Witch, her Victim, the Unwitcher and the Researcher: the continued existence of traditional witchcraft', *Witchcraft and Magic in Europe. The Twentieth Century,* p. 151.

parts is formulated as men having 'stronger blood running through their veins.'[369] In the Romanian witchcraft discourse, bewitched women accuse other women (imagined as witches or as clients of professional sorcerers) according to the principle of predominance of witchcraft accusations between peers,[370] while (male) Orthodox religious therapists are the ones to actively combat the magic aggressors in the victims' name. Unwitchers are always the shaping forces of the witchcraft discourse,[371] the ones generating and controlling the discourse and its ultimate position of authority. From a gender theory perspective, we can interpret the religious unwitchments of the Romanian context as processes through which, in the end, the formerly bewitched and now-cured women were progressively reconciled with the patriarchal order (which is the one always professed by the religious discourse), where their sense of personal satisfaction is supposed to exclusively derive from devoutly performing the social functions of worthy daughter, wife, and mother. Also, the (male) representatives of the Orthodox Church see themselves as perpetually engaged in an eschatological conflict with all representatives of the magic domain (sorcerers, witches, diviners, magic healers, clairvoyants, etc.), which in this discourse is perceived to be a deeply sinful, exclusively feminine domain.

These patriarchal elements embedded in contemporary witchcraft discourses are, on the one hand, a direct consequence of the rural-traditional core marking any scenario of this type. On the other hand, they equally represent only recent historical developments of the classic witchcraft accusations scenario. The paradox at work here might be able to shed some light on the internal tensions of the term 'tradition' and the way in which it can be conceptualized (against the more generally accepted idea of direct linear survivals and passive transgenerational reproduction of ideas, practices, and customs) as a generating dynamic core adaptable to various social

369 Dominique Camus, *Puteri şi practici vrăjitoreşti. Anchetă asupra practicilor actuale de vrăjitorie* (Iaşi: Polirom, 2003), p. 21.

370 André Julliard, p. 322.

371 Willem de Blécourt, 'The Witch, her Victim, the Unwitcher and the Researcher: the continued existence of traditional witchcraft', p. 184.

circumstances, able to gain new aspects while losing others at different historical moments and maintaining at all times an unmistakable identity. Or, as expressed by Kapferer: 'the concept of "traditional"—a thoroughly modernist notion—subverts the recognition that some practices which do have some historical depth, and maybe because of it, possess internal dynamics that make them always already modern.'[372] To be **traditional**, in this line of argument, means to have **historical depth**, and, therefore, the already very modern characteristic of being perpetually adaptable and relevant to newly emerging social and historical circumstances. The existence of some patriarchal elements within the two examples of contemporary witchcraft discussed in this book is one expression of this broader historical depth of the traditional European witchcraft discourse as more or less incidental quotations of the patriarchal order characterizing the preindustrial rural communities to which this discourse belonged in the first place. However, the patriarchal elements as such are not identical to those specific to their initial social context (for instance, the punitive potential of public witchcraft accusations to direct women to their 'proper' place in that society). In France, the profile of a predominantly masculine witchcraft, with men as intended targets and mostly men as unwitchers, is a recent historical development gradually gaining the shape of today throughout the 19th century.[373] In Romania, the fact that the unwitchment pole is nowadays dominated exclusively by representatives of the Orthodox Church is an even newer, post-communist development and part of the more general context of the Church's strategies to reimpose itself as a pole of authority on the public scene. And these changes highlight precisely the dynamic versatility of

372 Bruce Kapferer, 'Introduction: Outside all reason – Magic, Sorcery and Epistemology in Anthropology', *Beyond Rationalism. Rethinking Magic, Witchcraft and Sorcery*, ed. by Bruce Kapferer (New York & Oxford: Berghahn Books, 2003), pp. 1–30, p. 20.

373 Marie-Sylvie Dupont-Bouchat, 'Diavolul îmblânzit. Vrăjitoria reconsiderată. Magia şi vrăjitoria în secolul al XIX-lea', *Magia şi vrăjitoria în Europa, din Evul Mediu până astăzi*, ed. by Robert Muchembled (Bucureşti: Humanitas, 1997), p. 272.

the witchcraft discourse, which can, hence, be seen as traditional in type but already modern in structure. Throughout the centuries, various social categories exited the discourse, only to be replaced by others; women and men exchanged places they had traditionally played within the discourse, continuously shaping the gender distribution of roles; elements of the discourse always fluctuated and adapted to different technological realities (cars and mechanical tools of productions proved just as easily bewitched as livestock), to different social milieus (delaying of marriage imputable to spells became an equally satisfactory explanation for relationship failure in cities as it was in villages), etc. It looks as if the witchcraft discourse, based on the essential ambition to explain the otherwise unexplainable, might still have a part to play as one of the significant 'cultural repertoires'[374] of the European territory, predominantly reactivated at moments of personal crisis and deep social change.

There is one big difference too, often obscured within the social science texts that tackle these types of phenomena that I would like to draw attention to: The difference between what the witchcraft discourse might mean to outsider analysts, researchers, and producers of texts, and what it usually means to the actors directly involved in it. For the researcher (or analyst), contemporary forms of the witchcraft discourse require some sort of interpretation, if not explanation. Attempting to explain it away usually means searching for concrete reductionist reasons that could account for the persistence of witchcraft scenarios, sorcery, or magic practices within the settings of secular contemporary European nations, as if the root of inquiry is some sort of self-evident question such as: 'how is something like this still possible to occur in the territory and time of absolute (secular) civilization?'. Instead of trying to produce a unique theory that satisfactorily answers the aforementioned question, the more correct interpretation turns toward the analysis of the nuances of the investigated phenomenon in all their complexities, attempting to highlight the way multiple individual, social, historical, and econom-

---

[374] Willem de Blécourt and Owen Davies, 'Introduction: Witchcraft continued', p. 5.

ic factors intersect in order to perpetuate, shift, and create the local profiles of magic phenomena in contemporaneity. However, such interpretations, too, are ultimately reflections of the author's personal and professional sensibilities: 'witchcraft as resistance, witchcraft as the folk explanation of misfortune, or witchcraft and sorcery as types of social diagnosis (...). The practices are domesticated to the analyst's own sensibilities.'[375] More than that, even if interpreting might be, as an approach, fairer toward the investigated actors than any effort of explaining them away, more often than not it still is something very different from—and poses the danger of eventually obscuring completely—the actors' own exegesis of the phenomena they adhere to, create, and perpetuate.

For example, André Mary[376] interprets unwitchment processes of the French witchcraft discourse as ultimately resulting in successful transformations of the formerly bewitched, who before the unwitchment used to be opposed to globalism and modernity, into persons who are from then on better adapted to a world based on ruthless competition because during the unwitchment they had to empirically confront the fundamental wickedness of human relationships. Similarly, for the case of Romanian witchcraft, I can interpret the bewitched women's journeys of unwitchment under the authority of Orthodox clergy as resulting in forms of reconciliation with the patriarchal order always propagated by the Church, which is still functional in a society where the external avenues for women agency continue to be quite insufficient or dysfunctional. These interpretations do offer valid insights; however, they cannot represent ultimate truths (if there ever is such a thing in human matters), nor can they hold more value than the directly involved actors' points of view and interpretations. And, as stated already in the **Introduction**, no matter what terms we employ in order to best describe the

375 Bruce Kapferer, 'Introduction: Outside all reason – Magic, Sorcery and Epistemology in Anthropology', p. 20.

376 André Mary, 'Sorcellerie bocaine, sorcellerie africaine: le social, le symbolique et l'imaginaire', *Les Cahiers du LASA, Sorcellerie: bocage et modernité*, 17 (1987), pp.125–152, ‹https://halshs.archives-ouvertes.fr/halshs-00137125› [accessed 12 September 2015], p. 152.

contemporary witchcraft discourse (a cultural code; a 'province of meaning' counterbalancing the everyday life; or a particular transgenerational vision upon the world that a contemporary individual can access when in need), the fundamental value for the individual actors accessing this discourse is that of gaining a form of empowerment, eventually enabling them to fight off adversity in their lives and, in the end, to heal; or, in Galina Lindquist's terms, gaining an alternate avenue of agency allowing them to be 'walking the minefield'[377] of personal and social convulsive times of passage. Resorting to witchcraft discourse as a way to diagnose personal unhappiness and hardship is a matter of 'choice to interpret events in a particular way and to resolve misfortune.'[378]

Contemporary magic discourses and practices can be theoretically and rationally *conceived* as being something opposed to the institutionalized, sanctioned religion, or to the empirical scientific explanations. As participant to the contemporary complex society, each and every informant is fully aware of the conceptual dichotomies between the secular pole, the religious pole, and the magic pole. Nevertheless, this conceptual polarization does not seem to be as operational when examined in practice, in individual action. Especially in crisis situations, resorting to magic is not something *lived* by the actors, in the context of their own experiences, as actions dramatically contradicting the religious or scientific frames of reference—simply because such categorizations tend to completely lose their relevance when dealing with adversity. It is not a matter of ignorance or opportunistic shifting of allegiances on the part of the involved actors; it is simply an adaptation to circumstances,[379] a

---

377 Galina Lindquist, *Conjuring Hope. Healing and Magic in contemporary Russia* (New York, Oxford: Berghahn Books, 2009), p. 236.

378 Willem de Blécourt and Owen Davies, 'Introduction: Witchcraft continued', p. 7.

379 This is an all-encompasing approach also noted by Pina-Cabral for the Portughese peasants when facing adversity, especially illness. João de Pina-Cabral, *Sons of Adam. Daughters of Eve: The Peasant Worldview of Alto Minho* (Oxford: Clarendon Press, 1986), p. 187–188.

pragmatic attitude expected to increase the chances to succeed in restoring the normality of day-to-day existence.

ibidem-Verlag / *ibidem* Press
Melchiorstr. 15
70439 Stuttgart
Germany

ibidem@ibidem.eu
ibidem.eu